Consumed Nostalgia

Consumed Nostalgia

MEMORY IN THE AGE
OF FAST CAPITALISM

Gary Cross

Columbia University Press New York

Columbia University Press
Publishers Since 1893
New York   Chichester, West Sussex
cup.columbia.edu
Copyright © 2015 Columbia University Press
All rights reserved

Library of Congress Cataloging-in-Publication Data

Cross, Gary S.
Consumed nostalgia : memory in the age of fast capitalism / Gary Cross.
pages cm
Includes bibliographical references and index.
ISBN 978-0-231-16758-1 (cloth : alk. paper) —
ISBN 978-0-231-53960-9 (e-book)
1. Consumption (Economics)—Social aspects—United States.
2. Consumer behavior—Social aspects—United States.
3. Nostalgia.   I. Title.

HC110.C6C763   2015
306.30973—dc23   2014045595

⊛
Columbia University Press books are printed on
permanent and durable acid-free paper.
This book is printed on paper with recycled content.
Printed in the United States of America

c 10 9 8 7 6 5 4 3 2 1

Jacket design by Noah Arlow

References to websites (URLs) were accurate at the time of
writing. Neither the author nor Columbia University Press is
responsible for URLs that may have expired or changed since
the manuscript was prepared.

CONTENTS

Consumed Nostalgia

INTRODUCTION

Our Nostalgic
Novelty Culture

Strange isn't it? Many of us run after novelty and idolize youth;
quickly grow tired of our celebrities and look for new ones; and,
if we are old enough and (perhaps) fortunate enough, display pictures of our kids but not our parents, much less our ancestors.
Everything is ever new.

Yet those of us who have reached the "fullness of life" also collect the past, albeit often in the form of its novelties—G.I. Joes,
Barbies, and 1950s or 1970s kitchen knickknacks. Those who are
younger, say in their thirties or even twenties, may already be collecting the toys and dolls of their youth. Some may be unwilling
or just slow to empty their childhood bedrooms of their posters of
rock stars or sports heroes, school trophies, and video games when
they go off to college and beyond. And even if a lot of us didn't like
history in school and never read those historical markers along the
road, we may watch cable TV channels devoted to the past—TV

Land or even the History Channel (at least for the programs about the Wild West or World War II that may have fascinated us in our youth). We long for the past, no matter what our age. We moderns run away from the unmodern and embrace an accelerating pace of change, yet, at the same time, we crave what was once novel but what we long ago discarded. We are nostalgiacs.

Why is our novelty culture so fixed in our memory? Have we simply changed our minds and now turn what was once waste into want? Is the fast pace of our lives and culture just too great for us to cope with, obliging us to stop to catch our breath and maybe just to look back a little? Perhaps. But our longing to recapture the past isn't that simple or that easy to understand. The fact that many middle-aged Americans might be interested in somehow recapturing their childhoods by collecting toys may not surprise us, but shouldn't it? And the passion of collectors is often curious, even bizarre. In 2000, a founder of a software company, Brian Styles, had the time and money to collect seven hundred Lego sets and insure his lode for $60,000. Hot Wheels, a toy-car line popular in the late 1960s, has inspired a newsletter serving about three thousand adult subscribers and whose editor possessed nearly thirty thousand Hot Wheels. A few years ago, a rare pink VW Beach Bomb Hot Wheels toy was valued at more than $10,000. The crazy prices paid for injection-mold plastic knows no limit: Stephen A. Geppi, the CEO of Diamond Comic Distributors, paid $200,000 for the first handcrafted G.I. Joe.[1]

We can understand why a woman who, as a child, begged her mom for a Barbie doll as an adult might express a bit of wistfulness (along with whimsy) when she finds her ancient idol in her parents' attic. But why are there at least one hundred thousand avid collectors of these dolls (by the estimate of Barbie's maker, Mattel), whose average age is forty and who each spend nearly $1,000 per year to purchase twenty Barbies? And for the somewhat older "girl," there are the Ginny dolls, popular in the 1950s but still being manufactured more than fifty years later for adult collectors. Some people of the same vintage are drawn to Ding Dong School collectibles, from the totally uncool 1950s TV show for preschool children that featured the frumpy educator Frances Horwich. In time, the girls of 2003 or 2004 will collect the distinctive doll of their era—probably Bratz.[2]

No doubt the things of childhood touch a special sentimental nerve. But why would anyone but the curators of a computer history museum want to collect, repair, and display Apple I computers? Yet engineers sometimes do, even if an Apple I that cost $666 when manufactured in 1976 fetched up to $20,000 by 2005 but could do far less than the cheapest computer available at Best Buy.[3] The range of collecting is surely astonishing and amusing, and the media have often had fun ferreting out and reporting on the oddest: A recent article on collecting noted that among the "hot" items were muscle cars from the mid-1960s, televisions from the 1950s, metal-alloy Tootsie Toys, cast-iron miniature tractors and trucks, and Toni Dolls from the late 1940s and 1950s. What were "out" were cast-iron Britains soldiers, Crystal Oak furniture, and antique kitchenware and tools. Nostalgia, it seems, is ruled by the unfathomable dictates of fashion.[4] Often the campy prevails; how else to explain the lasting attraction to pink and turquoise Melmac—a brand of cheap plastic dinnerware popular during the 1950s? Aimee Cecil, a Los Angeles entrepreneur, has been able to resurrect the kitschy hobby of painting by number. Cecil sold about five thousand sets in 2006 at $90 each, though they cost $2.50 in 1953 when the craze began.[5] Often with the help of the Internet, others have made livings promoting collections of vintage napkin rings, aprons, toothpick holders, pencil boxes, and even sand pails. The eccentric and fashionable rich have indulged themselves. One paid $12,000 for a restored six-burner, double-oven Magic Chef range from the 1920s to give his kitchen that special retro look. Toasters have become collectibles, especially those from the 1920s and 1930s with unusual styling. Who could pass up the heart-shaped Universal Toaster of Landers, Frary & Clark?[6]

Much of this is the debris of a modern manufacturing economy that has an extraordinary capacity to produce endlessly changing lines of stuff, used briefly and sometimes not at all, before being discarded for new stuff. But many of us still want or even need to dig through the trash heaps to turn old novelty into new nostalgia. Some of this "junk" is collected simply because it is rare and thus valuable, often only because it was unsuccessful in the market back when. This is only one of the many curious properties of the nostalgia market.

At the same time, many items that seem to make the saved and savored pile help us recall the past, and these things may be in plentiful supply. Take, for example, old board games. The object of the nostalgia game is not to have the oldest or most original item but the game that brings back memories of a particular time and place. Beyond reasons of camp, why would anyone except a woman who was a "tween" in the mid-1960s want *Twiggy*—"a game that makes every girl like Twiggy, the Queen of Mod"—or *The Samantha and Endora Game: Bewitched!*? The same principle seems to apply to Gen-X collectors of *Pac Man*, *Demon Attack*, *Space Invaders*, and other Atari cartridge video games from the late 1970s.[7] More difficult to explain is the African American collector of race kitsch. Since 1984, the Greater Washington, D.C., Black Memorabilia and Collectible Show has exhibited a vast array of vintage toys, figures, and pictures. Many of these mementos feature African American sports, entertainment, and other heroes, but not a few depict degrading images of black pickaninnies, chicken thieves, and "coon jiggers," often in the form of dolls and toys originally given to white children. A very strange collection for middle-class, African American adults . . . or is it?[8]

A lot of this stuff appeals to relatively small groups of collectors, those people seeking a niche where they can specialize, stand out, tell a story, and perhaps have an opportunity to "catch them all," as advertising for Pokémon toys once urged kids to do. But the passion often goes deeper; it might even be akin to religious fervor. Who hasn't been astounded by Elvismania? Since his death in 1977, his widow and daughter have made a fortune from not just his songs (including now a satellite radio station devoted exclusively to the King) but also from his "relics." In the early 1990s Elvis's American Express credit card sold for $41,400, and Elvis-themed lipstick (Hound Dog orange and Love Me Tender pink) manufactured in the late 1950s found buyers at $350.[9]

Then there is Disneyana. A seat from the Dumbo ride in the Magic Kingdom cost an Orlando businessman $22,000 in 1993.

Such madness naturally sparked the Disney Company that year to create the Walt Disney Collector's Society to market reissued Disney memorabilia (pins, stuffed animals, animation cels, watches, figurines, toys, and much else). And private individuals with little if any financial stake in the Disney Company build their identities and spend their time around things Disney. Consider the Disney Tattoo Guy (covered in Disney characters) or the people who create websites around their favorite Disney theme-park rides. Werner Weiss's yesterland.com features rides and attractions long gone from Disneyland, and Jeff Baham's doombuggies.com is devoted to his obsession, the Haunted Mansion attraction at the Magic Kingdom. But Disney fetishism hardly ends there. If there are relic hunters of "sainted" Disney characters, there are also pilgrims to the Disney Jerusalem (or Mecca). Some fans visit Disneyland or Disney World twenty-five or more times a year, and Disney cultivates this market with special programs for this "elite."[10] What is particularly striking is just how specific and, well, "trivial" so many of these recalled memories are. It isn't surprising that the board game *Trivial Pursuit* (introduced in 1981) and its many variations and imitators have done so well ever since. Nostalgiacs not only collect; they also master the details, knowledge that many of us might consider "useless" but that is curiously empowering to those who have it.[11]

Nostalgia for our own pasts is about more than possession (or being possessed). It is also summoned by the senses. An obvious example is the fixation on the music of youth in the thousands of "oldies" radio stations, the recent renewed interest in vinyl records (those LPs that disappeared from stores in 1991 for CDs), and the frequent stories of has-been rock bands renewing their depleted fortunes with "comeback" concert tours. Added to nostalgic sounds is the appeal of half-forgotten tastes (revivals of long-defunct candy bars, for example). Sights, sounds, smells, and tastes all evoke memory and the desire to renew the sensuousness and emotions that went with it.

Enterprises, both public and private, have sprung up to meet the demand for nostalgia. Amazing arrays of sites restore, collect, preserve, and romanticize lost crafts and lifeways. These include not only local and specialized heritage and history museums but restored railroads and annual festivals of small towns. Perhaps the most successful are highly commercialized places, most notably many of Disney's theme-park attractions (beginning with Main Street USA). Nostalgia for the sounds, sights, and objects of the past has created a whole range of longings. And these have been excited and extended by all kinds of consumer industries—magazines, movies, comic-book stores, "retro" novelty shops, and old-time TV channels, not to mention numerous themed amusement parks, restaurants, and bars. The magic of consumer satisfaction makes nostalgia a major business. And like all entrepreneurial efforts to meet a demand, these impresarios of memory also create and channel that need, pricking the bud of desire, giving vent to its extravagant blooming, and shaping it in ways that increase sales.

VARIETIES OF NOSTALGIA

In retrospect, all of this is very strange. Fifty years ago, few behaved this way. Emotional feelings for the past were tied to communities, lost (and won) causes, and families. Nostalgia just isn't what it used to be. Taking a longer perspective, nostalgia in any form was practically absent from our ancestors of two centuries ago. Until modern times, few people traveled farther than a day's walk from their place of birth, and most lived much as did their parents or grandparents. Time was experienced mostly as a cycle of seasons and festivals, disrupted only by unwelcomed events like war or natural catastrophe. With little movement or change, there wasn't much to be nostalgic about. Moreover, people's memory of the past was vague; even "golden ages" were of uncertain duration and distance from the present. Our ancestors marked time by recurring festivals that magically captured "first" moments (origins of the cosmos or the birth of a religious founder, for example), most built around a "myth of eternal return."

Modernity began to change all that—and the first sign of this was increased travel. Change of place rather than time created the first nostalgiacs. In 1688, the word "nostalgia" was coined by the

Swiss doctor Johannes Hofer, meaning literally "longing to return home." This desire to get back to a faraway place and, with it, a long-lost time was rare and thus viewed as disruptive to authorities in the seventeenth century. No wonder. The first noted nostalgiacs were Swiss mercenaries in the French army who longed to return to their Alpine villages. Dr. Hofer believed that nostalgia exhausted the vital spirits and induced nausea, loss of appetite, cardiac arrest, and even suicide. He reported that those afflicted with nostalgia also heard voices and saw ghosts. Hofer thought that nostalgia was triggered when Swiss mercenaries ate "soups" and "village milk" from home or heard folk melodies, especially a "certain rustic can-tilena" used by shepherds to drive herds to pasture in the Alps. Hofer advised the usual cures (opium and leeches) but also sug-gested a novel solution—leaves of absence from the army to visit home in the Alps. Later, nostalgia afflicted other European soldiers and sailors in the many wars of the eighteenth century that took them far from home. Apparently the British, who were more accus-tomed to travel and colonizing distant regions, were less affected. But when farm boys made into soldiers during the American Civil War were depressed with a longing to return home, officers like Theodore Calhoun tried to shame them with bullying and manly marches (but also, when possible, with furloughs).[12]

Early nostalgia was a "problem" for only the few who were *dis-placed*. That would begin to change toward the end of the eigh-teenth century, when *time* sped up for many more, as revolutions, both political and economic, created deep discontinuities in life. Thus the old aristocracy became nostalgic for the Old Regime after the French Revolution. Later, Confederate soldiers longed for the Old South after the Civil War. Today, there are even Russians who look back romantically to the Stalinist era of the Soviet Union. Most people couldn't be nostalgic before the division between the "modern" and the traditional regime.[13]

Nostalgia also became more complex and subtle with techno-logical and economic change. Progress brought new possibilities for travel to distant places and new meanings of time. By the 1830s and 1840s, railroads and electric telegraphs were annihilating space and time, leading to an unprecedented uprooting of European people. Nearly half a century earlier, steam-powered machines were already beginning to make possible an extraordinary array and rapid turnover of goods. Everything was moving faster, bringing new things and new times. With a permanent state of mobility and transience, place and time become ever more elusive. Progress induced a sense of homelessness and forgetfulness. Eighteenth-century physicians of the Enlightenment thought the ailment of nostalgia would gradually give way to the benefits of progress. But by 1800 nostalgia was no longer restricted to homesick soldiers. It affected the multitude of Europeans with a longing for lost places and pasts.

Modernity meant disdain for tradition and the old and, with this, the worship of novelty and the young. But progress also made people nostalgic for what had disappeared. The modern world inevitably led to a reaction, the desire "to obliterate history and turn it into private or collective mythology, revisit time like place, refusing to surrender to the irreversibility of time that plagues the human condition," as the Russian writer Svetlana Boym notes.[14] Modern people discovered inexorable change and tried to get the past back as a possession.

The romantic movement, emerging at the end of the eighteenth century, rejected the Enlightenment's confidence in the rational future, ached for the disappearing world of the preindustrial village, and celebrated a longing for the past. One early manifestation was the creation by the rich of picturesque gardens with miniatures of ancient Greek temples, reflecting ponds, and grottos with statues of nymphs. In turn, romantic literati celebrated the worlds of peasants and artisans (think of the Queen's Hamlet of Marie Antoinette's in the gardens of Versailles). The object was to draw a contrast with the present world of machines and incessant change.

Nevertheless, both the Enlightenment progressive and the romantic nostalgic recognized that time was unrepeatable and irreversible. Gone were the old idea of cycles of change and the belief that the past returned naturally. Instead, people realized that the past was very different from the present. It had to be reconstructed, recreated through rituals, and symbolized in relics and mementos, sometimes displayed in museums or town squares but also hidden behind the walls of homes, sheltered from the transient world. Often history was encased and classified in the curio cabinet of the parlor. The past became a foreign country, as David Lowenthal notes, a place of "rooted legacies that enrich the paltry here and now with ancestral echoes. . . . Heritage aims to convert historical residues into witnesses that attest our own ancestral virtues," a place one toured and preserved but always kept apart from the real world.[15]

As progress advanced in the nineteenth century, so did nostalgia for lost communities. Memory settled in many places—in museums and monuments as well as schools where students were indoctrinated with national history and literature. Nostalgia was hard to separate from heritage—national, regional, ethnic, and religious. And many nationalists and other promoters of group identity had an incentive to preserve the memory of the tribe's origins, triumphs, and, often, humiliations. Public shrines and museums tried through words, symbols, and artifacts to replace lost sites of community—ancient neighborhoods, battlefields, or churches. This impulse has not only survived but flourished in recent years. Today, as we have finally abandoned the old faith in progress, nostalgia has become an even stronger theme in the cultural/political "wars" that divide us ethnically, religiously, culturally, and politically. It should not be surprising that 95 percent of existing museums date from after World War II, as people across the globe seek identities through the collected artifacts of the past. "Museum-mania" seems to be a direct reaction to the speeding up of life.[16]

But the longing for the past could also take a second, more private, especially familial form, evoked and realized through personal possessions. Sometimes these were handcrafted heirlooms or family portraits. Other times they were souvenirs brought back from a once-in-a-lifetime "pilgrimage" to a religious shrine but increasingly also to a World's Fair or even a seaside resort. Such acts of nostalgia were more domestic and personal than the grand gestures of monument makers. They promised to retain the memory of family. Preserving and displaying heirlooms and portraits was a practice long associated with the aristocracy and their claims of ancient lineage and authority. But in the nineteenth-century middle-class homes of the newly affluent, which had no claims of descent from William the Conqueror or Charlemagne, collections of memory were much more intimate—less about ancestry and more about relationships, existing or personally recalled. In fact, new technology, especially the camera (1839), fostered these personal ties to distant or deceased parents and prematurely departed loved ones, especially children and infants. According to Walter Benjamin, the bourgeois home of Paris a hundred years ago was a "miniature theater" of photos, furniture, and mementos that privatized nostalgia.[17]

A third form of nostalgia is for past fashion or styles that represent a former era. Distinctive patterns of design and construction of objects have a long history in elite cultures, but access to these fashionable goods trickled down to an emerging middle class during industrialization and the early stages of urban consumer society. Fashion nostalgia was based not so much on a feared loss of community or family but on an identification with the past in and through its distinct materiality—art, clothing, jewelry, furnishings, architecture, and artificial landscapes, for example. All this produced distinct forms of memory making, embodying particular pasts in particular possessions. And many of these goods were originally products of a commercial culture. Without doubt, nostalgia for past fads and fashions is hardly new. There have repeatedly been revivals of the styles of the past: neoclassical architecture in the late eighteenth century and renewed interest in American colonial furnishings in the mid-nineteenth century, for example.

But there is a fourth form of nostalgia that emerged in the twentieth century that I call "consumed nostalgia." Though sharing with fashion nostalgia an identification of the past with distinctly stylized goods, the consumed nostalgia of the second half of the twentieth century is about more than a revival of a style materializing a former era. It is a longing for the goods of the past that came from a *personal* experience of *growing up* in the stressful world of *fast capitalism*. Change was manifested in the increasingly rapid coming and going of things and experiences, especially manufactured commodities. By the twentieth century, these included, of course, cars and clothes but also entertainment, especially recorded music, movies, and, later, television. Modern fast capitalism meant fast consumption, a particularly intensive form of commodity culture, entailing the increasingly rapid pace of production and purchase, creating profit through the fast turnaround of investment. Even though this led to economic growth and increased comfort and variety, many people found fast capitalism disquieting. This stress resulted from a rather distinctly modern phenomenon—people found identity and meaning in specific goods but, as a result, felt that their selfhoods were threatened when those things disappeared. The nostalgic impulse came from a desire to get them back. Most important, this longing was often rooted in the formative years of consumers—childhood and youth.

So personal was this desire to recover a distinct childhood, that others, including family and friends, could not share in the loss of these consumed things and experiences and in the longing to recover them. Naturally, consumed nostalgia was difficult to pass down to the next generation. It was not based on the symbols and rituals of a longed-for community or family life. The recalled thing or experience, of course, might create bonds between often widely dispersed people who shared little but a common memory of consumption. But these communities of Model-T or Madonna fan clubs usually lack the duration, seriousness, and social breadth of groups memorialized in monuments or heirlooms—even though this "superficiality" usually spares adherents the exclusivity and ideological or tribal confrontation that divides participants in "culture wars" and, of course, real wars.

Consumed nostalgia shares much with more traditional forms of memory. In all four kinds of nostalgia—the communal, familial, fashion, and modern consumerist—the experiential quest is paramount. And nostalgia in the past like nostalgia today was rooted in objects. People have long needed material and sensuous markers to recall and get "in touch" with their social or family heritages. What makes consumed nostalgia different is not primarily its materiality or even its celebration of the time-fixed commodity (as in a past style or fashion) but its origins in fast capitalism and personal memories of the ephemeral commercial goods first experienced in childhood and youth.

One might assume that a "new country," presumably founded on the quest for the new, novel, and adventurous, might be immune to nostalgia in any of its forms. And it is true that some early Americans rejected Europe's "blind veneration of antiquity," as Jefferson noted. This, however, did not liberate them from the "disease" of nostalgia as "homesickness" because so many Americans were so frequently uprooted.[18] Americans certainly were not free from the monument or heirloom nostalgia of Europeans (just think about the extraordinary array of chiseled marble surrounding the site of the Civil War's Battle of Gettysburg or the clutter of inherited furnishings that once decorated late nineteenth-century American parlors). Moreover, the business in souvenirs memorializing a summer day with friends and family at Coney Island in 1900 flourished just as it did at European seaside resorts.

More importantly, Americans became leaders in this fourth form of nostalgia—without, of course, expunging earlier forms of collecting or passing on heirlooms, much less veneration for long-gone cultures or societies. Instead of grounding nostalgia in a canon of national literature and art as in Europe, American longings for the past often adhered to an ephemeral popular culture of youth that was closely associated with the precocious development of fast capitalism. As we will see, consumed nostalgia in the United States matures after about 1970.

PRELIMINARY THOUGHTS
ON CONSUMED NOSTALGIA

Whatever its form, nostalgia has earned the deep scorn of most intellectuals and the less open disdain of museum staff. Perhaps, as Svetlana Boym notes, nostalgia can make us "more empathetic toward fellow humans," all of whom experience loss in time (a reflective nostalgia). But Boym worries that when our longing for what is missing is replaced by a desire to belong to a group with links to the past, "we often part ways and put an end to mutual understanding." Thus we invent traditions to connect ourselves with a "past" that never was, and, more darkly, we fantasize conspiracies against our imagined heritage and home, be it a Judeo-Christian America or an Islamic utopia. As Susan Stewart writes, nostalgia lets us "authenticate a past or otherwise remote experience and, at the same time . . . discredit the present" that we find to be impersonal, artificial, or otherwise unacceptable. For these critics, nostalgia may no longer be a physical disease, as it was for Dr. Hofer in the seventeenth century, but it certainly remains a cultural malady, creating social division or escapist illusion.[19]

Intellectuals, particularly, have mocked the commercialized form of nostalgia that is often identified with the United States as inferior to the "cultured" heritage of Europe. Yet we need not make the smug contrast between England's Shakespeare and America's Mickey Mouse. While the critique of nostalgia is important and insightful, is it fair and complete? Does it really make sense of when, how, and why most people remember? Even more, does it address the way that many, if not most of us, express our nostalgia today and why?

We should always recognize that the public understands and uses the past in ways very different from the historian and often the museum curator. While historians study archival and other records to reconstruct the past and answer questions posed by other historians, the "public more often turns to memory, personal connections, and family stories" when approaching the past. Instead of an explanation of events or an abstract memorial, most people want to "experience" history (as is proven by the thousands of Civil War reenactors that flock annually to Gettysburg and other battlefield sites). For heirlooms to "work," there needs to be stories attached that touch the emotions.[20]

Even more to the point, we need to recognize how nostalgia has changed with fast capitalism and the modern fixation on personal experience in the formative years. Unlike the longing for the lost place and time that once was satisfied with public monuments or family heirlooms, many of us today recapture and relive the past in our own possessions, whose significance and attachments we seldom share with family members or the broad community.

Instead of seeking a lost community or cause, we recover our personal childhoods in a vast array of objects and recorded sensations. This essentially negates Boym's critique of nostalgia. Far from its leading us into a kind of intolerant tribalism or narrowly cast familialism, modern consumed nostalgia creates mostly an exuberant individualism. Critics miss how the new consumed nostalgia is liberating and, in fact, often fun. This is largely because consumed nostalgia is part of consumer culture, a phenomenon that makes things easy and pleasurable—albeit at a cultural and social price. We can even draw on the commercial culture that preceded us through viewing the movies or hearing the songs that were first popular in the childhoods of our parents or other ancestors. We can "regain" our childhood.

The most basic problem with these critics is their failure to understand just how unique this contemporary form of nostalgia is. It certainly has little in common with the experience of those poor Swiss soldiers or with those disaffected "Southern rebels" with their Confederate flags and stories of the "Lost Cause." We might all suffer from homesickness and a longing for our lost pasts and places. Many of us pine for a return to a lost culture and social order and divide ourselves politically over this desire. We often fret over and create romantic illusions about long-gone bonds of family. But consumerism has given us a new way of thinking about and coping with the past. We may and probably should find things about this new form of nostalgia to regret and oppose, but we need first to understand what it is.

Let me offer five ways in which today's consumed nostalgia is so distinct and so contradictory:

1. *Today nostalgia binds together not community or families but scattered individuals around seemingly ephemeral things that are meaningful to them personally.* How many of our holiday rituals today are really about religious or national ideas? Few of us celebrate ancestors, even our departed parents.[21] Much contemporary nostalgia is built on briefly popular consumer goods that unify, however loosely, narrow age groups. Instead of places or events shaping these brief "generations," goods link otherwise separated

individuals. Nostalgia today is increasingly about microidentities. In fact, consumed nostalgia lets us "put on" multiplicities of identities across the movement through life. It has been fashionable for a long time to call this postmodern, but what I am describing goes beyond plural identities and denial of universal "narratives" and national identity. These "postmodern" nostalgias are even more fragmented and ephemeral, constructed as they are around things, often very silly ones, and the memories and sensualities that these things evoke. They create personal meanings, but they also isolate and divide us.

2. *Today's nostalgia is less about preserving an "unchanging golden era" than it is about capturing the fleeting and the particular in its "authenticity."* In everything from our snapshots to our strange attempts to reenact the Civil War experience, we try to make the "there and then" into the "here and now" in pristine specificity and accuracy. We preserve that unguarded "cute" moment of our former toddlers in snapshots, not iconic family-portrait photographs shot by professionals. Reenactors wear wool uniforms in July encampments at Gettysburg, and some insist on not wearing underwear to capture the authentic experience. These activities have replaced the rituals of building monuments, attending ceremonies, and hearing inspired speeches as the reenactors' predecessors did a hundred years ago. We have substituted the "authentic" for the symbolic. Even more germane here: we no longer seek heirlooms (literally "a device for interweaving generations") as a gesture of family or group continuity. Because of weakened family bonds and the transience of things, fewer of us hand down household treasures to children. And these remembrances are far less standardized—gone are the stylized family photographic portraits, Victorian china cabinets, and ancestors' needlework. Something new has happened. Instead of symbols that link us across generations, we seek exact and personal remembrances of our own pasts or at least "authentic" representations of our families—informal snapshots and children's artwork, for example. This quest for the authentic is how we moderns cope with the fleeting—not by denying change and death in dreams of a timeless age but by capturing "our moment" in our snapshots, songs, dolls,

and cars. All this satisfies our longings for the personal connection, but it often is an authenticity impossible to share with others or to pass down to our children. And, I suspect, for many it is a poor substitute for the "eternal."

3. *All nostalgias consist of organizers and participants, but today the organizers increasingly are marketers (not officials), and participants are consumers (not members of organizations).* Our nostalgiacs bow not to the state, educators, museum curators, or National Park officials. Today, the nostalgic enthusiast more often responds to appeals of Disney, TV Land, and the thousands of pitches made by eBay merchants; publishers of those hundreds of collector's guides to Barbie Dolls, G.I. Joes, antique cars, and 1950s kitsch; and the DJs of oldie radio stations. This makes nostalgia less "political" and less confrontational than "heritage." At the same time, Hollywood does not offer a contemplative or "reflective" nostalgia (as advocated by Boym) that draws us to think about the ambiguities of change; instead, it presents us with a tangible, engaging, and even sensuous possession or experience. The success of nostalgia marketing varies a lot, and all this can tell us much about the workings of consumed nostalgia. Some obsessions with the past survive for decades (Disney is an obvious example). Others fade (circuses and many "heritage" museums). And marketers of memory are very sensitive to and even encourage fashion in nostalgia. All this makes consumed nostalgia both relatively benign (in part because it is so superficial) and dynamic, always changing. But it may only point to rather than fulfill our longings for memory.170

4. *Today's nostalgia seems to help us cope with the extraordinary speed-up of time by letting us return to our childhoods.* We no longer seem to need recurring rituals as did our ancestors in their rich traditions of harvest and other seasonal/religious festivals to fend off the terrors of time and the unshakeable truth that we all die alone, often unexpectedly. Instead of worshipping ancestors (or even seeking spiritual communion with the departed), we search for the "wonder years" of our own childhoods. We seem to find solace from the ephemerality of time in the nonephemerality of

things, an experience that seems to hide the deeper reality so well understood by our ancestors—the brevity of life. We cope with the ever-accelerating pace of change that continually robs us of our identities by creating a flow of selves over the years. We are continually drawn to root these selves in our personal pasts, in what seems to us as "timeless" but, in fact, is ephemeral, that is, our childhoods.

Experienced time is not like a walk along a road. While the present is often routine (especially after we have passed through childhood and adolescence), the future comes at us from behind (often unexpectedly) as the past recedes in front of us.[22] When this process is sped up as it is today, stress is added to the ennui of daily life. Nostalgia offers both an excitement missing in the everyday and provides a refuge from the fleeting in personal packets of childhood memory. Thus we lovingly recall getting our first electric train set, Barbie doll, or used car. In a world where many of the old glues of meaning and security have dissolved (family, work, and village/neighborhood, to name the obvious), these packed memories provide more than the symbolic and abstract representations of those lost relationships and experiences. They offer us the sensuous and material worlds of our particular childhoods, promising us personal meaning and emotional engagement, even if they isolate us from others.

5. *Today's nostalgia is rooted in special emotions linked to recovering memories distinctive to the objects of modern childhood and consumerism.* This suggests more than a regression into the superficial and puerile but instead a quest for an experience lost to today's adults. Emotions and sensuous feelings from the past are naturally evoked by encounters with "things." In a different age these may have been religions icons, ceremonial clothing or music, or monuments. Today they are mostly consumer goods from our youth; these give us a huge variety of hooks to hang our personal emotional hats on. As the anthropologist Mihaly Csikszentmihalyi succinctly puts it, "Our addiction to materialism is in large part due to a paradoxical need to transform the precariousness of consciousness into the solidity of things." Without stuff, there is little

to talk about, respond to, or recall, at least for most of us who aren't mystics or uncommonly introspective.

Today this stuff is mostly consumer goods and experience (like music and TV shows), and our nostalgia for them is associated with two stages of childhood—the emerging autonomy (and persistent memory) of primary-school-age childhood and the increasing consumer freedom and emotionally charged peer-group experience of adolescence. Broadly speaking, this is because over the past century our culture has favored youth over age, often making these years times of fond memory. That we might favor "first stuff," the things of our early years, may come from the simple fact that these things were new then and that with age and more things we become jaded. More particularly, many Americans experience pure delight (what I call "wondrous innocence") as six- or seven-year-olds in toys, dolls, and other fantasy goods given to them mostly by indulgent parents. The particular bond many have with the things (including cars, music, fashions, etc.) of their teens relates to the new choices and opportunities for self-expression through consumer goods that precedes adult responsibility.[23] All this adds up to far more than regression into the childish. Nostalgia for childhood things invites us to return to our years of wondrous innocence, but, in doing so, we may be merely "putting on" rather than "turning into" the child. Consumed nostalgia does not necessarily consume us. Such goods often help us define ourselves. We can play at being the boy or girl from the often whimsical vantage of the adult. But for all of the sensuous delight and personal meaning that these recollected consumer moments may provide, they do not take us very far into recovering or understanding past relationships or even the world of childhood wonder or of teenage self-discovery and emerging autonomy.[24]

So consumed nostalgia is very special, and its effect on us may well be very ambiguous. I think that we cannot dismiss consumed nostalgia as tribal, fake, merely commercial, or childish. But does it and can it ultimately satisfy? Modern nostalgia is a richly complex and even contradictory phenomenon that both opens and closes possibilities of understanding the past. The selling of nostalgia has met demand, perhaps even accelerated it, in many and diverse ways, but that commercialization has also channeled and constricted the meaning of memory. Many modern Americans seem to find identity in the past and find friends in shared passions; they even resolve festering "wounds" by revisiting lost times and places. This may be one of the joys of the man who "finally" gets that muscle car he dreamed about as a teen. Though often escapist, modern people find playful ways of returning to what was once serious (to the child). Packaged memory can give new meanings to the past, providing nostalgiacs new perspectives on growing up in the 1950s or 1980s, sometimes freeing them from old resentments and distortions.

Yet the commercialization of nostalgia may also accentuate escape, distort memory, and, in general, short-circuit the goals and potential benefits of recollection. I am not advocating a return to the tribal or ideological nostalgia of the past, but rituals of recall may need to go beyond associating the past with bought things and experiences. This involves more than challenging commercialization and its effects. It may require that we reassess why we go back (and what "past" we favor) and how we might do it better to deepen our understanding of the present and reveal new possibilities for the future. We may need to rethink and refeel our way through how we cope with the avalanche of change that swamps us, how we reconnect with pasts that continually leave us wondering where we are and who we are. We may need to seek alternative ways of relating to the past, ways that lead us to question our romantic memories, that introduce us to surprises, and that call us to see our childhoods with adult eyes. We may want also to find ways of making memory less isolating, less about "me," and perhaps more about a renewal of lost relationships and the creation of new ties across generations. Even more, perhaps we may need to reassess just what we should recall and where and when we need to forget. Like so many other commodities, consumed memory satisfies many of our longings, but it may reveal needs that bought things cannot meet and point us to what is still missing.

In this book, I will explore the fascinating, often curious and surprising phenomenon of consumed nostalgia. To understand all the richness of this topic and to make its telling engaging and persuasive, I will seek out the details, look for the unexpected, and in general approach it with a mind open to surprises and even the unexplainable.

I cannot consider all forms of modern nostalgia. Though they are interesting, I will not consider high school and family reunions or the now-common practice of using Internet-based social networks to contact old lovers and friends. Even though they may relate to childhood memories, these forms of nostalgia are only tangentially related to the world of consumption. Emphatically, I am not arguing that consumed nostalgia has displaced these other forms of memorializing. They all coexist today, though I would argue that consumed nostalgia has assumed a unique and growing influence.

Where possible, I will personally visit sites of commercialized nostalgia and, through interviews and observations, investigate their inner workings. My task is to seek a broad representation of players—organizers, participants, and, at times, outsiders. Adding depth to this reporting will be brief forays into the literatures of these nostalgias—old-car magazines and toy and period collectors' guidebooks, for example. I will also draw on the history, sociology, and even psychology of nostalgia. I will explore when and why these particular nostalgias appeared. At times, to add to the richness of the phenomenon, I will let the nostalgiacs tell their own stories.

I have identified seven distinct types of nostalgia. I begin with a consideration of some of the *objects* of memory: first, with those that shaped early childhood—toys and dolls; then those goods that defined the transition to adulthood, especially the teenage car; and, finally, the goods of the family and domestic sphere that framed a wider memory of childhood and youth. I will follow with two chapters that define *experiential* memory in the modern era—popular music and television. I end with a consideration of *sites* of nostalgia, cultivated places of heritage and commercialized places of fantasy (theme parks).

I approach this topic as a kind of outside insider. I am a baby boomer (senior class) who collects nothing (besides DVDs of old movies, and those not very systematically) but who is fascinated by those who do. For years, I have enjoyed going to "memory sites," including doo-wop concerts, heritage museums, and theme parks, but, like many readers, I have wondered why I and others enjoy them. Doubtless, the questions that I bring to this project will change as I met the unexpected, but I will address the following queries to understand this longing for a reconnection to the past: What sorts of pasts are desired, and which are not? What kinds of nostalgic offerings work, which do not, and for what people and why? How is this drive modern, and how it did take on the variety of forms and meanings with which we associate nostalgia today? How does the commercialization of nostalgia respond to needs but also short-circuit those needs?

So my task will be to hit the road (figuratively and sometimes literally) to observe and listen to today's nostalgiacs in all their diversity. At the end of this journey, which I invite you to join, I will sum up and evaluate what we have seen. I hope then that we will all understand much better this strange world of modern nostalgia.

1

Guys Toys *and* "Girls" *Dolls*

Nostalgia has long been about returning home to a place and time most people recall as happy, innocent, and full of promise. These returnings are sometimes also laced with melancholy and pathos; as Thomas Wolfe said, "you can't go home again."

No longer true. Today, we can get back home by collecting. Of course, it isn't the same experience exactly, but it may be the same "thing," and the thing collected, be it a toy, old car, or phonograph record, is now in our possession, and it won't go away, like our actual childhood worlds have. Many of us no longer want or need shrines and monuments to mark our crossroads or to be the destinations of our pilgrimages. Instead memory is now evoked by things, mostly manufactured, often in great numbers, things that can be purchased and collected long after we first encountered them. Sometimes these things relate to people, or even ideas, but often they do not, or only vaguely. And, unlike most souvenirs, they are not generally associated with a place or visit but with a time of life. These are the things of our "wondrous innocence," the very particular memories of a personal childhood and youth, and frequently memories of consumption. I begin this discussion with toys and dolls, not because everyone collects them but because they are often the objects of our earliest memories.

On the face of it, collecting the stuff of children's play seems absurd, even pathetic. In place of the majestic monumentalism of ancient cathedrals, we have the miniature; instead of the grandeur and national symbolism of the Lincoln Memorial, we have ephemeral bits of plastic, tin, cloth, and stuffing that we remember but that mean little to others, isolating us in our little worlds. Why has something seemingly as important as memory been reduced to the miniature? Still, how can it be otherwise when today memory has become so personal, so private, and so possessive?

Nostalgia for childhood stuff is an important form of the curious psychology of collecting, but it is also a significant deviation from that wide-ranging culture. To summarize briefly a large and complex topic, the impulse to collect art, artifacts, and curios had its roots in the modern but contradictory worlds of discovery, individualism, and preservation dating from the fifteenth century. Coming into full flower in the bourgeois world of the nineteenth century, this early form of collecting parallels the emergence of romantic nostalgia.[1] Usually wealthy collectors claimed status as custodians of timeless beauty, ancient crafts, and rarities. Today's collectors of Disneyana share the traditional quest for "completing" a series of related objects—Mickey Mouse figures, for example, rather than rare paintings or stamps. Their collections are attempts to tell themselves and others about themselves—their expertise, their taste, their stories. But the end goals of these two types of collecting are otherwise quite different. The object of bourgeois collecting was to define self through the aura of heritage (as in antique furniture and original art) and thereby to differentiate the refined collector from those lower on the pecking order. The goal of consumed nostalgia today is to collect personal remembrances and to find community with those who share those memories (sometimes even transcending social class). The pleasure comes not from an identification with the high culture of the past but from warm feelings about the stuff of one's own childhood, no matter if it's "childish" or even campy.[2]

The playthings that might affect us emotionally often do not affect others because these objects are part of that short time when we were children and others were not. These objects may separate us from our siblings, spouses, and friends even if they are only a year or two older or younger than we are. These things are small but consequently are personal and personally possessed. They represent a time that has only a very tenuous tie to our present—not to a lost golden age of culture but to a few seasons when we lived both in little worlds where our playthings made us feel big and in fantasies of adventure and caring that are long gone. These things and their magic have departed from our "dull" adult lives, and we want that wonder back. But, of course, the throngs who attend toy and doll shows may not be consciously aware of all this—and they have other things on their minds.

DOLL AND TOY STORIES

There is something curious about people in their thirties, forties, fifties, sixties, and beyond displaying and selling dolls. Many of the (mostly) women dealers that I talked with on an early Sunday afternoon in December 2010 at the Gaithersburg, Maryland, Eastern Doll Show were professional antique traders, some with years of experience in buying and selling objets d'art. The dolls, taken from their seemingly natural settings on the beds and in the arms of mostly little girls, are transformed by collectors, taking on the aura of antiques rather than playthings. Yet they were special because they evoked memories of childhood. This was an old show that once took up four buildings from the county fairgrounds but now is housed in just one, partially because of Internet shopping. Still, mostly middle-aged women came to see and sometimes possess the play figures of their own or someone else's childhood.

Every seller seemed to have a niche. I met a long-retired second-grade teacher at a booth whose claim to fame was writing a book

on Schoenhut toys and figures (an early-twentieth-century Philadelphia manufacturer of colorful wood play sets with jointed figures). A team of two women shared exhibition space, one mad
about baby dolls, the other preferring costumed, adult-like figures.
They joked that they "like to spend each other's money" by being
on the lookout for dolls that the other might want. Many seemed
to take the advice offered in books on collecting: focus on a time,
style, or type of doll; other collectors appeared to know only a little
about the histories of their collections.

But this was not true of Elinor Champion, a sixty-four-year-
old former officer of the United Federation of Doll Clubs, with
whom I talked at length. While her organization has tried to bring
together collectors across age and taste, she noted that many doll
lovers have split into their own clubs—fans of Barbie or Madame
Alexander character dolls, for example. She had a catholic perspective: she noted that "once you start collecting, it is hard to focus."
She admitted that "space is also an issue" and that "it's harder to
sell than to buy."

Champion insisted that many doll collectors possessed skills
and knowledge similar to connoisseurs of fine antique furniture or
paintings. Members of her United Federation of Doll Clubs share
information about doll history, the art of identification, and modes
of restoration. Some collectors inherited the hobby from their
mothers or mother-in-laws and then try to draw their own daughters into the tradition.[3] Serious collectors of fine French and German dolls conduct research into the corporate records of doll makers in Europe as scholars and curators. "It's just like going to the
National Archives," Champion noted. Collectors may start out trying to "regain their childhood," but soon they get into art, history,
and knowledge of the hobby. She made it sound almost professional.

But Champion also acknowledged that some collectors, especially younger ones, "actually play with their dolls." This play takes
many forms. A recent craze was collecting Bleuette dolls made
from 1905 to 1960. They were first manufactured for a French girl's
magazine, *La Semaine de Suzette*, as a premium to subscribers; the
magazine also published patterns for girls to use to make clothes
for their Bleuettes. Today collectors find these patterns on the

Internet and channel, as it were, those French girls of long ago as they make their own Bleuette doll clothes. Perhaps there is a snob's appeal in reliving a French girl's childhood; it happened far away and long ago, and this fact may make the fascination with the dolls seem less childish.

I persisted in my questioning, however, asking this doll expert to explain why women might play with dolls. Are these collectors regressing? Are they finding mothering substitutes for their children who have grown up or that they never had? She admitted that she found it "a little unnerving" and a "little creepy" when women dressed dolls in real baby clothes and treated them like newborns. "Something is missing" in the lives of these women, she concluded. Champion and other older collectors I met at this show still identified with the idea that they were private curators, preservers of a cultural legacy, and distanced themselves from the more recent trend of full-throttle identification with their inner child.

Champion expressed concern about the future of the hobby, especially in passing it on to the eighteen-to-thirty-five-year-old set. Young people don't collect as much, she noted, explaining why the people at this show were predominately over fifty. Some buy online instead, but her thirty-seven-year-old daughter was too busy with family to share her mother's passion. Some get into it as the "needs of mothering lessen." Still, she wondered if the next generation will embrace the hobby. She saw a gap between the boomers and the Gen-Xers. In particular she noted how many younger women now pass over traditional American dolls for Japanese ball-jointed dolls. Enthusiasts purchase customized dolls from a pallet of choices in body, hair, eye color, and facial expression, all designed to be posed and to project a personality. The attraction is not aesthetic or historical, much less nurturing or even a nostalgic return to childhood. Instead, the Japanese ball-jointed dolls today invite a new generation of young women to "believe in the power of play," as one doll company encouraged, rejecting the adult/child distinction. Some collectors of the ball-jointed dolls were not so much returning to a childhood memory but denying a departure from the play of children.

Moreover, the doll collectors at the Gaithersburg show were skeptical of other collectors in general. One woman called stamp and coin collecting a "cold hobby." She was there to sell dolls and make a profit, but she claimed that she received a "nice warm glow" when a customer told her a story about rediscovering the happiness of childhood in the purchase of an old doll or associated the doll with growing up in the 1950s. The women I met at Gaithersburg insisted that they collected differently from men. One noted, "Boys played with fun things. Girls played with what they were going to do": take care of babies, cook, or clean. Boys' toys were more childish, she suggested (thinking of balls and fantasy action figures rather than erector sets and miniature trucks). More revealing was the attitude of the two-woman team of doll collectors mentioned above: guys, they insisted, were more interested in the value and the hunt, not the personal memories or the shared love of playthings. Male toy collectors are into it for the "big bucks," Elinor Champion concluded. Listening to these female doll collectors, I wondered why they saw so little similarity with male toy collectors. It was almost as if the women were returning to the perspective of little girls with their dolls, mocking the play of boys with their toys.

How, then, did the predominantly male collector think about his toys? In the summer of 2011, I attended a "typical" toy show in suburban Pittsburgh, the Steel City Toy and Comics Show. As with the doll shows, this conclave for trade in memory seemed to be in decline, even though it appealed primarily to Gen-Xers rather than older collectors. If the toys of the majority of exhibitors were much more recent in origin than the playthings of the older female doll collectors in Maryland, their stories were similar.

Most exhibitors were in their thirties or forties, offering row after row of still-boxed *Star Wars* and other action figures ranging from the late 1970s to the first decade of the twenty-first century. There were a lot of action figures: Transformers and Marvel Comics figures but also Halo, Skeleton Warriors, and DC Universe. Several booths featured professional wrestling posters and action figures (popular in the 1970s on TV). Few exhibited anything costing much over twenty dollars. There was only a token display of plaything collectibles identified with females. An air of arrested male development and bonding permeated the scene. A group of five guys in orange t-shirts gathered around a Pittsburgh-area retro radio station's DJ, promoting monster movies and a "Monster Bash Oktoberfest." The DJ was about fifty and proudly admitted that his life was "music and monsters," passions he acquired when he was a preteen. Those interests lasted until he was sixteen, when he went through a decade-long obsession with girls and cars, after which he returned to his original true loves. Like others at this show, he had given up his childhood passion only briefly.

This fascination with monsters seems also to apply to the curious interest in muscled but obviously fake professional wrestlers. I met an interracial family with two boys, the elder of which was holding an Incredible Hulk figure. Asking about it, I found to my surprise that this toy belonged to his black dad, who at the time was off looking for other treasures for his extensive collection of wrestling and action figures. His indulgent wife explained that her husband (born in 1977) collected 1980s toys because they reminded him of his happy childhood before his parents broke up. These toys were what "he could count on." When he returned, he explained that he had been obsessed by WrestleMania since he was nine and that he had a basement room full of shelves of wrestling figures in classic poses (a photo of which his wife showed me from her phone). It seemed that he needed the miniatures to access the old emotional attachments of his childhood. Like many others at the fair, he was not a "loser" but a professional—an art teacher for young schoolchildren. His sons seemed to share his interest—as did other father-son pairs I saw throughout the show.

One forty-year-old dad with his eight-year-old son was at the show to collect Marvel comics. The dad recalled a weekly ritual with his father—going to the newsstand on Saturday evenings to buy a comic book—and went on to gather a large collection of comics, which recently he had had to sell during hard times. Now the forty-year-old dad was bonding with his son via the project of restoring his collection; the son also searched for action figures based on his dad's beloved Marvel Comics. All this suggests a curious pattern: a generation-niched crowd of men who never really gave up their toys and who defined (however obliquely and inexplicably) their ties to their fathers and connected with their own sons through the ephemerality of popular cultural objects. At least, this bonding is what they strived for.

While some certainly had supportive (or indulgent) wives, male aficionados of action figures and comic books showed no more understanding of female collectors of memory objects than did the female doll collectors of male connoisseurs of toys. The art teacher with his basement full of action figures, when asked about women posing dolls, had nothing more to say than "I just don't get it." When I told an older dealer in toy car and military figures what the doll collectors thought of male toy collectors, he admitted that male dealers were motivated strongly by the cash nexus. But he denied that male collectors lacked an emotional attachment: men were passionate about highly realistic miniatures of military vehicles and fully equipped toy soldiers and less about the "personalities" of the figures. Asian companies specializing in detailed reproductions of Vietnam or Gulf War figures attracted middle-aged men who remembered the machines, uniforms, and equipment of their adventurous youths and, in turn, associated these items with their long-scattered buddies in the military. These figures were, he claimed, displacing G.I. Joe figures that some of these men may have actually played with as seven-year-olds in the early 1960s.

All this may suggest that some men relate to and remember other men through the common link to *things*. The figures are mannequins for the uniforms and equipment that enchant these men and that express the shared memory of youthful male bonding (rather than to childhood, interestingly enough). Ties to the past and its people, be it to young childhood or young manhood, are mediated through very specific objects, conveniently reduced to toy miniatures. Was this just a male version of the female fixation on effigies and their costumes? Maybe it's a bit more complex than that. So let's dig a little deeper, first looking briefly at the history of toys and dolls and then at doll- and toy-collecting communities. I will draw on my own earlier research and reflections on the history of playthings.

HISTORICAL RETROSPECTIONS

Most toy and doll collectors have in common a basic emotional response to the things of their personal childhoods. But these childhoods differ, especially between males and females and, of course, across time. Playthings of memory are sharply gendered because, in part, as the first remembered possessions of five-to-ten-year-olds, these toys and dolls coincide with the child's full development of gender identity. Few adults collect the toys of toddlers (which tend to be unisex), probably because as adults they have no memory of them. Gender differences in toys have persisted for a long time. Boys' toy soldiers and girls' dolls' houses of the eighteenth century marked gendered spaces and activities, just as did nineteenth-century boys' miniature work tools and horses and girls' tin kitchen sets and dolls. Victorian work and transportation toys helped boys rehearse their future male roles of income-earning employment and symbolized for the boy his longing to escape from mother's apron strings and go out into the world. And, of course, these gendered playthings changed with technology. The male's toy horse was ceded to girls in the twentieth century with the arrival of the car and truck, which were passed on to boys in miniature. The play worlds of Victorian girls were far more confined than those of boys, but they were no less rich in tools and opportunities to rehearse anticipated future domestic and nurturing roles.[4]

In the twentieth century, these gender differences became, if anything, even sharper. In the three decades after 1900, boys' toys were often associated with scientific and economic progress and preparation for careers in business or engineering (construction play sets and electric trains, for example). Later they were linked with science fiction and fantasy (Buck Rogers in the 1930s and *Star Wars* from 1977), as boys' play became less closely tied to future roles and Victorian ideals of industrial progress. Girl's playthings became more nurturing (especially in dolls that looked like children and babies by the 1910s) and more fashion and consumer oriented (for example, with Barbie from 1959). Even as these toys upheld gender divisions, their changes reflected profound transformations in cultural and economic life, especially a shift from anticipating future maturity and work roles to adulthood-denying fantasy.[5]

And all playthings became far more ephemeral in the twentieth century. This coincided with the birth of the modern consumer economy in about 1900 and its ever-shifting range of goods. Along with toys and dolls, there was a continuous flow of new phonograph recordings, movies, novelties, and the emergence of annual model changes in automobiles and other consumer durables. This transition to fast capitalism promised replenished profit in the manufacture of durable goods, and it subjected consumers to an era of continuous change. It particularly shaped the experience of children: the array of playthings changed yearly, sometimes dramatically, along with the adult fashion and novelty industries. Beginning with the craze for Teddy Bears in 1906, toy and doll makers continually tried to create fads of must-have playthings that have marked and segmented a succession of childhoods.[6] Many other novelties followed, like the Kewpie doll, a childlike impish figure first appearing as an illustration in a story by Rosie O'Neill in *Ladies Home Journal* in December 1909 but soon licensed to doll companies.[7]

Fads were directed especially toward boys. The master of fad licensing was, of course, Walt Disney, who, in the 1930s, sold the image of Mickey Mouse, Donald Duck, and many others across the world.[8] Many character toys followed, becoming popular through comic books, Saturday matinee movies, and radio shows. Heroic radio figures like Tom Mix, Dick Tracy, Buck Rogers, and Superman offered boys a wide variety of fantasies. For example, the science-fiction world of Buck Rogers created opportunities to manufacture miniatures of fantasy weapons, vehicles, and characters, which were sold to eager boys in neighborhood dime stores. By the 1930s, boys' toys were less about their futures at work than they had been a decade earlier and more about what was popular at the Saturday matinee or what superhero was featured at the comic-book stand. This was a rapidly changing fantasy world from which parents, especially dads, were largely excluded, and their hopes for their sons (to become engineers and businessmen, for example) were forgotten.[9] Fast capitalism divided the memories and hopes of parents from the experience of their children.

Things were a bit different for girls. In the 1910s and 1920s, the childlike "companion" or "New Kid" doll partially supplanted the relatively formal Victorian doll, with her sometimes lavish wardrobe, fragile small head of bisque, and doll face (pursed lips and blank stares). The New Kids were made of composition (mostly glue and sawdust) and, later, hard plastic, and they were more sturdy to play and cuddle with than ceramic dolls. They were idealizations of the toddlers who owned them, exuding cheerfulness, energy, optimism, and "personality." Many companion dolls came as sibling sets (for example, the Patsy dolls of the 1920s), which encouraged little girls to rehearse family roles (and to pester parents for complete doll sets). Also new were the baby dolls (By Lo Baby of 1923 and the "changeable" Dy Dee Baby and Betsy Wetsy of the 1930s) that pushed girls toward nurture play at a time when birth rates were falling and little girls had fewer opportunities to learn mothering. Themed dolls (like those of Madame Alexander, first appearing in 1923) encouraged collecting because they were manufactured in a series based on fairy tales, literature, and film.[10] Shirley Temple dolls transformed the generic New Kid look by personalizing it in the form of "America's Sweetheart," shortly after the five-year-old Temple began her stunning career in movies in 1934.[11]

However, the 1930s produced fewer changes in girls' playthings than boys. The difference seems to be that girls in the 1930s were much more closely tied to the sentimental wishes of their mothers than boys were to the traditional values of either parent. Girls' play was less subject to the fad culture of fast capitalism. Mothers loved Shirley Temple dolls because these dolls reminded them of their childhood dolls. And this continued into the 1940s and 1950s, as mothers fondly recalled their own Patsies and Shirley dolls and saw their childhoods in their daughters' play with their New Kid–style Ginny dolls. But by 1959, girls were ready for a break from maternal expectations: Barbie. And this produced the same sort of rapidly changing consumer culture for girls as had existed for boys since the 1930s, a culture based on peer-driven novelty, often tinged with rebellion.[12]

At the beginning of the 1960s, novelty toys and dolls for both boys and girls were dominated by diverse action figures, led by G.I. Joe and the long but forever changing Barbie fashion dolls. Although Hasbro's G.I. Joe appeared first in 1964 as a miniature of the real soldier that most American boys expected to grow up to become (in an era of general military conscription), by the mid-1970s the Joes had become fantasy figures that changed continuously (first in the 1970s to "Adventure Teams," abandoning military themes during the unpopular Vietnam War, and then to miniature "Super Joes," science-fiction action figures in 1976).[13]

G.I. Joe's transformation was followed by a generation of action figures, beginning with the miniatures and props of George Lucas's *Star Wars* trilogy (1977–1983). Even more than the sci-fi play of the 1930s, *Star Wars* was a boys' peer-group fantasy, continually changing, as did the boys (mostly), who quickly entered and left the target age group. Unlike the westerns, whose stock characters and plots were shared by multiple generations of American males, *Star Wars* belonged primarily to the kids of that time.[14]

The action figure was not only a peer-driven kids' obsession, but it emerged from the quintessential ephemerality of a movie series. Though seen repeatedly by millions of children, the *Star Wars* movies were set in a particular time—a media moment in the fast capitalism of modern entertainment (that could be repeated in rereleases in theaters and on TV as well as on VCR/DVD copies), not a socioeconomic era. This was even truer of a new spate of TV action cartoons that, like *Star Wars*, spun off action figures and play sets: He-Man and the Masters of the Universe and the Transformers appeared in 1983, followed by the Dino Riders and the Teenage Mutant Ninja Turtles in 1988. It is toys like these, taken from the media moments of a generation ago, that draw the Gen-Xers to today's toy shows. Tomorrow's shows will be different. Fathers and sons may strive for shared obsessions (as evidenced by the Pittsburgh toy show above), but the narrow duration of the media moment of each fad limits cross-generational sharing.[15]

The girl's story after 1960 differed in many ways. In 1959, Ruth Handler of Mattel introduced a doll in Barbie that has dominated girls' play worlds over the past half-century far more thoroughly than did G.I. Joe. Handler found that when she abandoned mothers' memories of their own dolls and images of the ideal child, she could appeal directly to the modern girl's fantasy of freedom and fun. Barbie liberated the girl's play from maternal standards and introduced her to the wider world of peer consumerism.[16] Barbie continually changed her wardrobe, furnishings, vehicles, and "friends," resulting in a rich array of novelty for successive generations of girls. All this created an endless demand for Mattel's Barbie products, taking the doll line (as tentatively practiced in the Patsy dolls of the 1920s) to new heights of fast-capitalism sophistication. Even when she faced competition from Jem/Jerrica, Bratz, and the American Girl collection,[17] these doll lines too (eventually) imitated the Barbie model.[18]

These toys and dolls continuously changed and thus marked time. Though many to an adult's eyes seem similar, to the eight-year-old boy in 1990, the Turtles were cool and the He-Man of six or seven years earlier was dumb. Of course, the Lincoln logs and baby dolls of the early twentieth century survived for years. The Fort Apache play set, Louis Marx's soldier and Indian set, was sold in Sears's catalogs from 1953 to 1977. But these long-lasting playthings seldom inspire collectors. They don't identify any particular individual or any particular point in time because they crossed the years unchanged. Modern nostalgia segments the past because the rapidly changing world of toys has separated six-year-olds from eight-year-olds repeatedly since the 1960s.[19]

The increasingly speedy turnover of kids' stuff, thanks to the emergence of fast capitalism at the end of the nineteenth century and the continued divisions between girls' and boys' play(things), has had a long-term effect. A generation or more after first appearing in American toy boxes, these playthings divided collectors of childhood memories and even made them disdainful of one another. Moreover, in recent years, as I saw at Pittsburgh, the impulse has shifted from recollecting material memories of childhood in middle age to never abandoning that culture from childhood on. All this makes the worlds of both doll and toy collecting similar, but, still, differences remain. Let's take a closer look, by focusing first on collectors of girls' dolls and then on boys' toys.

THE CURIOUS MEANINGS OF DOLLS

Collectors do something unusual. They remove objects from where they were intended to be used and display them in a market and culture often very different. Doll collectors remove their prizes from the playful world of childhood and often imagine themselves to be art and history curators—as well as savvy speculative merchants. Nevertheless, for many collectors, dolls evoke feelings of nurture, emotions encouraged by mothers in their daughters' doll play.

Dolls, especially when collected by adult women, evoke astonishing and diverse emotional reactions from others: disdain, pity, and even disgust from most men and many (especially young and/or professional) women. Men as boys often belittled or even defaced and "tortured" their sisters' dolls. "Sophisticated" adults—men, but also women—have long associated dolls with "primitives" and today's doll collector with a pathetic effort to compensate for an emotional loss or simply with a desire to regress into a fantasy child's world. But, as the anthropologist A. F. Robertson notes in his extraordinary study of collector dolls, "The life of the doll and the child are intertwined, laying down complex layers of sensation and significance, from the erotic and maternal to the guilty and aggressive."[20]

One way of getting at this complexity is by examining the doll magazine. Like their toy-magazine counterparts, these periodicals offer readers guides to prices and information about clubs, conventions, and doll museums; they also feature the "histories" of various dolls. Typically included in magazines (*Doll Reader, Doll News, Antique Doll Collector, Doll World*) are articles on the origins of Ginny dolls, the range of Hollywood collectors' dolls from the 1970s, and the art of Mexican wax dolls.[21] Articles are specialized but often written in personal, affectionate tones, sometimes recounting the author's memories of loving a particular doll, losing it, and getting it back as an adult.[22]

Collecting these effigies of childhood has also often been fostered by people with strong personalities and unusual resources. Take, for example, Margaret Woodbury Strong, the daughter of J. C. Woodbury, a major investor in Kodak and other Rochester,

New York, enterprises, who, when she was widowed in 1958, devoted her energy and fortune to creating a "museum of fascination" based on the domestic goods and ephemera of the period between 1820 to 1930 and concentrating heavily on dolls. She had gathered about twenty-five thousand dolls by the time of her death in 1969. This extraordinary collection forms the heart of the Margaret Woodbury Strong Museum, which opened in 1982 and which today is a museum of play known simply as the Strong. Smaller and often ephemeral doll museums and exhibits sprang up from the 1950s. These included Greenwell's Antique Doll Museum of Florida, the New Britain Youth Museum (Connecticut), and doll wings of the Old Slater Mill Museum in Pawtucket, Rhode Island, and the Wenham Museum in suburban Boston. "Doll hospitals," shops for the repair and restoration of antique dolls, served an emerging collecting community at midcentury. The link between collector and private museum has long been strong as doll enthusiasts seek public recognition of their treasures and ways of displaying personal collections. Still, few enjoyed the endowment level of the Strong, and many closed after a few years.[23]

The heyday of modern American doll collecting began in the late 1930s and was organized nationally with the founding of the United Federation of Doll Clubs (UFDC), which has held annual conventions since 1950. The predecessor of the UFDC was founded in New York City in 1937, and scattered reference works by folklorists and craft advocates concerning doll making and collecting were published from the 1930s. The authoritative work by Dorothy Coleman and her daughters, *The Collector's Encyclopedia of Dolls*, published in 1968, is the culmination of this generation of collectors.[24]

Early doll clubbers did not openly and single-mindedly celebrate their nostalgia in the way that many do today. Mary E. Lewis, Janet Johl, Nita Loving, and other UFDC officials from the 1950s seem to have been typical white middle-class club women, free of career obligations and able to devote themselves to their hobby and to charity. Lewis, the founder of the UFDC, announced to the second annual convention that the group "promotes good will and advances the science of doll collecting through study and research." Johl called collecting an opportunity to "work for a better understanding among the peoples of the earth" and to "show the values and the privileges of freedom." From the beginning, UFDC members held doll shows to raise money for child welfare programs and to distribute small dolls and toys to the needy; they also offered parties for poor and disabled children.[25] The clubs continue a tradition of charity (now raising money today for battered women's shelters or providing dolls for orphans of victims of AIDS in Africa).[26] All this fits a pattern dating back to Victorian America, when relatively privileged women with time and money formed social groups that combined an artistic interest with charitable activities. But the UFDC went beyond the status-seeking goal of collecting rarities and bourgeois noblesse oblige. Despite the "grown-up" tone of its publications, the *UFDC Convention Journal* (1959) still expressed a common sentiment. Although a doll is a "little girl's dream come true," when she casts it off, the doll "waits patiently for she knows she'll be needed some day" when a grandmother will collect her for "the lonely days that come and go."[27]

The traditional doll collector at times expressed an almost religious feeling for the sacredness of the child and doll, an emotion rooted in romantic ideas from the early nineteenth century. In the 1980s, the personal stories of doll collectors and their childhood "first loves" with dolls were common in UFDC convention programs. For example, the 1986 convention featured a photo of the president when she was three years old holding her long-lost "Rena Marie" doll. The caption beneath was telling: "Oh, wouldn't it be fun to be a child again and enjoy the wonder of childhood?" This and other images of dolls and the little girls holding them were vehicles "for triggering a whole range of memories and emotions," writes another UFDC member, Dare Boles: "Seeds of shared childhood are in every photo. . . . We really do know these children of another time and place—they're just us in different guises at different stages of life."[28]

This curious evocation of the universality and thus sacred wonder of childhood echoes the romantic spirit of William Wordsworth in his famous poem of 1804: "Trailing clouds of glory do we come from God who is our home: Heaven lies about us in our infancy!" Yet Wordsworth laments that the divinity of youth soon fades away.[29] For the doll collector, it can be recaptured.

Still, the UFDC has tempered these personal sentiments with a devotion to preservation. Throughout its history, the federation has upheld the superiority of dolls made before 1945. Many members prefer French china dolls dating from as early as the 1850s. The UFDC's house journal, *Doll News*, regularly has featured late-Victorian dolls and their makers (Jumeau, Marseille, and Bru, for example). An article on the famous Tony doll of the Ideal Company (from the early 1950s) appears only in 1996. The previous year, a survey of preferences of UFDC members found that 76.8 percent favored antique dolls, but only 53 percent liked modern dolls, and of these 36 percent preferred "modern" dolls before 1960.[30] Although most UFDC collectors are too old for Barbie, nevertheless, contradicting my expectations, many of them don't favor dolls of their own childhoods but prefer far older ones.[31] These antiques, of course, enjoy the patina of heritage and antiquity, but they also represent a culture that these collectors associate with the ideal childhood that they wish they had.

Closely related to the antique doll is the porcelain collector doll (PCD), which were copies of Victorian fashion and early-twentieth-century companion dolls. A market for these dolls appeared in the early 1970s. Appearing quite naturally as rising costs of antiques priced many would-be buyers out of the market for "original" dolls, the PCD also offered women the representation of a dependent child. PCDs captured both the style of the past and the "timeless innocence" of childhood. In fact, PCDs were often "better" than their antique sisters because they were more realistic (made of porcelain, a material that produced a more exacting replica of the "ideal" child's complexion and expression), especially when compared with the now-aged composition or hard plastic dolls that date from the 1920s and 1930s. By 1983 there were already thirty rival manufacturers of PCDs (including makers of commemorative coins like the Danbury Mint). These manufacturers grossed $7.6 billion in 1993, compared to $30 million a decade earlier.[32]

Advertised as a cute and irresistible addition to the family as well as a wise investment, (at average prices of $108 by 2003), these dolls combined emotion, status, and financial value. Manufacturers successfully employed the sales tactic of "line extension" by promoting "families" of dolls and theme sets to encourage multiple purchases.[33] Advertisers of PCDs used an appeal to the supposed "neediness" of these dolls to attract empty-nest mothers seeking an emotional reconnection with memories of infant care or with recollections of childhood doll nurturing. This approach also won sales from childless women, who later in life may regret not having experienced motherhood at first hand. Three-dimensional and poseable dolls provided expressions of iconic moments of childhood—"A Christmas Prayer" (featuring a five-year-old girl doll dressed in a nightgown and on her knees), "My First Tooth," and "I'm a Big Boy Now!" (posed for toilet training).[34] All this "neediness" in the dolls has appealed to women who feel the need to be needed. After all, an American woman born in 1951 can expect to live fifty-two years after the birth of her last child and twenty-five years after the birth of her last grandchild. The PCDs give women permission to do what children do: personify effigies and project dependency on them. These dolls provide their owners with narratives of mommy care by inviting purchasers to talk to their dolls and make them family.[35]

PCDs look lifelike but escape the truth of life that change is unavoidable and youth and childhood fleeting. In fact, these dolls represent "children who were never born and children who have grown up." An extreme variation is the My Twinn doll (1998), which offered collectors custom-made replicas of themselves as children (fashioned from a personal picture provided by the purchaser). This curious appeal to nostalgia but also narcissism confirms Robertson's thesis: "denial of mortality seemed to be central to the passion for dolls."[36]

BARBIE'S "GIRLS"

Most doll collecting seems to recall a childhood and nurturing past, and it certainly attracted adult women born before the 1960s. But perhaps something has changed in the rising cohort of the nostalgic collector.

An early marker of this generational break is the Modern Doll Convention, initiated in 1979 by younger enthusiasts whose childhoods were filled not with Madame Alexander dolls from the 1920s on but with Ginny dolls from the 1950s and, later, Barbies. In 1984 the UFDC finally established a modern doll division (dolls manu-factured after 1945) and appointed A. Glenn Mandeville, an advo-cate for collecting Ginny and Barbie, as the judge in show competi-tion. This was a long time coming. Though Mattel had advertised in UFDC publications as early as 1971, the federation was reluctant to embrace Barbie (even publishing an article in 1974 that aired com-mon critiques of Barbie as a threat to girls' creativity and for rush-ing girls too soon into sexuality). And, while *Doll News* occasionally featured Barbie and other modern fashion dolls from the 1980s, clearly the majority of doll collectors in this "establishment" group continued to favor more traditional dolls.[37] And, interestingly, key players in publishing "professional" articles about these modern dolls (including eventually Barbie) were men, such as A. Glenn Mandeville and John Axe. Nevertheless, the dominance of the "golden age" of antique dolls was beginning to be challenged.[38]

Ginny represented a transition as a fashion doll, but she still remained in the companion-doll mold. However, Barbie took doll collecting (as it did doll play) in a new direction. Barbie was dif-ferent from the childlike dolls of the past. As we have seen, she was an adult and, even more, an independent and infinitely self-transforming fashion model and ardent consumer. The opinion of one of Robertson's research assistants is revealing: "Barbie is a sol-itary individual, missing ties to both past and future. . . . Barbie's boyfriend Ken and little sister Skipper are mere accessories, and her relations with them vague and insubstantial. Barbie switches roles and identities with breathless ease, astronaut one minute, doctor the next, all with a change of clothes."[39]

Adult Barbie collecting can be like the Barbie play of children; it is centered on acts of fantasy living through Barbie's freedom as a consumer. Barbie collector conventions are not just about buy-ing, selling, and collecting Barbies (though the 2011 convention included esoteric workshops on identifying "Ponytail Barbies" and the various looks of Ken) but also about *becoming* Barbie—dressing as and partying to a Barbie theme. In 2011, the convention's theme was "Barbie® and Ken® Spring Break 1961" (the convention was held in Ft. Lauderdale). Included in the events was a birthday party for Ken. The convention website encouraged participants to "Dress to impress in your favorite party gear. You can select a Ken® doll fashion from your favorite era or maybe coordinate with someone else to come as Barbie® and Ken® dolls in those wonderful coordinating outfits."[40] In 2014, the convention was called "Every Day's a Holiday with Barbie®," with a pronounced pitch toward consumerism: "You can shop 'til you drop in the Presidents' Day Salesroom" or "stock up on the unique, ultra-limited souvenirs in the Memorial Day Souvenir Shop."[41]

The Barbie generation is certainly large, or at least potentially so. Not only did 90 percent of American girls five to eleven years of age own at least one Barbie in 1974, but Barbie fan clubs had been larger than any other girls' club (other than the Girl Scouts) in the early 1970s.[42] Unlike the nurturing memories of earlier dolls (and the retro PCDs), Barbies were about helping "young ladies make the transition from pig tails to pony tails and on to the hip hop and retro styles of today," as Mandeville put it, a shift from dependence and "cuteness" to style-conscious teen. The key, he notes, is that "the history of Barbie is the history of style" then and now, for Barbie is about memory but also about keeping up. Moreover, collecting Barbie entailed more than recalling childhood. It was about high-end fashion realized not in wearing a designer gown to the charity ball but by displaying it in special-edition Barbie dolls. When the fashion designer Bob Mackie (of Dior) began providing stylish mini-clothes to Mattel, specialty stores began selling limited-edition Barbies as high-end collectibles. By 1989, FAO Schwartz had contracted with Mattel for the sale of "Barbie Doll Exclusives" for an upscale market (for example, the limited-edition "Night Sensation in Black Taffeta").[43]

I saw an example of this unique approach to memory in a conversation I had with my lawyer in August 2010.While signing a will and other papers, I mentioned that I was writing a book about nostalgia. My lawyer, a woman in her early fifties, launched into a detailed, animated discussion of her own Barbie collection, which she sets up every Christmas on a special bookshelf near her family's holiday tree. Not only does she have Barbie, Skipper, Midge, and Scooter (her mother didn't let her have Ken), but she told me about how she sets up her display in a kind of tableau vivant around different themes—one year, going to a football game; another year, to a pajama party (the latter with cups and saucers for cocoa, a telephone for the "girls" to call their friends, pillows, and much else). She was particularly proud of her outfit for Skipper—"town togs," a costume that she described to me in loving detail. In the middle of this, one of the office staff came in to witness the documents. And naturally she joined the discussion, which sounded to me, at least, like two eight-year-olds comparing their doll collections: one bragged that she had a Barbie wedding gown, the other that she had a really cool Francine doll. My lawyer is normally very serious and socially and politically rather conservative. But to her this bit of midsummer midday regression was anything but strange. The Barbie display "takes me back to the fantasies of my youth," she said. When she set up her collection, she "can forget about the 4 am calls from clients. What other way is there to get back to childhood?" At the time, I wasn't sure if these women were just having fun with me, putting on their eight-year-old selves, but now, after going to a number of toy and doll shows, I think that they were expressing a comfortable and comforting part of themselves, one emerging briefly from their adult, serious shells.

It shouldn't be surprising that doll nostalgia often takes the form of rehearsing doll play or that this play would differ across generations. But it is striking how different the nostalgic play of Barbie's girls is from their elders' goals of returning to early childhood or to motherhood. By "putting on Barbie," these middle-aged women expressed a seeming longing to reconstruct (or even hold on to) the fantasy world of freedom, youth, fashion, and self-indulgence that Barbie represented.

OLD BOYS AND THEIR TOYS

In the gendered world of nostalgia, mostly male toy collectors tell a rather different story than do the largely female doll collectors. One of the masters of early collecting was Louis Hertz. As early as

1937, he was writing articles for *Model Craftsman* about collecting late Victorian tinplated train miniatures, and in 1947 he published one of the earliest reference works, *Handbook of Old American Toys*. By 1969, when his definitive work, *The Toy Collector*, appeared, he represented an established tradition. He eagerly defended toy collecting from snobs in the antiquing community who defamed his treasures as insufficiently old and significant and even more from the "do-it-yourself psychologist" who mocked grown men collecting toys as "merely a retreat to childhood on the part of those with immature minds." Hertz insisted that collecting miniatures (vehicles and tools but also milkmen in Edwardian garb and even cartoon figures like Happy Hooligan) recaptured the recent past "as well, if indeed not more successfully than any other medium." These collections reflected an "appreciation of American industry" and a celebration of progress. While sharing with traditional doll collectors a defense of the hobby as culture, not regression, Hertz took a distinctively modern approach to preservation in his focus on date-specific toy novelties. While museum curators may acquire and display folk toys as illustrative of traditional artisanship and the distant past, Hertz desired only manufactured toys that closely replicated the mechanical world they represented and could be precisely dated and otherwise definitively identified. The object for Hertz and other modern toy collectors was to capture a precise point in time, not a romantic notion of an "era." Thus the miniature train became a collectible whose value increased proportionately with exactitude, rarity, and purity (and innocent of signs of ever having been played with and thus adulterated by time).

Hertz's generation recognized the rapid transformation of recent history and expressed the modern desire to recapture the "moment." But it is not just a specific time of manufacture that is captured in the antique toy but the collector's "time." It is no surprise that some of the earliest collectors of rare mechanical toy banks from the 1880s were bankers who probably had played with them as kids (gathering them in the 1920s when they were in their forties and fifties). In his 1969 work, Hertz insisted that antique toys had more than monetary value; playthings are valuable also because they are "the windows through which the child first sees and realizes his full-sized world, and toys mold the viewpoints and ideals that are later carried into adult life." Playing with erector sets from the 1910s and 1920s actually did spark careers in engineering. But this was not an endorsement of regression to that formative experience. Even though Hertz admitted that the "interests of many collectors frequently center on the toys they remember having owned or seen," nostalgia for childhood, he claimed, was still "comparatively minor." As if to ward off critics that toy collecting was somehow unmanly, Hertz emphatically denied that "real" collectors would "re-dress" their toys by restoring or modifying them, as did female doll collectors.

His book's purpose was to inform collectors but also to set rules. Collecting required "uncommon discipline"; serious participants in the hobby had to specialize, become experts. The object was not primarily to collect memories but to master a category, often abstractly defined by material (tin, cast iron), function (transport, guns), or country or manufacturer of origin. As a defender of a genteel tradition, he disdained those who collected with sight merely to future value.[44]

A far different perspective appeared forty years later in 2008, when Harry Rinker, an appraiser of antiques and collectibles, whose writings and media appearances make him a leading authority, published *Guide to Toy Collecting*. For Rinker, "toys and childhood memories are inexorably linked," and like Charles Foster Kane in *Citizen Kane*, we all seek the "Rosebuds" of our lives, maybe not the sled of Kane's childhood, but some toy or doll fetish. Gone is Hertz's effort to legitimize collecting as historical preservation or a quest for intellectual mastery. Rinker saw no shame in playing with toys at any age, and from that desire came the motive to collect. From nostalgia for that special toy sprang the desire to collect others, Rinker noted, and, with it, the thrill of the hunt, growing expertise, sociable encounters with other enthusiasts, investment possibilities, and, most important, a greater sense of self. What had not changed since Hertz's 1969 manual was the quest to categorize and specialize insofar as Rinker offered a comprehensive list of toy types. Gone with Rinker was the focus on Victorian and early-twentieth-century mechanical banks and trains that had obsessed Hertz's readers; he added categories like Disneyana, action figures, and TV-character toys, for which dozens of well-illustrated price and identification guides had been published, often by hole-in-the-wall presses from small towns in Wisconsin, Pennsylvania, and Kentucky.[45]

Hertz's personal history mirrors the early history of toy collecting. This craze took off in the 1930s, and with good reason. The generation of boys born between 1890 and 1910 was the first to experience modern consumer culture (the introduction of brand goods in food, drink, cosmetics, appliances, cars, commercial music, and, of course, toys). Memories of these distinct wonders of manufactured playthings became an obsession thirty or forty years later when these boys had become middle-aged men. They began collecting toy savings banks; miniature horse-drawn vehicles such as carriages, fire pumps, delivery wagons, and circus bandwagons from the 1890s; and the somewhat later tiller-steered automobiles, quaint delivery trucks, and especially Lionel electric trains. Comic strip–character toys such as Happy Hooligan and Andy Gump reminded these men of their earliest fantasies, and the naiveté of these playthings served as a contrast with modern toys. From the 1930s on, this was a slow-growing (and probably for many an embarrassing, thus secret) hobby.[46]

Most of the early and most energetic collectors specialized in toy soldiers and ships. Early in the twentieth century indulgent dads and uncles gave boys sets of toy soldiers made by companies like Mignot (French), Heyde (German), the American Soldier Co., and especially Britains (English). Later, these toy soldiers became collectors' items. The publisher Malcolm Forbes and his son, Robert, legitimated this seemingly childish pastime by displaying their extraordinary toy soldier and boat collections at the National Geographic Society in Washington, D.C., in 1982.[47]

Even earlier in 1970, toy collecting had grown enough to have its own magazine, *Antique Toy World*, and through the 1990s it was a major promoter of Victorian and early-twentieth-century toys. The magazine regularly featured the writings of Al Marwick, a promoter and enthusiastic collector of pressed-steel toys from Buddy L (quality truck, car, and construction-machinery miniatures from the

1920s) as well as late Victorian navy ships from the German Märklin company. A car dealer from Kansas City, Marwick's real passion was hunting for the rare quality antique. It was the "hunt" that was fun, and he insisted that "a natural curiosity for the origin and history should always accompany the collector of toys." Marwick and other middle-aged men in the 1970s gleefully wrote their own stories, presenting themselves as fun-loving guys living ordinary, even humdrum lives, who found adventure in trolling the back roads of rural America looking for that special Bing miniature battleship that was for them the fulfillment of a life's dream. *Antique Toy World* made room for Japanese robot toys (from the 1950s) and even conceded mention of "Disneyana" toys, but this traditional toy magazine mostly featured only the older and rarer Disney toys from the 1930s. *Antique Toy World* was the bible of the older and probably wealthier collector in the 1980s and 1990s who still shared Hertz's belief that collecting the miniatures of technology (even if wrapped in nostalgia) was an intellectual and preservation-oriented task. In this, they shared the views of the UFDC's *Doll News*.[48]

Whatever the collectors' obsession, these toys brought back memories of a particular childhood. In successive years, not only did the older toys (like mechanical savings banks) grow too expensive for average collectors, but new types of toys began to attract the next wave of men trying to recapture their boyhoods. Robot toys of the early 1950s became popular collector's items by the end of the 1970s, and toys based on TV characters from the late 1950s and early 1960s attracted attention by the early 1980s. Each consumer cohort (defined almost by the years that a particular toy line was sold) collected their own childhood memories. A toy expert could practically determine a collector's age by his enthusiasm. Who but men born in the late 1940s like me would be interested in Davy Crocket toys (a craze of 1954)?

Rinker is clearly more reflective than Hertz of the toy collector today and probably of enthusiasts since the 1980s and 1990s. Like the emergence of the modern doll collector (of Barbies or ball-jointed dolls), it is no longer childish (and for males "unmanly") to admit to collecting and even playing with the things of childhood. Moreover, the old identification of miniatures with steady technological progress has been replaced with the recollections of media moments of objectified fantasy. This describes the baby-boom collector of TV-driven toys. A typical toy collector from this era is Tom Frey, of the Pittsburgh area, who caught the toy bug in 1981 when he bought a Roy Rogers Chuck Wagon at a flea market, hoping to give it to his son. Naturally, in those golden days of *Star Wars* figures, his boy was totally uninterested in a 1950s toy based on a cowboy TV show. But soon the father was "recollecting" his own childhood rather than trying to relate to his son's. Frey filled his own toy box, eventually writing a column in *Antique Toy World* about "classic plastic toys" from the 1950s and 1960s.[49]

Many of these toys were manufactured by Louis Marx, famous for his practically endless array of cheap sets of dinosaurs, cowboys and Indians, soldiers, American presidents, Roman centurions, and medieval knights. These figures reached far and wide into the psyche and media culture of boomer children. In 2001, Francis Turner opened the Marx Toy Museum in the small West Virginia town of Moundsville, the site of a long-defunct factory that had manufactured an extraordinary range of play sets in the 1950s and 1960s for Louis Marx. On display are not just the relics of boomer childhood but also manufactured goods just as they appeared on store shelves. They recall less the experience of the toy box and more the shopping trip and the anticipation of the purchase.[50]

Also popular with boomers were collections of toy vehicles, especially Matchbox and Hot Wheel cars. In 1953, an English toymaker, Lesney Products, produced die-cast replicas of a wide variety of cars, replicas small enough to fit into a matchbox and thus cheap enough to be accumulated in large numbers by British and even American boys. Matchbox vehicles prevailed until 1958, when the giant American toymaker Mattel looked for an alternative to its faltering cap-gun business by introducing a line of miniature cars called Hot Wheels. Though similar to Matchbox in size, Hot Wheels featured piano-wire axles that turned the cars' tiny wheels quickly, allowing their youthful owners to hurl the cars across wood and tiled floors and on tracks. Annual model changes marked differences between one cohort of boys and the next. And this vast variety later provided the once child, now collector, with status as an expert in the esoteric knowledge of identification and appreciation of rarity in these toy cars. At a convention of Hot Wheel enthusiasts in 2003 in suburban Los Angeles, almost three thousand collectors (almost all men over thirty) paid a sixty-dollar registration fee to see and trade Hot Wheels for four days.[51]

Male boomer collectors abandoned Hertz's curator role and no longer were embarrassed by regressing into childhood. Instead, they embraced childhood memories of play, memories materialized by fantasy objects that were animated by characters and stories from the media. Of course, these men might have strong emotion-laden memories of grandmothers and caring (or harsh) teachers or coaches. But the rituals of recollection were less often built on relationships (as was clearly the case with doll collectors of the same generation); they were centered on very particular playthings. And again unlike the traditional doll enthusiasts, whose love of Victorian and early-twentieth-century dolls reflected a "timeless" view of wondrous childhood, these boomer toy collectors focused on the "media moment" in fashioning their nostalgia.

BOYS WHO NEVER GIVE UP THEIR TOYS

Boomer nostalgia for toys was still a recovered memory. Toys were abandoned by age eleven or twelve for sports and girls and later for career and family. Like the women who collect PCDs in their middle age, these men saw their collections as a return to a past that had past. But a younger generation seems to have introduced a new factor—a tendency never to give up their playthings. This I saw at the Pittsburgh toy show. When Jeremy Padawer said in 2007, "What I think has happened is we've been unable to let our childhood go," he may have been speaking for his company, Jakks Pacific (maker of a variety of licensed toy figures *for adults as well as children*), but his comment may apply to at least some Gen-Xers. By 2007, about a third of action figures ($1.5 billion worth) were bought by and for males over the age of fifteen. This trend began in the early 1990s and helped launch companies like Jakks Pacific and Mezco Toyz. The NECA (National Entertainment Collectible

Association) since 1985 has featured action figures based on movie themes like *Pirates of the Caribbean* and *Nightmare Before Christmas*, many of which were taken from stories appearing long after the target collectors were children. Mezco Toyz prospered with a line of *Family Guy* action figures, based on the adult TV cartoon, and with figures combining humor and horror (especially the Living Dead Dolls). Adult collectors may not (openly) play with these figures the way they did when they were children, but the act of collecting and staging action figures seems to continue from boyhood well into adult life. In 2003, Jakks Pacific added a new dimension to Gen-X nostalgia with plug-and-play TV versions of early video games like *Pac-Man*, *Centipede*, *Pong*, and *Asteroids*, which originally had been played on Atari game consoles back in the 1970s.[52]

The drive to "play through" into adulthood seems to characterize at least young boomers and the Gen-X cohort of collectors (similar in age to younger Barbie's girls). Brian Styles may be representative. In 2006, Styles was an owner of a successful software company with a wife and son but still was a nearly lifelong collector of Lego building sets. Though he abandoned the practice at sixteen, he returned to Legos at twenty in 1988 and by 2006 had seven hundred Lego sets.[53] Styles saw no contradiction. Why ever give up the joys of childhood if it doesn't interfere with successful adulthood? What for some boomers was rediscovered in middle age was enjoyed by some Gen-Xers without any wait. Collecting past fantasy culture might once have been a "utopian refuge" that required various forms of "legitimation" to transform what others saw as time-wasting activity into an art.[54] Hertz's generation and even older boomers held onto childlike things in self-delusion and sometimes in secret. Today, a younger generation can brag about it. Still, both boomers and Gen-Xers shared that "utopian refuge" that at least began in the "wonder years" of the six-to-twelve-year-old. In modern times, these are the years when not only is everything new but when freshness and delight is intensified and highly individualized by makers of playthings who know how to excite wonder and sustain desire. It's no surprise that these wonder years are recalled in fondness or never, or only reluctantly, given up.

RETRO AND THE DISAPPOINTMENTS
OF SHARING MEMORIES

Despite the pleasure gained by these collectors, it's hard not to notice some disappointments, and they seem to have grown over the years. In 1994, about ten thousand men showed up at a G.I. Joe collectors' convention commemorating the thirtieth anniversary of the G.I. Joe doll—or action figure. Many, often more modest, gatherings followed. One of the leaders of the "movement" was Vincent Santelmo. In 2009, at forty-eight years of age, Santelmo claimed to own "99.9 percent" of every Joe figure, uniform, accessory, and other piece of equipment manufactured in the 1960s and 1970s—all in the same mint condition: "My collection is priceless." But the appeal of Joes and conventions devoted to Joe collectors may have peaked by 2006, with the Joe Show of the New York collector James DeSimone, who had organized up to ten G.I. gatherings a year up to that time. The recession of 2008 and rise of eBay dramatically decreased crowd size (by 90 percent), and DeSimone finally abandoned this business in 2009. Santelmo too had decided to close the books on his hobby (and promotion of G.I. Joe through his numerous publications). G.I. Joe may return, of course, or take on a different form in the Internet age or in a later revival. But, like other consumed nostalgias, Joe may be a wave that has hit the beach. It will be just a matter of time before another wave appears for the following generation, but probably with even less lasting power, given how fragmented collecting culture has become.[55]

Toy companies have repeatedly revived old lines of playthings, both to sell nostalgia but also to win the imaginations of a new generation. In 2002, for example, Hasbro featured Mr. Potato Head (on his fiftieth anniversary), and Mattel offered a "Matchbox Across America" series (with a car for each state). That year, Mattel's Masters of the Universe line was also reissued for a retro twentieth-anniversary "celebration." A Japanese company relaunched the most popular toys from the Transformer line two decades after they first appeared. This was not merely a lazy marketing ploy to sell the tried and true (a motive behind the endless array of movie sequels and copycat TV shows) but an effort to tap into the nostalgia boom while simultaneously drawing in new kids who hadn't been born when the toy or doll first appeared. As the Vivid Imaginations chief executive Nick Austin, a promoter of retro toy lines, noted in 2003, "You get a multigenerational groundswell of affection when you relaunch the properties."[56] New versions of 1950s-era Radio Flyer vehicles were introduced in 2001, including tricycles, foot-powered scooters, and wagons. While designed for kids, Robert Pasin, a company executive, admitted that the line was intended to appeal to boomer grandparents and other gift givers who had owned Radio Flyers as children. This continued throughout the decade as other toys reached their twentieth anniversaries (Cabbage Patch Kids, My Little Pony, and Care Bears, for example). This suggests a "twenty-year nostalgia cycle that's built into the pop culture in the twentieth century," notes Gage Averill of the University of Toronto, as toy (and music) makers tap into the "vivid" impressions of those who were children a generation ago.[57]

These retro duplicates point to the desire of adult buyers to share their memories with the kids in their lives. These grownups try to regain their inner child in the expression of delight in their giving of gifts to actual kids. Toy makers hope to profit from this impulse. But does this fantasy of cross-generational gift-mediated bonding happen that often, and, if not, what does this say about commercialized nostalgia?

Perhaps typical is the response of the daughters of the journalist Peggy Duffy in 2001, when she gave them new Barbies clad in neon-orange bikinis and dragged out a box of her old Barbie doll clothes that her mother had saved to share with them—her memories of doll play. Not surprisingly, the girls were unimpressed. "They looked at each other, sharing something unsaid between them. It was that generation thing. We all felt it." Duffy recalled that she "wanted to pass along those hours of pleasure and somehow forge a link between my childhood and theirs." The daughters accommodated her for a few months when she bought them some new Barbie outfits, but without the same excitement that she recalled, mostly "mixing and matching the new clothes with the old, creating some wild, eclectic attires."[58]

Duffy was lucky: her daughters might have tossed out the Barbies, demanding Bratz dolls instead. This line, appearing first in 2001, had a vaguely ethnic look about them: big, almond-shaped eyes with heavy shadow and lips painted with bright gloss. Bratz dolls offered the same array of fashion and consumer themes as Barbie had done for decades, but to many parents, including women who had played with Barbies, these new dolls seemed suspect, even "whorish." Probably without full awareness, modern girls' fascination with Bratz dolls is an expression of youthful rebellion similar to that of early Barbie enthusiasts.[59] In another twenty years, the girls, who may have abandoned Barbie for Bratz in the first decade of the twenty-first century, will recall Bratz dolls not as the streetwise anti-Barbies that offended their mothers but as cherished memories of childhood, and their daughters might well look to something else in their quest for identity and independence.

But elders still try to win the young to their way of collecting memories. After giving a talk at the Heirloom Doll Club of Kansas City, in November 2011, I chatted with a group of about twenty women, mostly in their fifties, sixties, and seventies, about their efforts to get their children and the younger generation interested in their hobby. One woman declared that members of the younger generation "don't have the connection" with their elders' dolls; understandably, they look back not on "my childhood" but on their own. Moreover, the motivation of younger collectors is surely different from the middle aged. Consider an older member who started with hard plastic Madame Alexander dolls (from the 1950s) but, when she later encountered the dolls that her mother and grandmother had as children, switched to collecting these much older antique dolls. Even though she never met her grandmother, she "got to know her" by collecting dolls and making clothes for them just as her grandmother had. She seemed to think that she somehow enhanced her grandmother's memory by owning dolls that her grandmother might have wanted but couldn't afford. Her motive was to link with the past. This was no longer the case with the young. She and other members noted that younger women don't have our "downtime" because today there are "so many stimulants." There was room in the club for women who identified with Barbie and even the "interactive" ball-jointed dolls from Japan discussed above, but there was only one such member, and she was a newcomer.

The problem of winning younger members to replenish the ranks of older doll collectors has increasingly obsessed the UFDC. While membership grew from 7,263 in 1976 to about 17,000 in 1986, by 2011 club membership had dropped to 10,381 (and of these 1,333 were at-large members who signed up online but did not take part in local club activities). The mean age in 2002 was sixty-four, and a recent administrator, Teresa Faller, estimates that it was about seventy-three in 2011. Clearly, women collectors have less time and willingness to join local doll clubs (a problem shared with other volunteer organizations). Moreover, the leadership no longer consists of affluent homemakers with a lifelong dedication to club activity but instead recently retired professionals or small business owners.[60]

The UFDC also has been trying to address the other problem—the seeming break in generations where mothers and grandmothers today seem less able (or willing) to recruit their young to their fascination with antique and increasingly old "modern" dolls from the postwar era. Of course, they have found room for Barbie in *Doll News*, but then Barbie was a half-century old in 2009. Instead of trying to appeal to that young-adult generation, the UFDC has taken a different institutional approach: encouraging clubs to sponsor "junior doll clubs" for girls up to seventeen and to open the convention to girls from eight years of age, all in an effort to instill memories of doll wonder early in life so that it might be picked up again in adulthood. Clubs not only teach girls about classical dolls (no Barbies or Bratz) and the arts of sewing doll clothes and making dolls, but the annual convention has held a "tea party" for junior collectors since 2003. Club leaders, it seems, hope to duplicate themselves in the wonder years of today's girl, not to address the challenge of "Barbie's Girls."[61]

While I saw men sharing their nostalgia for Marvel comic action figures with their eight-year-old sons at the Pittsburgh toy show, the past is too personal and the cultural gap across generations still too wide for many to bridge. In this era of fast capitalism, playthings change too often (though they may well share common purposes) for kids from one year to the next to share common memories. This is one of the great disappointments of commercialized nostalgia, as the following chapters will show. Despite all the other things that divide enthusiasts of memory, their obsessions are not much ado about nothing but guys' toys and gals' dolls. They are witnesses to a modern quest, a return to a childhood long gone, a childhood in many ways irretrievable but still sought in the certainty of possession and collection.

2

Lovin' That '57 Chevy (or Whatever Was Your Favorite Car at Seventeen)

On a warm Saturday afternoon in June 2011, I found my way to the fairgrounds of York, a small city in south-central Pennsylvania, for an annual Street Rod show. Hundreds of men, mostly grey bearded and pot bellied, some with female partners, had gathered in groups of two or three around their prides and joys—restored and modified hot rods packed along parking lanes for easy viewing by strolling crowds. Some of these cars had once been raced on drag strips or even on public roads (as in *Rebel Without a Cause*), but now they are just "street" rods, parked and polished displays of acquired taste, often representing years of hard work and achievement. Few of their owners were under forty; almost none were black or Hispanic. Many have or had jobs in skilled manual trades, often in the metal or automobile industry. Some cars had been given cute names like "Driving Miss Daisy" or "Troy's Toy," simple expressions of individuality that sometimes surfaced in conversation in the form of antigovernment sentiments, expressions of a vague but hardly ideological conservatism.

The prevailing mood on the scene, however, was one of nostalgia—from the sounds of the Beach Boys' "Good Vibrations" playing in the background to remind all of a youth lost forty or more years ago, to the stories of serendipity in the endless hunt for the perfect car, to the pride in transforming a rusted pile of parts into a work of art. Until 2009, these shows were restricted to pre-1948 "rods," but few were actually restorations. Many retained, say, a Deuce Coupe body (a metal roofed, 1932 Ford V-8) but had long lost the original motor and chassis and had been transformed from an uncomfortable and underpowered relic into a modern marvel with add-ons like radios, CD players, cushy seats, air conditioning, and automatic transmissions. The body could even be a fiberglass replica without any shame felt by the owner. For street rodders the idea was not to restore cars to their factory-fresh condition. Their nostalgia came from returning to the look of the 1940s and 1950s hot rod, itself an ersatz creation: young men of that era had transformed ordinary used cars from the 1930s by "chopping" (reducing the car's height), "channeling" (narrowing the body), "raking" (lowering the front end or raising the back), and much else. Memories were evoked via the unique artistry of the rod; parked with the owner stationed nearby, the rod became a conversation piece, providing an opportunity to tell stories of the hunt for that rare engine or body part, to share the decision-making process in choosing this or that "crate" (newly manufactured) engine or even door handle, and to acknowledge the hours consumed and the skills displayed in the sawing and sanding of metal to give the car its distinct lines. The pre-1948 rule had excluded the long, low, and finned cars of the 1950s and later models. But, with the rescission of this rule, a handful of these beauties made a tentative appearance. Many of the older street rodders didn't like this intrusion, even though those daring few "modern" car owners (like the 1959 Ford man I talked to) were grateful for finally being allowed in. The more pragmatic of the old guard admitted that compromises were required for the rod world to survive. There was a vague scent of melancholy in the air as these men lamented that they had failed to convince their adult sons to follow in their footsteps, even though some sons may have taken up the hobby but with a car closer to their own memories (say a '55 Chevrolet, a 1960s muscle car, or even something sporty from the 1980s). Nevertheless, the average age of participants seemed to rise every year as older participants retired or passed on. Unless something changes, it is just a matter of time before the street rod is gone.

It's not that street rodders are necessarily that conscious or articulate about their culture. Tim, a sixty-one-year-old, claimed that he just "likes the look" of his 1938 Chevy rod and is proud of its 1967 Camaro frame (a good ride), new powerful engine, air conditioning, automatic transmission, Cadillac seats, and of how he removed the rubber running boards (for a "cleaner" look). Tim also admitted to owning three other rods as well as a Jeep, all of which he stored in his six-stall garage. He couldn't count the number of cars that had passed through his garage, even though a restoration might take five years. One of his earliest was a Model T, but he admitted that few men alive today could relate to them (having last been manufactured in 1927). Over the years he "graduated" to his dream car (the '38 Chevy). But each vehicle had a story that helped him mark time and feel that life was progressing. And subtly intertwined in his car memories were his relationships with family and friends.

Gary at sixty-three once had four rods. When I met him at York, he had none. A somewhat obsessive collector, he admitted that he seldom kept a car more than a year or two and has owned at least one hundred cars. In this he was but an extreme version of a pattern common to the American way of consuming cars. He admitted to being "easily bored" and was at the show "maybe" to buy back a street rod coupe he had sold four years ago to buy a convertible. As a teen, he drag raced a 1965 Pontiac GTO and wrecked it. Gradually, like so many others, he switched to "beauty cars" and raised a family. In 1997, then in his fifties, he got into street rods. Now, he confessed, he is less interested in them, lamenting that the friends he made in a dozen years of attending street-rod shows were no longer coming.

But Gary still identifies with his tribe. He likes the self-expressiveness of the street rodders. "Nothing has to be right."

They are not picky, as are the "experts" who collect antique cars and mock you if you have "even a bolt out of place." Yes, the antique car crowd is "book learned," but the rod guys will help one another, he said, recalling how, when a man's engine failed at last year's show, a crowd of street rodders helped him install a new one on the spot. This was a tale of a modern barn raising, of men with ready skills and an appreciation for the fixes guys get in willing and, in fact, eager to break the routine of the show with a collective (perhaps even competitive) effort at "helping the other guy."

Gary's wife, Laura, seemed to love old cars almost as much as Gary did, but for a different reason. They were a substitute for her kids, who had now grown up. Sometimes, however, husband and wife competed. Standing out in the crowd were Laura and Tim, the owners of a green fiberglass Model A Ford (1928) "themed" with the image of Kermit the Frog. While Tim regaled me with information about how, with his crate engine, his Model A could go 75 miles per hour and how he had spent thousands of dollars and hours over five years to make it all new, Laura took me aside to display her album of photos of plush-doll Kermits posed on the car at various shows.

Another common family unit at the York show was father and adult son, like Paul and his son Tim (now forty-three), the elder a mechanic and the younger a car-body man. Tim had lived at home until twenty-nine (not as unusual as it once was) and despite his having had a long string of "girlfriends," some live-in, he never married even though he now owns a house, perhaps to shelter his six cars and motorcycles rather than a wife and children. He admitted that "cunts and cars" have competed for his attention. Guess which won out?

Another much older man that I met later simply said, "cars outlast kids and wives." He told me a sad story of how his adult children tried a few years ago to sell his collection of fourteen rods (which he had begun collecting in 1953) and locked him out of his garage. Having been through a long series of marriages, for him, "wives are thieves." But he was not a Grumpy Gus in this crowd. In fact, he was somewhat of a celebrity: he seemed to know everyone who came by, and he topped it all off by wearing a well-worn top hat, a common affectation among street rodders. He owned a shop employing sixteen men. When his employees asked that he get rid of the Confederate flag decal on his truck, he agreed after his men said that they would comply with his dress code. All very guy-like.

I met this man in a crowd around a "rat rod," which, with its unpainted body and its seemingly haphazard cobbled-together parts, is a curious parody of the street rod. The crowd enjoyed identifying the oddities, including an old Coke machine panel for the rear door, "Southern Comfort" printed on driver's door, a beer keg in the trunk bed for the gas tank, a hand grenade's handle for the hood, and brass knuckles mounted on the back to open the tailgate. Topping it all were the words "yes, it's finished" posted on the windshield.

Although most of the rodders I met at York were working-class men, including not a few misogynists like Tim, I did encounter exceptions, such as Paul, a sixty-nine-year-old rodder from New Hampshire. He had been rodding since he was fifteen, when he chopped and channeled a 1934 Ford, but he sold it at nineteen to go to college to study industrial engineering. He estimated that only 20 to 25 percent of rodders were professionals like himself. Like so many others, he left the hobby when he married, started a family, and moved up the career ladder. But he picked it up again when his son (also at fifteen) decided to restore a 1969 muscle car, which prompted the father to take on a 1932 Ford—both father and son opting for a car of his own generation. Eventually the son followed the father's path, losing interest and lacking time for old cars with the coming of work and family. The car-based father-son bond was short lived. But Paul had no regrets, and, unlike others, he was comfortable within his consumed nostalgia, perhaps because it did not consume him.

THE MAGIC OF THE FIRST CAR

This was not my first visit to car shows. I've been wandering through them for years and have long enjoyed the variety of cars displayed. But this visit to York made me much more aware of the variety of people who restore cars and what their nostalgia for cars says about their lives, relationships, and perspectives. It's about much more than old guys going gaga over old cars. The car and its at times yearly redesign is a quintessential example of fast capitalism, tying successive groups passing through that adolescent moment of possessing their first car to a vehicular memory.

Often cars and their owners seem matched by age. At a small show in July 2007 in central Pennsylvania, I met a sixty-four-year-old man with a particularly beautiful '57 Chevrolet hardtop. As I expected, he told me that he had a '57 Chevy just like it when he was a seventeen-year-old, when he and his wife were dating. I wasn't surprised to hear how his younger brother wrapped his car around a tree; he had been trying to get another like it for years. A nearby farmer had just the one he wanted in his barn, and the collector pleaded with the owner for twenty years before he was able to buy and restore it. This is a common pattern: fixation on the car of youth and romance, the loss of that special vehicle, the long journey through marriage and family in search of getting it back, and a joyful climax in recovery and restoration in late middle age. The prize was not only the machine but youth.

I've seen many variations on this theme. In May 2010 at a small show in Palmyra, Pennsylvania, I met a relatively upscale early boomer (about sixty-four) who owned a black '57 hardtop Chevy. He and a friend who came by shared the same obsession and had joined a Chevy collector's club, which sponsored yearly tours. Members were issued a booklet that could be stamped for taking different trips; when a member takes the car five hundred miles, he gets an oval sticker to put on the car. The tours went to various landmarks and were conducted in family groups. The second man recalled being a teen: "I looked out the window and saw the '57 Chevys come by. What kind of kid had twenty-five hundred dollars back then? I had just got my driver's license." But he finally got his '57 Chevy three years ago.

While the Chevy clubbers seemed pretty social (with a hint of Boy Scout conventionality), moments later I met a Ford guy who was far more individualistic, though about the same age. Somewhat grizzled and wearing a top hat, he stood by his 1958 Ford

Edsel station wagon. Compared to the mid-1950s Chevrolets, the Edsel was rare because it was a stylistic and marketing disaster, and thus it had been manufactured for only two years. Of course, I expected him to realize this and also expected that he would tell me about how he really likes the oversized oval grill that so many today find grotesque. But the man told me his version of the oft-heard "search-for-one-car-only-to-discover-accidently-a-better-one" story. At seventeen, he owned a 1957 Ford, which he bought for twelve dollars from a cousin who had blown out the engine. My top-hatted friend restored it and kept it until a few years ago, when he "got behind on his taxes" and had to sell it. Last year, he was back in the hunt for another 1957 Ford. But seeing an "all-original" 1958 Edsel station wagon for sale, he bought it cheap. He knew everything about car restoration and offered me plenty of details about fixing the brakes and Edsel features (like the push-button transmission on the dashboard). All this was expected. But then he casually mentioned that his dad had an Edsel. I probed, asking him if he thought it was significant that he was following in his dad's footsteps, "graduating" from the 1957 Ford sedan he had as a kid to a 1958 Edsel as an older man. He didn't bite. Maybe his fixation on Fords was somehow related to his family ties, but all he said was that the Edsel "fit right in there" with his niche car, the 1957 Ford. He was a Ford guy, not a Chevy guy like "everyone else," and his favorite years were 1957 and 1958, when he was a teen. The car defined him and his guy group, a "community of consumption" with or without his father.

This pattern is repeated in different age groups at these car shows, echoing the annual model changes of the car industry, which produced narrow and often isolated cohorts of youthful enthusiasm and, later, middle-aged nostalgia. The next obvious group was enthusiasts of Mustangs and especially the muscle cars from the mid-1960s to early 1970s. These cars were part of an effort on the part of Detroit to appeal to the hot-rod crowd. By 1960, competition between the Big Three car companies led to three-hundred-horsepower ratings and by the 1970s to four hundred plus, true "factory hot rods." Car designers from GM went down to Woodward Avenue in Detroit to watch and learn from the kids cruising in stock cars with overpowered engines the youths had installed and modified themselves. In 1964, GM simply dropped a 325-horsepower V-8 engine into Pontiac's lightweight Tempest, producing the GTO, the first muscle car. The Chevrolet Camaro and Plymouth Barracuda soon followed. Ford went in a slightly different direction with its Mustang, a relatively inexpensive sporty coupe with a long hood, short trunk, and many options, marketed to young singles. Despite their success in appealing to American youth's love of auto power, these muscle cars didn't drive out the rods; instead they became a favorite in old-car shows when the generation that grew up with them in turn became nostalgiacs.

Men who had been youths in the early 1970s (when the muscle cars were entering the used car and thus youth market) chafed at the downsizing of American cars in the wake of the energy crisis of 1973. A decade later, now in their thirties, some became nostalgic for the four-hundred-plus-cubic-inch V-8 muscle cars of their youth, which they felt were the true symbols of the American way of life. And they stuck with them through adulthood.[1]

I met one of these muscle-car men in the summer of 2005. He owned a 1965 Camaro but also favored Pontiac GTOs. He had a visceral disdain for the then ascendant Japanese cars that so attracted younger men and proudly sported a "Rice Burners Suck" sticker on his engine, in reference to Asian sports cars. This militant defense of the American power machine was surely a protest against the decline of the American car industry (and manufacturing might in general) since the mid-1970s, when fuel-efficient (and many say better-made) imports began to triumph.[2] For the muscle-car generation, the gas-guzzling behemoths of Detroit without all the pollution controls and fancy computer modules represented not only their innocent youth but the golden age of American power.[3]

A final age group was born in the 1970s and early 1980s. There aren't many of these guys at the typical local show yet. But I met a couple of them several years ago who told me that they favored 1980s Japanese sports cars because of their fascination with the action film *The Fast and the Furious* (2001), which featured Japanese cars.[4] I bet they will become more prominent at car shows in the next decade.

GREASER RODS AND BOURGEOIS ANTIQUES

The main difference between old-car guys is what was hot when each of them was young, but there were also cultural and class-driven clashes. I opened this chapter with the story of the street rodders, mostly men of working-class backgrounds with pride in their manual skills and dragster memories. They don't much care for the "experts," mostly of more solidly middle-class origins, who prefer their old cars to be "perfect" and "original." Street rodders are sentimental about the look of the "rod," for many years favoring 1930s car bodies. But as I discussed above, that's as far as "authenticity" goes. The engines, chassis, upholstery, transmission, and much more are usually modern, and the bodies are often radically modified and painted in colors that Henry Ford would never have approved of (his Model Ts were mostly black). The idea was to combine old parts that "look right," maybe adding an REO truck grill to a Chevy Coupe, within which would be mounted a Buick nail-head V-8 engine.[5] This was not nostalgia for the pristine restoration but for the craft, wit, and individuality of the hot-rod culture of their youth.[6] Car nostalgiacs divide not only over different car memories; they also relate to these cars in contrasting ways. Let's briefly consider the history of the street rodders, the antique restorers, and others.

Street rodders trace their origins to the amateur customizers and racers between 1910 and 1940. Adding components and increasing top speed and acceleration eventually went together. As the historian Kathleen Franz notes, Americans reveled in their knowledge of and control over their vehicles, treating them as "personal technologies" by modifying and adding to their vehicles. This appeal explains the popularity of *Popular Mechanics* and *Fordowner* in the 1910s and 1920s, which were filled with ads from aftermarket companies, providing early car owners with add-on headlights, trunks, oil gauges, speedometers, and camping and tourist gear. By 1930, manufacturers had upgraded their vehicles to include many of these add-ons. But the impulse to customize and personalize had hardly disappeared.[7]

Instead, tinkering became much more closely linked to the quest for speed and youth. After 1930, used Model Ts and other mass-produced cars (manufactured in large numbers in the 1920s) were cheap enough for young working-class American men to own. In fact, many owners were teenagers. These kids sought not comfort or safety, as did the older, middle-class tinkerer, but rather modifications that would make their jalopies go faster. The "Ts" were a gift to the creative improver. Not only were they easy to modify thanks to their simplicity and plentiful parts, but there was a lot to improve. Their cast-iron pistons and weak connecting rods meant low performance and maximum speeds of perhaps forty miles per hour. But youthful tinkerers found that retrofitting a standard Model T with lightweight, balanced aluminum pistons and rods enhanced performance, as did installing larger carburetors to allow more fuel and air to pass into the cylinders. Similar equipment was available for the "T's" successors, the Ford Model A and V-8s in the 1930s. These became the first hot rods.[8]

Youth found freedom from childhood dependency and maturity's burdens under the hoods of their hot rods and in competitive racing. While the automobile has long been associated with the responsible male provider, it became so ubiquitous in America that in some forms it could also express a rebellion against that culture. This happened as early as the mid-1920s in southern California, when young men began to customize hand-me-down cars. By 1931, they gathered on the dried lakes that stretched across the Mojave Desert from Los Angeles to Muroc to race their high-performance Model Ts. In 1937, a growing craze for racing led clubs to organize the Southern California Timing Association (SCTA) in order to set formal rules. The SCTA organized competitive races. Another goal was to modify cheap and plentiful old family cars to give them a distinctly defiant look by chopping, channeling, raking, and much more.[9]

In 1942, the racing clubs broke up when the men were sent to war. But sixteen-year-olds remained, and during and after the war they didn't bother with going to the dry lakes: "Wild eyed kids in hopped-up jalopies" roared "up and down the streets . . . at dizzy breakneck speeds," *Colliers* reported in 1947.[10] These races were reported in magazines and newspapers in the late 1940s across the country. They inspired sensationalist films like *Rebel Without a Cause* (1955), *Hot Rod Rumble* (1957), and *Dragstrip Riot* (1958). Panic over dragsters led to numerous state and local laws restricting hot rods.[11]

However, returning veterans attempted to legitimize the hot rod of their own teen years. SCTA officials and Robert Peterson's *Hot Rod Magazine* (beginning in 1948) denounced street racing and promoted safety and cooperation with law enforcement. The National Hot Rod Association, founded in 1951 by Wally Parks of Los Angeles, encouraged hot-rod clubs throughout the nation that policed their members and engaged in local charity work. These clubs built special-purpose "drag strips" of asphalt (a quarter of a mile long with a timing trap at the end for single-car speed tests) as safe and sane alternatives to paired competitive street racing. *Hot Rod* and its many offshoots became commercialized, featuring articles on expensive "aftermarket" accessories and, through advertising, the companies that made them, promoting an increasingly diverse hobby that had nothing to do with foolhardy kids playing chicken with their illegal cars.[12] *Hot Rod* and the clubs nevertheless retained a rebellious streak, mocking the lack of imagination in standard production cars of the 1950s and glorifying the hard work, creativity, and skill of customizers. This set the stage for generations of hot-rod enthusiasts and later for street-rod nostalgiacs.[13]

Perhaps the most famous of these customizers was Ed "Big Daddy" Roth (1932–2001), whom Tom Wolfe in *Esquire* (1963) called the "most colorful, the most intellectual and the most capricious" of the car customizers.[14] Born in Los Angeles, Ed Roth was brought up in the world of customizing, beginning with his first car, a 1933 Ford Coupe, acquired at the age of fourteen. Like many others, he dreamed of making a living from his hobby, and he succeeded by painting customized cars and making "Weird-O" T-shirts he sold at drag races. He built his own often bizarre vehicles, like the bubble-topped Beatnik Bandit (1961) and the surf buggy Surfite, which was featured in the 1964 film *Beach Blanket Bingo*. These were designed more to be "cool" and to mock Detroit's conventional styling than to be practical. Dressed in outlandish costumes and with a signature top hat rakishly perched on his head (a fashion choice others soon emulated), Roth became a celebrity at races, shows, and in the hot-rod magazines.[15]

But when Roth hit his thirties in the mid-1960s, the hot-rod culture declined sharply, and Roth, identified with motorcycling and the Hell's Angels, was delegitimized: aging enthusiasts settled down with families, and younger men embraced other forms of rebellion. We should not be surprised, however, that hot rodding experienced a renaissance in the early 1980s. Men now in their fifties and sixties, who twenty, thirty, or even forty years before had been rebellious teenagers who had souped up and raked down Model A Fords, returned to the obsession of their youth. Too old and wise for the rigors and dangers of drag racing, they collected and rebuilt the hot rods of their teen years, reducing them to *street rods* because they were driven on "cruises" through town and displayed in old-car shows rather than at drag strips. Naturally, a variety of magazines like *Rod and Custom*, *Hot Rod*, and *Street Rod Action* (many of which had earlier served a mostly youth market), books, and aftermarket-parts companies served this community. Power was the key to the memory of youth, but so was the look of the old rods. This was the mostly working-class crowd I saw at the York Street Rod show.[16]

A second group, the collectors of "antique" cars, come from very different backgrounds, and their nostalgia produced different longings. They are folks that the street rodders at York derisively called the "experts," and they are, by and large, more middle class than the rodders. One of the best places to see them is in mid-October in Hershey, Pennsylvania, home of the Antique Automobile Club of America (AACA) and one of the largest sites for the display and sale of restored old cars and the parts that make them "original" again. The show has been an annual event since 1954, now on the grounds of Hershey Park, a popular theme and amusement park. The show offered 10,400 spots to vendors in 1999 and up to 250,000 attended, but the advent of the Internet has reduced the need for this most traditional of marketplaces. Still, a decade later there were plenty of opportunities to buy parts for Model Ts

as well as far more exotic ancients. Three days of buying and selling is followed by a grand parade of cars beginning with Stanley
Steamers, Rolled Dash Oldsmobiles, Hupmobiles, and the simplest
of one-cylinder horseless buggies from the beginning of the twentieth century. Following down the line are the Model Ts and their
now almost forgotten competitors from the 1910s and early 1920s.
Attracting special attention are the extravagantly luxurious Due-
senbergs and sixteen-cylinder Marmons and Packards from the
1930s (now called "classics") and their poorer but enduring cousins, the rare and streamlined Tuckers, Grahams, and Henry Js,
as well as more modest and ordinary Chevrolets and Plymouths.
Later appear the fins and chrome of the 1950s and the muscle cars
of the 1960s. Finally, the latest antiques (defined as being at least
twenty-five years old) from the 1970s, though these are small in
number, and many participants see them as merely "used" cars.
What all of these old vehicles share is their owner's obsession with
returning their automobiles to factory-fresh condition.

The AACA, the pioneer promoter of pristine restoration, origi-
nated in 1931 at an antique auto show (of cars twenty-five years or
older driven to the site on their own power). It was sponsored by
an organization of Philadelphia car dealerships to drum up business in the depressed car market of that time. At a subsequent
Annual Antique Automobile Derby in January 1935, area collectors disgruntled by the lack of prize money and the disorganiza-
tion of the event decided to form a permanent club of antique auto
owners, publishing a bulletin in 1937 to publicize events and share
information. This was part of the bourgeois world of largely suburban and small-town professionals and entrepreneurs, much like
the Kiwanis, Elks, and the other fraternal clubs that had flourished
since the mid-nineteenth century. The enthusiasm may have roots
in youth, but not in the sometimes rebellious world of the working-
class hot rodder. The first members owned an unusual collection of
Wintons, Waltham-Orients, and Oldsmobiles dating from 1902 to
1915, not Model Ts, souped up or otherwise. By 1947, the AACA had
formalized rules of competition, dividing old cars into four categories and eleven classes to distribute awards (a big part of the club's
activities). By 1952, there were eighteen categories to accommodate

newer cars and a more refined view of difference. After 1975, to adapt to younger collectors, separate classes were created for Ford V-8s, Chevrolet Corvettes, Ford Thunderbirds, Ford Mustangs, and even 1955–1957 Chevrolets, all reflecting the popularity of these models. Many old-car owners brag about their awards and claim that they enhance the value of their cars, but others see them as excessive, almost a nuisance, and even meaningless because there are so many prizes for so many "classes" of cars. Membership in the Antique Automobile Club of America was only 850 in 1948, growing to about fifty thousand by 1985, but the AACA claims that since then "growth has remained steady," perhaps reflecting the aging of the hobbyists and the rise of independent clubs.[17]

Devoted to rescuing the dream machines of their youth from rust and restoring them to full authenticity, antique car enthusiasts have long had a reputation for a detailed knowledge of their vehicles and a willingness to engage in the often time- and wealth-consuming task of finding the correct part for a perfect reconstruction. This group is much more diverse than you might think. At the Hershey AACA meet in 2010, I met a man of forty-seven who was a Model T enthusiast. I wondered why a person born nearly forty years after the last "T" rolled off the assembly line would be interested in such things. Even odder, he was looking at a 1923 Ford "TT" fire truck. He explained that his father had bought a chassis and part of a body of a Model TT dump truck but had died at forty-seven without having had the time to restore it. As a way of honoring his dad's memory, he completed the restoration. Inevitably, he took me through the details of how TT trucks differed from the regular Model T cars (gearing on the back wheels for uphill loads, a longer wheel base, etc.). Like other "T" people, he enjoyed talking about how simple the car was: the brakes were not on the wheels but on a band on the transmission, and the fuel tank under the seat, lacking a pump, sent fuel to the carburetor via gravity, requiring drivers to back up hills when low on gas.

The Model T, of course, has had many generations of enthusiasts and even its own bimonthly magazine, *Model T Times*, featuring biographies of particular Ts and their owners, advice on restoration, details on transmission and carburetor assembly, and reprints of Ford Service Bulletins from the 1920s. Much of this information is practical, but it also pays homage to the lives, times, and characters of these ancient Fords and those who loved them.[18] While the forty-seven-year-old I met at Hershey owned cars more "appropriate" for his age (Camaros, Road Runners, and other muscle cars), he liked the old Fords best. In fact, he had two Ford TT trucks and went on road trips with his two brothers (one of whom has a Model T car) along the back and coastal roads of Massachusetts. The old Ts, he said, are "fun to drive," but the tribute to the father of the three is also part of the experience.

More typical than the Ford Model TT enthusiast was a fifty-year-old Californian. He was the owner of a construction company, but his real identity was as a shepherd and rescuer of Mustangs. I met him looking at a 1964½ Mustang, one of the first that appeared in April 1964, months before the common 1965 Mustang and thus more valuable, he explained. His knowledge of Mustangs was boundless (including how to identify the correct match of parts and model year by number and what taillight assembly went with the 1966 convertible). At the time of our meeting, he owned four Mustangs. He had many other cars, and he claimed to feel no particular nostalgia for the Mustang (in fact, he noted that they weren't really very good cars—bad handling, etc.). But he disdained the street rodder's neglect of the details of ordinary nuts-and-bolts restoration. He had a sense that installing the "wrong" motor or part was a kind of defilement. And he would never buy a Mustang that had filler or other mere cosmetic repair to the body. Restoring the car to its exact original condition was for him a service to heritage.

The old-car books and magazines have long shared this enthusiasm, dedicating themselves to stories about how, for example, a 1935 Packard, for forty years untouched, was found in an Iowa barn or Brooklyn garage. Some, like Richard Lentinello, the editor of *Hemmings Motor News*, went so far as to say that old cars should "proudly wear their wrinkles" without any restoration. Their pitted chrome, faded paint, and even worn upholstery are a witness to history, untouched by human interference. But this is an especially purist perspective. Still, the quest for authenticity can be very specific: owners of pre-1935 cars with wood-spoke wheels take much pride because few have survived humid summers and unpaved roads. And for insiders there are a lot of dos and don'ts. Two-door sedans are "better" and thus rarer than four doors. Convertibles are highly desirable, and so are "woodies"—fine finished panels in wood, often customized station wagons.[19]

These biases were and remain common among the antique-car crowd. Over and over I heard men offer detailed knowledge of distinguishing characteristics of their favored car and model years (even when they often knew little about cars outside of their "specialty"). At the AACA meet, I chatted with two men in their seventies admiring a 1915 Model T, each offering bits of information about when the headlights changed from all brass to mixed metal and from chemical to electric. Having it right was crucial. A retired owner of a propane business from Florida was proud to know that his 1932 Ford Coupe was the first to lack five windows but to have a cigarette lighter. One of the functions of the Antique Automobile Club of America is to reward such diligence with prizes for authenticity.

PRIDE IN THE CLASSICS, BEMUSEMENT IN GREMLINS

The pride in getting it "original" was common with the men who did their own work, and it was certainly important to anyone trolling the car carrel at Hershey, looking for that "investment" in the perfectly restored and rare antique. But there were differences between the Model T and Mustang guys and those in the market for a Duesenberg or other rare and outrageously expensive luxury beauties, the "classic cars" built between 1925 and 1948 (though this term is flexible).[20] These classic antique cars and their enthusiasts form a third group of car nostalgiacs. Among the classic cars at Hershey were a 1936 Lincoln with a rumble seat and a rear side door to store golf clubs and a 1947 Packard "woodie" station wagon in pristine condition. (It had had only one owner and a sign announcing that the owner "must sell"—but also insisting on a $300,000 "firm" price).

In fact, the motive for collecting these "classic" cars may be closer to the tradition of elite antique collecting than to nostalgia for youth. When the Chicago financier Richard Driehaus bought a $410,000 Lincoln, which was customized by the famed 1930s designer Raymond Loewy, to add to his collection of forty Duesenbergs, Packards, and other antique cars from the 1930s to 1950s, he obviously wasn't buying his teen experience. He was affirming his taste for the unique, often Art Deco styling of such luxury vehicles. Such collections may also give the modern investor the sensation of participating in a tradition of wealth display, identifying with his forebears who hadn't gone broke in the crash of 1929 and who had especially enjoyed flaunting their riches during the Depression years. Perhaps it is fairer to say, as does the classic-car insurer Jill Bookman, that the collector's classic "represents his or her path to success." But love of the "classics" might also affirm memory. This was the case for a fifty-six-year-old executive from Chicago who said in a 2008 newspaper interview that "classic cars bring me back to that time when I was growing up. . . . It's the feeling you get when you smell cut grass or burning leaves," as he waxed nostalgic about the 1949 Cadillac limousine that his father had bought years earlier from the McCormick estate.[21] The affluent can be nostalgic too.

And many feel at least curious about the celebrity auto of yore. Such certainly was the appeal of the 1940 Packard at the 2010 Hershey show, a stunningly long and luxurious vehicle obviously designed for a chauffeur and elite passengers. But, of course, what made it stand out was that it had been owned by the movie star Cary Grant, a gift from the Woolworth heiress Barbara Hutton (famed in the tabloids of the 1930s as the "Poor Little Rich Girl"). This is a nostalgia several times removed from the memories of most people living today, but the car, especially the luxurious "classic," can physically embody the aura of the celebrity, especially the long-gone "star," remembered through endless reruns on the Turner Classic Movies cable network. Many today are nostalgic about the nostalgias of those who came before them (as we'll see again).

Certainly this distant nostalgia is part of the explanation for the continued interest in the Old Car Festival held every September since 1950 at Greenfield Village in Dearborn, Michigan. These people might be said to form another, separate group of old-car nostalgiacs. Appropriately located at Henry Ford's homage to industrial heritage, the Greenfield Village show is open only to cars built before 1932. Of course, the premium at the Old Car Festival is rarity. Typical entries were long-forgotten makes like the Northern, Toledo, Franklin, Falcon-Knight, and Jackson, as well as the better-known curved-dash Olds, Stanley Steamers, and Ford's N, R, and S models, which predated the T of 1908. Despite the cost, difficulty in finding replacement parts, and the struggle just to get these relics to run, owners seem to feel as if they are part of a heritage. They share in the "spirit" of those auto pioneers who a hundred years ago braved rutted roads and nearly nonexistent service stations to take their buggies for a spin.[22]

At the other end of the spectrum are a fifth group of collectors, devotees of the relatively modern vehicle, those built after 1970. Though fitting easily within the twenty-five-year rule as "antiques," older collectors (from Greatest Generation enthusiasts for the Model A to late-boomer boosters of muscle cars) find it hard to understand why anyone would collect those "junky" 1970s cars. This is the era of obvious decline in America's car culture: recall if you can those early-1970s "boats," those monstrous cars guzzling gas at eight or ten miles per gallon (the Ford Torino Squire station wagon, e.g.) or the late-1970s attempt to "downsize" following the gas-price crisis of 1973 that led to those not-always-so-reliable Ford Pintos and American Motors Gremlins and Pacers. But then, for those who were teens in the age of disco and bell-bottomed pants, these cars inevitably evoked nostalgia when they began appearing at the shows. McKeel Hagerty, an insurer of vintage cars, noticed that 1970s cars began appearing in 1999 at car shows. "Nobody could figure out what would happen when we hit the seventies, because they were really hideous. . . . They were the worst cars ever made in America." But this hardly deterred collectors of a certain age bracket. In fact, for them, "When it comes to these cars, the kitschier the better." Steve Green, a New York real-estate developer and owner of twenty-eight AMC cars, found that their designs were so bad that they became wondrous in retrospect. The American Motors Matador coupe, Green noted, "was known as the car that sank AMC. . . . It was the car that was so hideously ugly that it was thought to be a mistake." But he proudly owns the last one to come off the assembly line. Some might identify these cars with the energy crisis, Watergate, or the excesses of *Saturday Night Fever*, disco, and peach-colored suits—and want them simply because that was "their time." Others even claim that these cars anticipated styling later copied by the Japanese and thus are important artifacts in automobile history. But behind such rationalizations is the fun of watching the startled look of passersby or just of reconnecting to memories of the smell, sound, and feel of cruising along with disco in the cassette player.[23]

Through all the variation, it always seems to come down to this: these men related to their pasts and to other people through their machines. That these machines are often cars is no surprise. Automobiles represent (and deliver) power; they are mechanical extensions of the self that take men where they want to go. They fill the role that horses once provided many Americans, but sometimes now with four hundred of them.[24] And with the turn of a key and press of a pedal, sparkplugs fire, pistons pulse, crankshafts turn, and wheels spin in an amazing harmony. Acceleration and speed meant power, even if that power didn't translate into control over everyday life. Cars liberated Americans from the constraints of home and work, even if the car was used mostly to get to and from those constraining places. The male love affair with the car is understandable, especially when it is associated with that most romantic of times, the rite of passage from childhood to adulthood in America, which all comes together in the rituals of getting one's driver's license and first car.[25] These memories were recaptured in a variety of ways: some collected old cars and made them new again, others returned to that rebellious creativity of their youth by making old cars different through "rodding," still others identified with the unrestrained luxury of classic cars or the pioneering ingenuity of the first generation of car enthusiasts, and, finally, a few even embraced the embarrassment of

1970s cars because they were of their generation and expressed their aesthetic of camp.

These men are all individualists who distinguish themselves by their cars. But these vehicles also help their owners relate to one another and to the people in their pasts, even if not always optimally. Old cars make otherwise private men social. Much of this is in the display: guys showing off their creations or possessions, letting others know what they have done and how special they are. But car shows also offer opportunities for exchanging information about rare skills and elusive car parts. Some join with others in proudly being stewards of tradition or even in seeing beauty or fun in what others see as junk.

Sometimes the man's nostalgia is joined by his wife or partner. She may help him sand rusted car bodies or hand him wrenches while he is replacing a carburetor. Sometimes the wife's creativity parallels that of the husband. At a show about five years ago, I met the wife of a fifty-year-old man with a restored pink 1961 Studebaker Hawk. She decorated the interior for shows with teddy bears, handmade with baby Alpaca wool from her own animals on their farmette in central Pennsylvania. Another couple, displaying a 1955 Chevrolet sedan (with a bright yellow exterior and a purple engine block with pink hoses), took pride in the fact that they spend two evenings a week on this and other cars they own. It keeps him "out of the bars" and her "away from the malls," they gleefully observed.

The couples who "share" this mostly male nostalgia, however, seem to be older, in their fifties at least. Younger men seldom appear in the shows with women: at a 2010 show, I asked a thirty-year-old man with a 1948 Chevrolet pickup (including a hand-restored wooden truck bed) if his wife or girlfriend worked with him on the truck. His reply was that he was divorced and happy to devote his time to restoring trucks and other vehicles. After all, "cars don't run away." This chap seemed a lot like the single young man I met at York who had given up on women. Both lacked an "understanding female mate" and seemed less mature than their dads had likely been at their age. Perhaps the two phenomena are related?[26]

CRUISE "NITES," BENCH RACING,
AND BOWDLERIZED REBELLION

Whether old cars nurture or undermine the pair bond, they definitely help men relive the social rituals of youth. This is seen best
in cruise-ins. In many ways, these are simply more informal forms
of car shows, held often weekly in warm weather at convenient
drive-in eateries, which make their parking lots available in hopes
of increasing business, or in conjunction with small-town or
suburban festivals. Some are sponsored by old-car clubs. Larger
cruise-ins offer raffles, collect for charity, and hold contests (like
who has the highest beehive hairdo for the women). On an August
evening in 2005, a mix of fifty antiques and street rods ranging
from a Model A to a 1963 Ford Fairlane gathered around the Happy
Day Diner on Route 40 near Baltimore. Technical advice, as well as
memories of when they raced there as teens, were freely shared
before many left to go to another drive-in. Some inevitably engage
in "bench racing"—that is, where old-timers retell racing stories.[27]

Many cruises are held in small towns where mostly lifelong
residents relive memories. Since 1993, Payson, Arizona, with the
sponsorship of the local old-car club and business groups, has
held the Beeline Cruise-In Charity Auto Show, a two-day event in
April. Civic boosterism, no doubt, prompted the town of Tupelo,
Mississippi, to sponsor the Blue Suede Cruise, combining the
usual car show with vintage rock bands, appropriate for Elvis's
hometown. In 2003, the Tupelo show was held in early May in five
different commercial districts of the town to maximize commercial exposure of entrants and visitors. In Hastings, Minnesota,
a small town about thirty miles south of St. Paul, a cruise-in on
Main Street was careful to prohibit "tire burn outs," roller blades,
and alcohol as well as "hydraulics" (used mostly by Latinos on
"lowriders"). Such rules excluded "outsiders," especially kids and
"alien" ethnic groups. Other cruises were sponsored by local radio
stations (often those playing "oldie" songs). One station in central
New York featured a round of biweekly "cruise-ins" at the parking lots of a retro "soda fountain" and pizza parlor. The etiquette

for cruising has long been established: organizers negotiate with a restaurant—not a bar—for sponsorship. Success required rules prohibiting alcohol, loud radios, pets, or burnouts. To keep these events comfortably middle aged and to discourage the young from coming, cruise-ins often banned SUVs and mini trucks.[28]

More elaborate events include August Nights, organized by Reno, Nevada, tourist officials. Originating in a retro-rock concert held in August 1986, which attracted vintage car owners who more or less stole the show, cruise events dominated subsequent August Nights. Over the years, there have been auctions, swap meets, and even drag racing. August Nights extended over a week, usually in early August, in part to fill the gap in the gambling business during that month. By 2013, August Nights had become a series of programs beginning May 22 and ending on October 5 for those diehards who needed still a final "Show-n-Shine" display of their vintage cars at the "Fall Frenzy" held at the Circus Circus Hotel and Casino.[29]

Probably the biggest event is the Woodward Dream Cruise in suburban Detroit, dating from 1994. At first, it was a neighborhood fundraiser to build a soccer field, but the event very quickly included most of the towns along Woodward Boulevard as well as numerous corporate sponsors. Shorn of its lawless associations with street racing and bathed in the nostalgia of youth, the Dream Cruise has become a major tourist event every August. Much to the surprise of sponsors, the first cruise, in August 1995, attracted ten thousand cars and about one hundred thousand fans. By 2004 there were forty thousand vintage vehicles entertaining 1.5 million car lovers, turning the event into a carnival. With increasing complaints of public drinking and cars parking on lawns, the authorities cracked down in 1999. But, despite this and persistent conflicts over which cars should be allowed to participate, the Woodward Cruise remains a major event in Detroit.[30]

Today's cruises, like most nostalgic events, have a history. In contrast to drag racing (or illegal street racing), car cruising emerged as a modern adaptation of the promenade around the town square or up and down Main Street. Auto-mobile youth gathered at car-based places—drive-ins and parking lots—and instead of walking, they drove slowly, up and down a wide, usually straight street, ideally with many stoplights to facilitate opportunities to meet other cruisers or bystanders. The two principal goals of social interaction were meeting, flirting with, and getting phone numbers of the opposite sex (although in Los Angeles gay cruising became common in the 1980s) and encountering (mostly male) competitors for exchanges of boasts and barbs about one another's cars and their customizations. A few would challenge others to short races, often after the cruise or on a relatively deserted road. All of this is depicted and sentimentalized in George Lucas's *American Graffiti* (1973), recalling cruising in 1962. In 1964, as a seventeen-year-old, I recall seeing dozens of teenagers' cars on Friday nights crawling in a circuit down Riverside and up Main Street in downtown Spokane and feeling left out because all I had to drive was a 1956 Ford station wagon (no chick magnet for sure, unlike the much favored Chevrolet sedans of the mid-1950s). At the Library of Congress I met an African American librarian who had the same experience "proming" in a small town in Alabama. We called it "tooling the town" in Spokane. Although mostly monopolized by white kids, zoot-suit-wearing Chicano youth in their low-riding Chevys cruised "slow and low" down the main streets of southern Californian towns in the late 1940s, a tradition that was resurrected in the 1980s in East Los Angeles and that still survives on Santa Clara Street in San Jose.[31]

Although cruising took place across the country, here we will focus on Detroit and Los Angeles. There has been cruising along Detroit's Woodward Avenue since 1926, but cruise nights on warm weekend evenings had become so popular by the 1950s that the street looked like rush hour. A similar story was the tradition of Wednesday "cruise nights" on Van Nuys Boulevard, north of Hollywood in Los Angeles, with distant origins in the 1911 "carriage parade."[32]

The key nodes of the cruise were drive-in eateries. With roots in the early days of auto touring (dating from 1921 in Dallas and expanding dramatically after World War II with the arrival of franchise drive-ins like A&W but also independent hamburger joints), these sites became ideal for parking; conversing with the opposite sex; showing off oversized rear tires, customized tachometers and floor shifters, racy hubcaps, and noisy mufflers; and perhaps getting a cheap meal or soda. Kids from different high schools gathered at one drive-in or another. Locked out of bars until twenty-one, these places were the only opportunity for casual socializing. And because Detroit's youth easily found jobs in the car factories, car ownership (even of new cars) was easily attained.[33]

It's no surprise that adults might be nostalgic for cruise nights, especially when they have largely disappeared and thus can be romanticized. Memoirs of Woodward Avenue cruising claim that the era declined in the early 1970s with the rise of gas and car prices, the beginning of the decline of Detroit's dominance of the car industry, and the subsequent decline of factory jobs for unskilled youth. The key reason for its waning is that cruising threatened the adult community, especially because it contested commercial space—interfering with shoppers along the cruising route. As early as 1967, "No Loitering" signs were posted in Detroit drive-in parking lots. By 1968, popular drive-ins were charging entrance fees (redeemable upon purchase).[34]

From the early 1960s, commuters in greater Los Angeles complained about the slowdown of traffic caused by cruisers, and police worried that streets clogged with kids' cars would impede the movement of emergency vehicles. Underlying these concerns was the fact that auto-mobile teens were often unknown to adult authorities. Cruisers could and often did come from other neighborhoods and even distant towns. They could gather and disperse quickly. In the 1960s, reports of cruising bands of teenagers harassing customers at widely dispersed shopping centers as well as violence between carloads of warring gangs appeared sporadically in the press.[35]

However, accounts of crackdowns by the authorities in Los Angeles appear mostly from the mid-1970s. At least some part of this crackdown is attributable to the resurrection of the Latino tradition of "low riding" along Whittier Boulevard in East Los Angeles and the suburbs of Orange County.[36] Inevitably, as the authorities cracked down on cruising along one street, it reappeared on another. Auto-mobility made it easy for cruisers to shift to other routes. This led to a sort of "whack-a-mole" game: the police beat down one cruise site only to see the emergence of another on another Los Angeles boulevard. This kept going until 1986, when law enforcement used a new tactic, the checkpoint system, prohibiting cars from passing a checkpoint on a cruise route more than two times in three hours, a tactic widely adopted across the country. Although cruising has survived in some small towns, it has largely disappeared from the American weekend scene.[37]

Curiously, though cruising came under attack in the 1970s and 1980s, it was also during this period that nostalgic cruising exploded in California. But, as we know, in this form it was very different than the original. At the height of the crackdown in 1981, groups of men in their forties were gathering around drive-ins in souped-up old cars, not in defiance of the elder establishment but often with its express blessing. That January Dave Gibson, a forty-two-year-old chiropractor, organized the Orange County Cruise Night to be held not on a street but at an A&W drive-in for the first Friday every month. Posting a newspaper ad for old-car enthusiasts over the age of thirty-five who were interested cruising "like we did in the fifties," he received an overwhelming response: 140 cars showed up.[38]

In fact, the gathering of older hot-rod enthusiasts had been going on since 1966, after which organizations like the Roadster Roundup, Early Times, and '40s Limited (from Los Angeles), the Minnesota Street Rod Association, Mid-Western Rod Run (Wisconsin), and others appeared. The hot-rod clubs that formed in the 1950s were usually led by teens and young men and usually disbanded when leaders were inducted into the army or went off to college. By contrast, the new clubs were organized by men in their thirties, often married and with children, who had once belonged to these older clubs. The new clubs were about reviving memories of hot rodding but from an adult perspective. Members gathered for family picnics, swap meets, parades, and "Show and Shine" events in parking lots, where they displayed their chopped and channeled prizes.[39] As the *Rod and Custom* columnist Tex Smith noted, the old clubs needed to diffuse public hostility and so promised to stop street racing and curb lawlessness among youthful hot rodders. By the late 1960s, all this had changed: clubs now consisted of "settled family men" with money to equip "properly" the Deuce Coupes from their youth. There was no need for the defensiveness of the old clubs. "Now a fenderless '29 [Ford Model] A roadster is 'cute'" and no longer a symbol of teenage defiance.[40]

Several of these new clubs from California and the Midwest joined with *Rod and Custom* to promote and publicize the First Annual Street Rod Nationals (held in Peoria, Illinois, in August 1970). Out of this emerged the National Street Rod Association (NSRA). Unlike the National Hot Rod Association, which promoted drag racing and a wide range of often exotic vehicles, the NSRA favored customized but street-operable cars with pre-1948 bodies (but often much later and more powerful drive trains). By the 1990s, the NSRA Nationals were attracting ten to twelve thousand street rods at midsummer events. This success, in fact, led to the division of the NSRA into ten regional organizations, each with their own annual gathering in 1983. The street-rod meets consisted of "regular guys" who had often spent years in their garages piecing together old car parts in an effort to return to or perpetuate the craft culture of their youth. Moreover, the meets were supposed to be informal and family friendly. The first Nationals set the tone by including not a speed race but a Streetkhana. This was a revival of a skill and reliability contest (gymkhana) from the early years of the automobile and that adult authorities sometimes organized for teen hot rodders in the early 1950s (often called "roadeos"). The Streetkhana was an obstacle race, timed, but with points lost for hitting pylons on the serpentine course. And, like the Antique Automobile Club meets, there were a lot of prizes given, ("Best 3-Window and Non-Ford Car," e.g.). The second Nationals in Memphis in 1971 featured a turtle race, a greased-pig contest (involving women), and other family-friendly activities.[41]

Not surprisingly, the nostalgic cruise-in movement of street rodders had no time for the cruising movement of youth in the midst of its repression in the 1980s. A merchant's group on Van Nuys Boulevard in 1986 sponsored a "classic car parade" even though five years earlier it had pressured officials into banning teen cruising. Intent on not resurrecting the old tradition, the leaders still admitted that cruising was an essential part of what made their street famous, and thus cruising had to be included in a seventy-fifth-anniversary festival for the boulevard. But only the old cars of adult collectors were to be included, requiring an application and picture of the car, obviously with the purpose of excluding lowriders or other "gang-type" vehicles.[42] The officials, of course, conveniently forgot that their predecessors a generation before probably saw their candy-apple red 1940 Fords as of the "gang type."

As in so much nostalgia, the elder cruisers, who gathered in old-fashioned, custard-serving drive-ins to show off their 1931 Model As or 1949 Lincolns, had forgotten or romanticized their old rebelliousness. When they were young in the 1950s, these folks were greasers. Yet, thirty or more years later, they groused about how the young had no respect, even as they relived their teen years of freedom and romance through a car and the experience and things that went with it—the drive-in, back when a hamburger, fries, and a Coke could be had for about a half-dollar. Yet many still wanted to share their memories with the next generation. In a 1989 interview, a forty-four-year-old mother of two from suburban Los Angeles who met her husband cruising boldly asserted: "I have to bring my kids and show them what happened in my day. I know they'd love it."[43] Sure.

Cruise Night groups took on distinctive casts reflecting the age and social background of their members. In Milwaukee, they varied from the subdued surroundings of the antique cars gathered at a middle-class restaurant in the mostly white northwestern side of town to the more lively working-class Latino bunch in the south-central part of the city, with "lowriders" bouncing on their hydraulic pumps and speakers on their car hoods loudly playing rap and salsa music.[44] But behind all of the posturing and braggadocio, shop talk and sentimentality, competition, and class, age, and ethnic divisions was a culture that binds men and memories to their machines.

All this suggested to me a curious parallel: Halloween, long an occasion for pranks and vandalism by teens and young adults, had been bowdlerized in the 1940s when it was transformed into "Trick or Treat" for costumed small children.[45] In this case, though, the shift from the rebellious to the maudlin went from the young to old. Cruising, with all of its youthful challenge to authority, was transformed into an evening of middle-aged couples showing off the cars of their youth while sitting on lawn chairs, stuffing themselves with greasy food, and getting "lost in the fifties."

But it may be all too easy to reduce this to a social or cultural analysis. There was something poignant about nostalgic cruisers and their quest. At the end of my visit to the York street-rod event, I came upon a family group— elder parents, their fiftyish-year-old son, and his wife, about the same age. I asked the wife what she thought of the rods; she said that they were "dumb," admitting, of course, that she had one in her family garage. I figured that she was one of those put-up-with-the-boy-man-to-keep-him-out-of-trouble types, and she admitted as much. But she went on to say something else—how she hated the changes that had come to the street-rod culture that she and her family had known for many years. She lamented the passing of the family games of volleyball and horseshoes that took place in the evenings as entrants camped out at the site (a custom gone four years earlier). She talked about how much fun it was to go to the cruise-ins nearly every weekend in the summer at well-known local drive-ins like the Red Rabbit and the Tropical Breeze. The street-rod shows, she complained, had become more commercialized. The granddad chimed in that he hated the new guys who didn't know cars, hired out the work, and ordered parts on the Internet. He had been hot rodding since 1957, when he was a teenager and still had a 1937 Ford rod. But he resented the changes. The old swap meets had disappeared. He especially hated the new rule that let in post-1948 cars. Cars with fins couldn't be rods! All this, of course, is the lament of the old-timer, a member of the in-group whose identity lies in the old rules of inclusion and exclusion but also in defending a tradition of craft. But there was more. The wife saw a decline of a family experience, the bringing up of her son in and around a tradition that had been passed from grandfather to father. However, her twenty-one-year-old son, after having driven his dad's customized rod a few times, quickly lost interest. He wasn't at the show, and the mother now wanted to sell the husband's rod and "maybe go traveling," though she had no particular place in mind.

This family saw a culture in decline just as they saw a break in a generational chain. I could have said something to them like, "in the modern world of continuous change, this is to be expected." But of course, I didn't. Instead I thought to myself how much this consumed nostalgia gave to this family and how much it couldn't.

Car collectors are tribal. They share not a common ancestor or allegiance but similar interests and obsessions, a common lingo, and mutual practices. That bond may be sustained by reading the same car-collector magazines and going to the same car shows year after year, but ultimately it is assured by possessing the "right" kind of car—often rooted in a common experience with the ephemeral and ever-changing automobile industry. Owning, but also customizing, was the ticket to belonging. What made that car correct was its past and how it was part of the collector's personal initiation into the man's world of vehicles. This loyalty could make "friends" of men who had little else in common (though different types of collecting reflected the different class cultures of participants). But it also makes for "enemies," those post-1948 street rodders who dared pollute the grand tradition, for example. The right car had also to be "authentic," and the quest for exactitude permeated old-car culture: the perfect restoration of the Mustang, down to the last bolt, and the reincarnation of that old spirit of rebellion and skill that shaped the culture of the original hot rodder. In a sense, the old-car scene is a form of "reenacting" reminiscent of those who put on the uniforms of Civil War soldiers. Old-car men ignore or even protest the fast-paced world they normally lived in by fixing on a sliver of what was once part of the almost equally fast-paced world of their youth. They found a way of coping with fast capitalism by arresting and possessing a moment of it in the past, thus making their obsession "timeless." Their cars gave these nostalgiacs ways of making their lives and relationships meaningful. Recall the man who comfortably saw himself as a '57 Ford guy. We must not be too quick to mock this claim of selfhood.

Yet we may also wonder if this identity doesn't hide and obscure a broader and less material individuality beyond that '57 Ford. Of course, many car guys weren't so individualistic. Many longed for social links through their cars—ties to fathers and old friends long gone or to memories shared with others who had the "right" car. However, these links seem to be less than secure, less than what these men (and their families) needed. This is a story of fulfillment and disappointment as people seek an elusive past, and we will see it again and again in the following pages.

3

(Re-)Living That Golden Decade

I have to admit that I have a bit of nostalgia for the 1950s and the 1960s. Were I thirty years younger, I doubtless would feel the same for the 1980s and 1990s. The 1950s was the decade of my childhood (turning four in 1950 and thirteen in 1959), and the 1960s was the decade of my teens and youth (fourteen to twenty-three). Memories of the 1950s turn around the things that my mother and grandmother surrounded me with: yes, a few toys, but mostly objects that expressed their tastes and needs, and those were very different: my mom's living room was as avant-garde as she could afford, being a single parent of four with a two-bedroom 1950s ranch home that she bought new: Danish modern dining-room set (and a Formica-top kitchen table with stainless-steel legs and blue plastic-covered chairs), sectional sofas, a suspended light with oval-shaped paper lampshade, and even a "butterfly" chair (black canvas over a wrought iron frame that some wags called an ass tray). She would have loved the living room at Fallingwater, built by Frank Lloyd Wright in the 1930s, but, of course, ours was a tract house with store-bought furniture. At Christmas, she sometimes had us children spray flock (a mist of sticky white stuff that was supposed to look like snow) on the tree, but as an added touch she tinged the flock with orange coloring and insisted on only plain globe ornaments. This was her way of updating the traditional green tree smothered in tinsel and garlands. I recall being grateful that she didn't go for the aluminum trees lit by a small colored spotlight from below (as was popular at the time). She was an art teacher and painted in the abstract expressionist style. So quite naturally she embraced what today is called "Midcentury Modern."

My grandmother's small two-room apartment was cut out from the front parlor of a fine "Victorian" home built around 1900. Even if she could have afforded to "modernize" her place (she was a laundress), she would not have. Her furnishings were probably typical for her age (she was born in 1898): formal dining set in cherry wood, ancient couch, lace curtains, and lots of doilies both displaying her skill at crocheting and covering worn spots on the arms of the sofa. Looking back today, her tastes were retro-Victorian, with all the dignity that a single woman earning forty dollars a week in 1958 could afford. Yet what I recall most about her apartment is the Sunday dinners of roast beef, mashed potatoes, gravy, and bacon-grease-soaked green beans that we ate off TV trays in front of her nineteen-inch TV set while watching westerns, Disney, *The Loretta Young Show*, and *Alfred Hitchcock Presents*. All of this too was very 1950s.

My memory (and affection) for the 1960s is less vivid. Oh, I was very much a part of the "countercultural revolution" (well, as much as I was likely to be, coming from a provincial place like Spokane, Washington). And I certainly participated (at least absentmindedly) in the new fashions of the late 1960s and early 1970s. I love to tell my stories about the triumphs and follies of being an "organizer" in the movement against the Vietnam War. But I have less of an emotional attachment to the smells and sights of the sixties than the fifties.

This is, of course, a very subjective story. But that has been a major point of this book. Memories are particular, and no more so than today. My strong recollections of domestic spaces in my early childhood may correspond to the simple fact that my life in the 1950s was more contained than in the 1960s. Anyone born a few years later (like my younger brother) would have very different recollections. And when I get nostalgic about the 1950s, I'm thinking of the second half, mostly (which merges vaguely into the early 1960s). And, the 1960s really begin (for me) in early 1964 (when not only did the Beatles rock America on the Ed Sullivan Show but when I was liberated from the horrors of high school). All this suggests that the designation "the fifties" or "the sixties" is arbitrary and ambiguous, yet it is somehow still necessary even if and even because we each give "our" decade personal meaning. In fact, nostalgia invents periods like "the 1950s," reducing a complex and contradictory decade into an image that says almost as much about when the decade was "invented" in nostalgia as about the decade itself.[1]

An afternoon meeting with a central Pennsylvania family in late August 2011 at the annual Grange Fair of Centre Hall reminds me of the power of 1950s nostalgia for many a half-century later—even if they sometimes have no personal memory of that decade. On the fairgrounds organizers rent 950 tents to families who gather together the last week in August to acknowledge change and recall the past. The fair dates back to 1874, and many participants can recall how this custom has been passed down three or more generations.[2]

The site, which I have visited for many years to attend doo-wop and other retro concerts, has a Brigadoon time-out-of-time feel about it, as if it truly is "lost in the fifties." Though it dates from much earlier, the 1950s seem to be the base decade of nostalgia today, in part because it is the fringe of the memory of the now dominant boomer elders. Of course, helping form this impression are the pavilions displaying traditional rural crafts and barns full of prized cows, rabbits, and sheep; the midway of traditional carnival fare; and the tables of fairgoers eating dinners of chicken, gravy, and waffles. But the most unusual and retro feature of the fair was the tent-dwelling families. Other fairgoers go modern and camp in recreational vehicles and trailers on the edge of the grounds. But the diehards insist on the traditional, uniform, dark green rectangular tents. Some fairgoers personalize their tents by outlining their open fronts with strings of colorful lights (a recent addition are lights in the shape of toy tractors or other themes of a fading farm life). Other tents are fronted with miniature white picket fences, and passersby can easily see the tent furnishings within, which are often surprisingly homey. While some use utilitarian garden and patio furniture, others bring dated upholstered chairs and carpets, old TVs, and even what appears to be the rocking chair of a grandparent, perhaps long departed.

The family that I visited went a little further, carefully decorating the tent in 1950s kitsch. The matriarch and patriarch of this clan were in their early sixties, lifelong veterans of the Grange Fair; the tent a hand-me-down from the maternal side. It was a work of love for the mother, Debbie. The dad had his own nostalgic hobby—model trains—but he was, of course, cooperative. Her display included the "essentials": plastic Melmac dishes in pink, olive, and peach; a Formica kitchen table; a turquoise-colored rotary phone on a phone seat and table combo; ceramic lamps shaped like panthers; Danish modern chairs; a display of 1950s women's hats and gloves on a screen; and even a hidden CD player adding a background of 1950s rock music. When I asked Debbie why she collected the 1950s, she offered a surprising answer: "because Kris [her daughter] likes old stuff too. When I'm no longer here, she can have it." Of course, these things still evoked a personal feeling, reminding Debbie of her childhood and of her parents and their generation. But for Debbie, that wasn't enough. Her fifties collection needed to be heirlooms—not because of their intrinsic or market value or because they had been in the family a long time (they had been recently collected at auctions and antique and junk shops) but because they represented her and her childhood to her daughter and perhaps later to her granddaughter. Her collection was to be a gift of herself across the generations, perhaps even a way of extending her life through the ephemerality of a presumed era that marked her identity. The Grange Fair tent and its decorations were the mom's projects (just as was her house, except the basement, where the dad and his extensive collection of miniature railroads reigned). Debbie had become increasingly skilled at her collecting, especially at reupholstering chairs and restoring pillow covers in authentic fabrics. She had her eye out for Eames furniture (one of the classy brands of the era) and had learned about the range of the fifties look by perusing vintage magazines and advertisements. She was proud of the valuable pieces she obtained cheaply because others at the auction were not as knowledgeable.

It is hard to say whether the mom's strategy has or will work and whether her heirlooms really will weave the generations together. The daughter Kris certainly marveled at Jell-O ads from the fifties and found it hard to believe that women really would make such strange concoctions from flavored gelatin. And 1950s kitsch provided an occasion for the women to talk about home and changes in homemaking. But the "boys" in the tent weren't much interested. The dad (a retired computer technician) was bored by fashion-dated artifacts, though he admitted that he might want to take apart the vintage telephone or explore how the ball disc gear worked in old mechanical calculating machines. The Grange Fair tent may be an extension of maternal space, in this case, at least. That certainly was the impression I got from watching Debbie sit in the center rear of the tent, as if holding court, as her cousins, nieces, and nephews and their families arrived throughout that afternoon.

As Kris said, "It's all about the family coming back together." Tensions between family members were minimized because no one was confined to the tent: the fair's carnival grounds provided a ready escape. Until recently, most campers came from nearby Penns Valley, but now with the decline of farming many make pilgrimages from more distant towns back to Centre Hall to pay their respects to remaining parents and renew memories that often date back to the 1970s, 1960s, or even 1950s. Debbie's 1950s kitsch and her hopes of passing it down are part of the hard work of keeping tradition alive.

I learned quickly that nostalgia for that special decade was a lot more complicated than some shallow fixation on the oddities of the past or even distorted memories of families and the "way we never were."[3] So let's look a bit more closely at fifties and sixties nostalgia, when and why it came and the kitsch that represented it.

RELAUNCHING THE FIFTIES

It is hard to date the beginning of fifties nostalgia, but conscious-ness of the decade surely was formed by media representations of it.[4] While the 1960s certainly produced disdain for the 1950s as an era of conformity, Cold War conservatism, and male chauvinism, fondness for the decade emerged by the end of the 1960s. As early as 1969, following an era of turbulent politics, social disruption, and radical counterculture, fifties icons like Elvis Presley returned to the stage in Las Vegas to sing before a middle-class, middle-aged crowd (see chapter 6).[5]

In 1972, cover stories on fifties nostalgia appeared in *Life* and *Newsweek*. That year *Grease*, a celebration of early rock, appeared on the stage and began a long Broadway run. It was only one exam-ple of selected and romantic recollections of the 1950s, especially of youth music and fashion and a focus on a handful of media icons: Marilyn Monroe, Marlon Brando, and James Dean (two of which by then were conveniently dead), were glorified for their represen-tations of cultural archetypes rather than for what they did or who they were. The 1974 nostalgia book, *The Happy Years*, represents the 1950s not as a series of evocative events but as endearingly sweet and even goofy, an America at peace with itself.[6]

Following on the 1950s rock revival was a series of sentimental films and TV shows with 1950s themes: *American Graffiti* (August 1973) offered a lament on the end of the lively but also naive cruis-ing and drive-in world of white working-class teens of 1962, and the next year the TV situation comedy *Happy Days* entered Amer-ican homes with a more sentimental treatment of the teen and his oh-so-understanding family, the opposite of the tale of youth alienation and familial dysfunctionality in the 1954 film *Rebel Without a Cause* and its many successors. The greaser character, the Fonz, was hardly the drag-racing juvenile delinquent or the switchblade-carrying gang member of 1950s movie dramas, *West*

Side Story, or *Blackboard Jungle*; instead, he was a harmless wise-cracker, cool, but always respectful of the parents of his middle-class buddy, Richie Cunningham. By the end of the series, he had evolved into a shop teacher and school administrator. The Fonz became the 1950s. Like many sitcoms, social and familial differences were made humorous or glossed over. And reruns of family sitcoms from the 1950s (*The Adventures of Ozzie and Harriet*, *Father Knows Best*, *The Donna Reed Show*, and *Leave It to Beaver*) reinforced the positive image of the decade as a time of wholesome, middle-class scenes—white picket fences, small-town neighbors, and ideal families—when kids were cute if continually confused and in need of bemused and gentle guidance from parents, especially from the dad.[7]

If music and TV nostalgia shaped sentimental views of the 1950s in the 1970s, the 1950s were resurrected more subtly as a "cool" decade, and the heart of this "coolness" was a series of new technologies that radically transformed the look of stuff. A lot had to do with plastics, so often maligned at the time as cheap and flashy. Though rooted in the 1870 invention of celluloid, derived from plant cellulose,[8] plastic would come into its own only after World War II, with the introduction of malleable but sturdy plastics like polyvinyl chloride (PVC, which is used as pipes but also a substitute for leather on furniture) gradually removing the prejudice against plastic. Melamine (for dinettes and dishes) and Formica (for table and countertops) made kitchens far more colorful and easier to clean. Key was the development of a practical mass-production injection-molding machine in 1937 for plastic that enabled rapidly changing and flexible design—replacing craft with a machine-based aesthetic.[9]

Other postwar advances were perhaps less dramatic but no less important: molded plywood, fiberglass, foam rubber, and cast aluminum—allowing designers of furniture to break from the traditional shapes of chairs, tables, sofas, and lamps to produce an array of space-age forms and styles previously unimaginable. The American architect Charles Eames was notable for molding plywood. Eames's armchair constructed from a glass-reinforced polyester (fiberglass) shell on steel struts was all the rage when manufactured by Herman Miller in 1948. Combinations of plastics, aluminum, and plywood offered extraordinary possibilities in molding radios, clocks, phonographs, and TV sets. The modern art of Mondrian and Calder inspired suspended lampshades in the form of mobiles and palette-shaped coffee tables. Meanwhile, the streamlining designs developed in the 1930s for locomotives and cars by the noted American industrial designer Raymond Loewy were adapted to home appliances like vacuum cleaners and refrigerators. The Finnish émigré Eero Saarinen designed cheap and comfortable chairs of molded plywood. Finally, Russel Wright introduced American modern dinnerware in 1939 with his practical and simple designs of mix-and-match colors, and in 1953 he produced his Melmac line of dishes made of melamine resin plastic.[10]

These styles were popularizations of often experimental and elite designs from the 1920s and 1930s that ordinary American consumers had once shunned in preference for traditional wood furniture and cloth-covered furniture, often in ornate styles. But in the "conservative 1950s" the consuming masses (though few from my grandmother's generation) embraced Art Deco's sleek and geometric lines, the austere and functional designs of Bauhaus and the International Style, along with its American variation, Machine Age Modern.[11] The success of these innovations was a classic example of fast capitalism: the profitable marketing of novelty and the consumer's embrace of change for its own sake.

Why was there this upsurge in "modern" styles in a decade seemingly dedicated to cultural retrenchment and retreat? To be sure, the upheavals of the depressed 1930s and war-torn 1940s induced Americans to be "homeward bound," as housewifery, motherhood, and male corporate conformity were extolled in the media and as the Red Scare produced cultural and political reactions to the avant-garde. The 1950s produced a *Reader's Digest* world of neat rows of suburban tracts and "the family that prays together stays together" sentiment that inspired the construction of family/fellowship additions to churches. But inevitably all this led to its opposite—a minority world of the hip and beat in literature, jazz, and dress (mildly manifested by my mother's taste). But the modern also went mainstream.[12] Tom Hine argues that the appeal was to a popular quest for the new and novel after nearly a generation of austerity; a lusty, giddy embrace of change almost for its own sake and the redemptive promise so often made at the New York's World Fair in 1939 and then repeatedly through the war that the future would bring new and exciting conveniences. As Hine puts it, by the early 1950s,

> the objects people could buy took on a special exaggerated quality. . . . They celebrate confidence in the future, the excitement of the present, the sheer joy of having so much. . . . Each household was able to have his own little Versailles along a cul-de-sac. . . . Products were available in a lurid rainbow of colors and a steadily changing array of styles. Commonplace objects took extraordinary form, and the novel and exotic quickly turned commonplace.[13]

This cornucopia was not available to all and was largely confined to the suburbs, but it reached beyond the comfortable middle class. The 1950s were not only a decade of domesticated women and corporate-conformist men but the era of the space race and abstract painting. And all this modernity was lionized in the mainstream magazines.[14] Even more, it was the era of popular luxury (Populuxe, in Hine's terminology), delighting Americans tired of austerity and enriching merchandisers.

Still, why should this contradiction of modern styles and traditional values and behaviors appeal to nostalgiacs like many hip merchants of 1950s' kitsch a generation and more after the 1950s? Part of the answer, repeated by collectors, is the charm evoked by the almost childlike attraction to the new in the 1950s. This produced a strange sort of nostalgia for an age when people believed in and embraced the "future," presumably in contrast to the jaded pessimism that followed and continues today. This fascination with the "past futuristic" is not limited to nostalgia for old science fiction or 1950s fantasy about future jet travel and space flight. It also was expressed in the allure of the "atomic kitchens" of that era, interestingly also sites of activity for the "traditional housewife." Ads for appliances and home-improvement goods in the 1950s promised the glittering newness of the "ultimate in Space Age modern convenience, ease, and beauty." At the time, this may have been an attempt to persuade women to return and stay in the home and give up dreams of fulfillment in the wider world, as Betty Friedan in *The Feminine Mystique* argued in 1963.[15] Still, collectors a generation later or more admire what they see as the "optimism that housewives held for the future" in the 1950s: the promise of liberation from time-consuming chores and for replacing the "stodgy old stoves and refrigerators of a few years earlier . . . with the color and chrome of a new model festooned with the latest features and doodads."[16]

This enthusiasm for the new in the 1950s had been fostered by corporate spectacles hyping the home of tomorrow. The Chicago Century of Progress Exposition in 1933 featured thirteen model homes built of modular steel, artificial stone, and glass; the New York World's Fair of 1939 offered glamorous displays of GE's streamlined all-electric kitchen. Disney's Tomorrowland in 1957 presented curious tourists the Monsanto "House of the Future," with its four cantilevered plastic bays radiating from a small central core, and the Whirlpool corporation set up a traveling "miracle kitchen," complete with a center console where menus could be planned, food supplies inventoried, and, with a TV monitor linked to cameras at the front door and in the nursery, home activities observed. In the age of the Cold War and nuclear brinksmanship, designers "took the button that everyone feared and put it in the kitchen appliances."[17]

Yet for all the stress on the gadgets and the mystique of progress in convenience and push-button power, nostalgic collectors look back on the "atomic kitchen" as also a time of aesthetic innovation. As one writer put it, "creative boundaries were expanded using wall-to-wall color, accessories, and spatial drama that appealed to the senses and provided a lift from normal kitchen routines." The kitchen was to not to be like a jet cockpit or NASA control room but closer to a modern art gallery or hotel lobby. It was to be a "comfortable zone" to do chores, a "suitable space for family and friends to congregate and feel part of the activities." And the formality of the long-surviving Victorian dining room with its breakfronts, cherry or oak dining tables, and upholstered wood chairs of often elegantly turned legs were finally replaced by casual furnishings of easy-to-clean but also comfortable modern materials. Even though Pennsylvania House, Old Colony, and Bassett continued to manufacture colonial-revival dining-room sets (which often inhabited seldom-used dining rooms, especially in more affluent 1950s homes and after), these are not collected (though they are passed down). Rather, the informal and often playful furniture of the "kitsch-en," with their Formica tops, chrome legs, and bright vinyl chairs in pink or turquoise, attract nostalgiacs. Traditional cream-colored china with delicate designs has been passed over by the new 1950s look of Fiesta, Harlequin, and Riviera ceramic tableware in bright and cheery canary yellow and seafoam green. Adding to the glistening modernity were blenders, toasters, and coffee percolators in chrome. By tumbling so much into the woman's workspace, once a site of drudgery and then a place of isolation from the wider world, the dream engineers of the 1950s created an aura of sensuality, convenience, and even familial happiness. They offered women "an adventure not unlike reaching for the frontiers of space."[18] This was promise of a carefree and happy future when Americans believed both in progress and the restoration of "the happy home." This powerful affective combination in Midcentury Modern seems to have been lost and thus draws later generations.

But the attraction to 1950s domestic stuff went well beyond the sleek lines of Eames design and futuristic appliances. It included many consumer goods that can be broadly incorporated under the label "kitsch," decorations and novelties that sometimes conflicted with the principles of Midcentury Modern values. Kitsch is "over the top" in its use of color, novelty, and playfulness, often so much so that today it often seems garish, tasteless, and even bizarre. In fact, during the 1950s, the modernist sophisticates (like my mother) deplored kitsch as cheap, commercial, and crass. However, since the 1960s, the appeal of "camp"—an attraction to popular "tastelessness" as an antidote to elite "quality"—has made kitsch cool for a new generation of sophisticates. A tongue-in-cheek enthusiasm for camp was perhaps best expressed in the hit TV show *Batman* (1966–1968). Originally intended for a juvenile audience, *Batman*'s comic-book plots and dialogue attracted millions of young adults. A knowing but bemused distance from the popular cultural icon is required to appreciate camp.[19]

This may explain the revival of the 1950s "paint-by-numbers" fad legitimized by an exhibit of this phenomenon at the Smithsonian's National Museum of American History in 2001. Paint-by-numbers sets offered untrained "artists" the opportunity to paint colors in predrawn shapes on a board following a numerical code, thus recreating pictures suitable for framing. Highbrow moderns disdained this craze when it first appeared in 1951 (published by Palmer Paint): Paint-by-numbers sets were uncreative, sentimental, mechanical, and merely "decorative" (a favorite put-down of my mother and her painter friends) because most of the sets featured realistic landscapes, kittens, puppies, sailboats, and sunsets, romantic images that appealed to the middlebrow masses who lived in crackerbox houses. Yet, this craze revived fifty years later, supported a number of paint-by-number entrepreneurs. In 2006 Aimee Cecil sold about five thousand kits at ninety dollars each.[20] It is hard to explain the appeal except by the charm of camp. Another category of 1950s kitsch were "head vases" and "figural planters," curious colorful, even garish, ceramic vessels in the shape of Nubian slaves, Spanish dancers, or black leopards into which flowers and plants were displayed. Still other forms of kitsch/camp were canisters and other kitchen ceramics that were embossed with colorful images of poodles, cats, or owls. Collectors rediscovered these bits of bric-a-brac in the mid-1980s, leading to price increases and even the production of two books touting their wonders to collectors in 1996 as the speculative market merged with an emerging nostalgia community.[21]

Perhaps even stranger is the enthusiasm for 1950s Christmas kitsch. Travis Smith in his *Kitschmasland* finds that there is a sort of natural history of Christmas decorations—first Christmas kitsch appealed to Americans as novelty, then it was rejected as tasteless kitsch, and finally it returned as "camp" and ultimately as a cult. What makes aluminum Christmas trees, for example, succeed as objects of nostalgia is that they can be "whimsical, sentimental, and even beautiful." Consider the ornamental glass balls inspired by the Sputnik satellite or even the A-bomb. The contrast of today's generic chains of tiny lights with the bubbling "electric candles" of the 1950s creates a special appeal. And the decorative—yes, perhaps gaudy—beaded egg ornaments or reindeer candle holders have attracted collectors because they remind them of their childhoods. Smith continues: "As a culture we may be in danger of becoming too jaded and sophisticated to appreciate these designs from our not too distant past." Focus on the good design of Eames or Saarinen, Smith concludes, is incomplete. The ironic stuff of dime-store Christmas says as much about our history and culture. "We have to realize that kitsch is . . . us."[22]

While much Midcentury Modern and 1950s kitsch appeals to women, men collect the 1950s too, but once again very different stuff. Men have been attracted to first-generation hi-fi sets, a memory of that distinctly male accessory (at least in the view of Hugh Hefner and readers of *Playboy*), but some also have collected space toys, the complement to women's space-age kitchens. A similar attraction to the futuristic naiveté of the 1950s seems in play, but in this case what is prominent is an especially childlike delight in collecting "B" sci-fi movies and the often garish posters advertising them. Interestingly, there seems to be little interest in the actual American space program of the 1950s and 1960s. Rather, the now campy icons of 1950s (and early 1960s) TV and movie fantasies of space travel have drawn collecting crowds. Among the most popular were toy ray guns, robots, and rocket ships, as well as lunch boxes, figures, and other memorabilia depicting TV programs like *Space Cadet*.[23]

The evocative appeal of kitsch is so powerful that it has long been a customer-pleasing décor for restaurants and other commercial gathering places. These are not just old diners who have refused to update. They are modern facilities (including McDonalds franchises) that have been "theming" their establishments, built in or since the 1980s, with 1950s celebrity posters, especially rock stars such as Fabian, Buddy Holly, and Little Anthony and iconic TV images of Ralph Kramden and Ed Norton, characters from the *Honeymooners*; oversized fuzzy dice; advertisements with distinct 1950s styling; and, of course, photos or miniatures of red-and-white 1958 Corvettes. Typical also from the mid-1980s were Jim Dandy's Rockin' '50s Restaurant, in Hobart, Indiana, with its turquoise booths, pink-topped tables, and a black-and-white-check floor, and Ed Debevic's (a California and Chicago chain), which featured singing and dancing wait staff. Sonic drive-ins, with origins in Oklahoma in 1953 and success in the lower Midwest in the 1950s, expanded nationally in the 1980s, trading on its 1950s space décor and design.[24]

More recently, the Internet has produced websites like "Baby Boomer Memories—Nostalgic Gifts for Boomers," offering an array of gift ensembles to "trigger" memories of a 1950s childhood. These include coffee-table picture books like *Recollections: A Baby Boomer's Memories of the Fabulous Fifties* and *The Oldies Music Aptitude Test: Trivia Fun for Armchair Deejays*. Also offered are the "Hometown Favorites 1950's Nostalgic Candy Gift Box," a three-pound collection of vintage candy, and even a 1950 Time Capsule. This and similar websites attempt to create a sense of boomer nostalgia built on childhood memories of toys, games, and music.[25]

Fifties domestic collectibles may be, but generally aren't, "heirlooms," and thus they are seldom something that can't be let go because that would mean a final loss of a loved or respected one. Instead, these collectibles seem to be valued as representative of a lost time. They represent what we are no longer—or what we learn secondhand—even if we embrace this materialized memory with irony.

THE SIXTIES, COUNTERCULTURE, AND CULTURE WARS

Just as the early 1970s began the 1950s revival, the mid-1980s launched the nostalgia for the 1960s. While the high-school setting of the 1970s musical *Grease* marked a cheerful memory of the 1950s, *The Big Chill* (1983) sparked a somewhat more ambiguous recollection of the 1960s: it depicted a reunion of sixties college radicals reflecting on how the world and their values had changed since their youth. The contrast between the movies illustrates differing memories of the two decades: the first, a reprise of a naive, if exuberant, first age of rock music and the budding of sexuality in a "typical" 1950s high school; the second, bittersweet reminiscences of older, middle-class Vietnam-era protesters who had participated in the drug and sexual revolution of the late 1960s. The difference anticipated a more controversial treatment of 1960s nostalgia even as 1960s nostalgia shared a similar focus—that is, not on events but on consumption.[26]

The impetus of the 1960s revival was, of course, the maturation of older boomers, especially those who entered adulthood in the second half of the 1960s and who by the end of the 1980s had reached their forties. By then, this group not only had money for memories but sufficient distance from their youth to be intrigued by it—or, at least, by sentimental treatments of it. Younger boomers, of course, recall the 1960s as their childhood and are nostalgic for the decade in very different ways, identifying it with toys, for example. In 1989 NBC ordered two TV pilot programs on the Vietnam War: *Shooter*, based on combat photographers in Vietnam, and *China Beach*, which featured three women stationed in South Vietnam during the war. That same year ABC planned *The Wonder Years*, a sweet series about a twelve-year-old boy growing up in 1968. It is revealing that *Shooter* was never aired; *China Beach* ran only from 1988 to 1991. *The Wonder Years*, by contrast, was a hit that aired for six seasons with much success thereafter in syndication.[27]

Advertisers also recognized the potential of 1960s nostalgia in the mid-1980s. Sam and Dave's 1967 hit "Soul Man" sold Campbell's soup, and the California raisin industry animated humanized raisins to dance to the 1966 hit "I Heard It Through the Grapevine" in an oft-seen ad. Although rights to old songs cost up to $200,000 compared to the price of a jingle written for a commercial, which typically ran from $10,000 to $50,000, advertisers were willing to pay extra to reach the twenty-five-to-forty-year-old baby-boom generation.[28] As the media scholar Daniel Marcus notes, these ads evoked "feelings of childhood security and joy." But they did more than tap into sentimental nostalgia:

By associating products with styles once cherished but that also had gone through a period of relative obsolescence,

> merchandisers introduced kitsch as a primary element of
> 1980s consumption. Kitsch offered assertive simplicities
> to sophisticated consumers, taking them back to the days
> before their taste became educated . . . offer[ing] consumers
> the opportunity inversely to display their cultural knowing-
> ness by feigning innocence.[29]

This was a selective embrace of the 1960s that avoided both its traumatic events—like the Vietnam War—and its achievements—like
the civil rights and women's movements.

In many ways, the material memories of the 1960s were less
distinct than the 1950s, certainly in home furnishings and appliances. Yet there were obvious flashpoints in clothing that evoked
late-1960s nostalgia (because the early 1960s were really culturally part of the 1950s). Perhaps inevitable was the revival of fads
like bellbottom jeans as well as the geometric, multicolored print
dresses inspired by Emilio Pucci's designs.[30] Inevitably other "far-
out" representations of 1960s clothes appeared. By 1990, flea-
market dealers across the United States reported renewed interest in 1960s countercultural makeup and clothes in day-glo colors.
Antique and art dealers, unable to unload truly old furniture or
paintings, found that they could sell cheap collectibles from the
1960s. Tube-shaped desk lamps covered with psychedelic designs
were popular, as were the odd shapes formed in lava lamps (a fad
from 1963). In 1995, even a large New York exhibition hall could
present the program "Psychedelic 60's: Pop, Op, and Peace," featuring collectible tie-dyed T-shirts, tricolored crocheted vests,
and other outfits from the 1960s to nostalgic consumers. All this
appealed to the romantic memories of boomers who in the late
1960s went to the "head-shop districts" of cities to purchase their
tokens of quasi hippiedom. It also attracted much younger consumers seeking to "channel" the 1960s. Miniskirts, pantsuits, and
other clothes inspired by Mary Quant of London's Carnaby Street
became collectible in the 1990s, as did tie-dyed shirts, patchwork
velvet dresses, embroidered jeans and denim jackets, chain belts,
flowery ties, Indian kaftans, love beads, and even fringed buck-
skin jackets.[31] Shortly after 2000, fad candy from the 1960s (and

1950s) was popular enough to spur Internet sites (groovycandies. com, sweetnostalgia.com, and oldtimecandy.com). Even Wal-Mart offered an array of Pez and other novelty candies for boomer adults.[32] Once again, time-bound novelty returned as nostalgia.

Child "foods" like candy were especially likely candidates for nostalgia, but so were TV shows, which are so often pinpointed to memories of special times of growing up. This is particularly easy to do because TV-themed kids' stuff was so common in the 1960s. Thus lunch boxes and posters featuring characters from *Star Trek* and TV sitcoms became hot items at collectible shops like that of Herb Hastings' Way Back Machine, a store in Cleveland opened in 1984. Not surprisingly, in 1994 merchants in towns near the site of the Woodstock rock festival capitalized on the twenty-fifth anniversary of the infamous gathering of sex-and-drug-crazed hippies by stocking their stores with 1960s memorabilia. By the late 1990s, dealers in collectibles found that the Internet had greatly expanded their market, allowing them to abandon expensive storefronts necessary to attract street traffic for cheaper warehouses from which to distribute their wares. As Boston's Rudy Franchi, the owner of the Nostalgia Factory, noted, "The number of orders we get from the boonies is unbelievable. It's all these people who are stuck out there in the middle of nowhere" who want a bit of a lost or imagined lost youth back.[33]

By 2011 the link between the time-tied TV show and retro fashion was again realized in the commercial collaboration between the clothing chain Banana Republic and the costume designer for the hit show *Mad Men* (aired on American Movie Classics), a series based on the Madison Avenue world of advertising in the early 1960s. Banana Republic offered a limited-edition collection of "Mad Men" clothes and accessories for men and women, including everything from "leopard print pumps to a navy shawl-collared suit jacket for men."[34]

Despite all this, collecting the 1960s and sentimental attachment to that decade met with greater hostility, both by those who lived through and rejected that decade and by its generational successors. From the first signs of boomer retro (in 1986), the press sided with "all those who are suffering from the current nostalgia for the 1960s and the alleged culture of that time."[35] Critics complained of the selling of a sanitized 1960s that ignored the stress and conflict of the era. As one journalist noted, "The period's current incarnation is largely a feel-good phenomenon, long on youthful fun and freedom, reducing the entire decade to a kind of continuous rock 'n' roll sound track."[36]

1970s RETRO

Inevitably, 1960s nostalgia was followed by 1970s nostalgia, which was well underway by the end of the 1990s. However, even for those for whom the 1970s was formative, it is hard to give this decade a definite "brand" culturally or politically. It was, by most accounts, a decade of disappointments, noted for Nixon's disgrace, defeat in Vietnam, the humiliation of the Iranian hostage taking, and inflation, ending with President Jimmy Carter's famous speech about America's national "malaise." The popular clothes styles (white polyester double-knit leisure suits and gold chains, as in John Travolta's *Saturday Night Fever*) and those "swooping wings" on women's hair (Farrah Fawcett) and big mustaches and long sideburns were easy to mock later, as were sappy songs like "You Light Up My Life," corny slogans like "Have a Nice Day," and fads like mood rings and citizens' band radio ("ten-four, good buddy, I copy you"). In contrast to the idealism of the 1960s (whatever one thought of it), the 1970s was tagged as the "Me Decade" of self-absorption.[37]

And this was not the opinion merely of the 1960s crowd. "Happy-face buttons replaced clenched fists," as Pagan Kennedy writes in her memoir of growing up in the 1970s. She recalls her frustration at missing all the fireworks of 1960s youth rebellion and notes how the political edge of the 1960s was blunted by commercial cooptation ("Black Is Beautiful" jeans patches and mass-produced peace-sign medallions) and that the idealism and pride of the civil rights struggle degenerated into the gangster sex and violence of the blaxploitation movies of the 1970s. All this made the "seventies generation" sometimes envious, even resentful, of the sixties boomers but also defensive of the contributions of "their decade."

Probably more common was to adopt an ironic, unsentimental nostalgia that celebrated the 1970s with a heavy dose of whimsy, cynicism, and self-referential and self-deprecating humor—with few claims of "their decade's" moral superiority. Even more than in the 1950s and 1960s, 1970s nostalgia celebrated camp. Complicating the picture more was the curious fact that the 1970s was often remembered for being a time that recalled the decades that preceded it. "It's hard to get nostalgic about a decade that itself was nostalgic" and that, at the time, many believed was a fall from the golden age of the 1950s.[38]

Moreover, not much held these memories together, and the 1970s, even more than other decades, didn't fit a clear pattern: when did it begin? Not in 1970, when the psychedelic sixties (which began in earnest only in 1967) was still in full flower. The 1970s left some distinct artifacts: a cult of macramé wall hangings, houseplants, redwood-slab coffee tables, mushroom-shaped cookie jars, crocheted afghans, and avocado-colored appliances. But, unlike Midcentury Modern, which often represented the promise of progress and plenty in postwar America, the 1970s issued a plethora of fads and fashions without any clear social or cultural meaning. As Kennedy speculates, "It was perhaps the stunning array of disposable, faddish products designed to do nothing but help the buyer feel hip that characterized the seventies." As often noted (see chapter 5), after 1971, TV shows became more youth-oriented than ever before (given the networks' obsession with selling ad time to companies seeking that demographic). But like so much in that decade, "controversial" programming, designed to appeal to a new generation, was "nonthreatening theater where new social values—proposed by the women's movement, the civil rights movement, and the sexual revolution—could be explored and laughed at" (e.g., *The Mary Tyler Moore Show*, *Sanford and Son*, and *M*A*S*H*).[39] Detached from or only vaguely linked to events and broad historical trends, the kitsch of the 1970s was fragmented and noted mostly for having once been a craze.

So it isn't so strange that many 1970s collectibles are campy fads especially associated with popular TV shows: sitcoms like *The Brady Bunch*, *Laverne and Shirley*, *The Partridge Family*, and *The*

Beverley Hillbillies but also action shows like *Starsky and Hutch* and *Charlie's Angels* are all "immortalized" in toys, coloring books, paper dolls, games, posters, school supplies, and lunchboxes. "It takes about twenty years for items to become collectible, and items with TV's *The Brady Bunch, CHIPs,* or *Three's Company* have taken off thanks to reruns," said Charles Criscuolo, the owner of Flashback Collectibles in Chicago, in 1993. So it's not surprising that colorful (and, to a later era, garish) platform shoes from the 1970s were also selling again in the mid-1990s.[40] In 2001, the *Wall Street Journal* reported with glee that for several years tuxedo suits in powder blue, sunshine yellow, and peachy peach from the 1970s were the rage for high-school proms as well as for costume and Halloween parties in California.[41] The retrospective campiness of 1970s fashion and culture was even more dominant than its 1950s and 1960s predecessors.

But 1970s retro differed in still another way: nostalgia for the quintessential novelty of that decade, the video game.[42] A couple of newspaper interviews of men who grew up in the 1970s suggest a trend: In 2003, Mark Murawski, a software engineer from suburban Pittsburgh, saw nothing odd about collecting the Atari 2600, a game that first appeared in 1977 when he was five. But he also owned subsequent video-game systems, including the Nintendo NES (1985) and Sega Dreamcast (1998), as well as later devices (the PlayStation 2, Nintendo Game Cube, and Xbox). Located in a basement "man cave,"[43] these games constituted his private museum, a record of his entire life's dedication to gaming. "It's not a child's toy you're going to grow out of," declared Murawski.[44] In 2002, a graphic designer from Decatur, Alabama, Rodney Siddall, then thirty-five, acknowledged to a reporter that he was a 1970s junkie with collections of yellow smiley-face cookie jars, Hot Wheel cars and track sets, and magazines featuring Fonzie from *Happy Days* and *The Six-Million-Dollar Man.* He rarely listened to music not from the 1970s and loved *That '70s Show.* He was particularly fixated on his first Atari 2600 and his *Pac-Man* game cartridge, which he got in 1977 when he was ten. But he didn't give up gaming when he left childhood. During his teens and twenties, he bought all the trendy game systems. In the 1990s, still in his twenties, Siddall "returned" to the video-game systems of his childhood, collecting Atari 5200, Atari 7800, Mattel's Intellivision, and more than four hundred Atari 2600 cartridges, as well as later systems. Siddall insisted, "I don't think collecting this kind of stuff means that I don't want to grow up. I just think it is part of a way of capturing a piece of my childhood."[45]

But these Gen-X men were doing something different from the boomer collectors who tried to recover childhood memories in middle age. They retained, continuously, an infatuation with the video games of their 1970s youth, never, or only for a short time, abandoning their enthusiasm as they matured. I saw a similar pattern at toy-and-comic-book shows: male collectors who grew up in the 1970s told me that they gave up their childhood obsessions only for a few years in their late teens and early twenties (when school and women replaced their childhood obsessions). This is hardly the old nostalgia. Moreover, these Gen-X video collectors don't seem merely fixated on the past: they are also trendy adherents of subsequent video novelties, riding the wave of fast capitalism in this most dynamic of late-twentieth-century industries. What explains this generational difference?

It may have something to do with the particular history of video games and the generation that was first raised on them. Computer games began as diversions of the digital engineers who invented Pong, a crude electronic tennis game (1958), and Spacewar!, where dashes of light representing missiles were annihilated with blips of light across a black-and-white TV screen (1961).[46] It was only in the early 1970s that companies like Magnavox and Atari and later ColecoVision and Mattel's Intellivision commercialized this technology with digital arcade machines and home consoles and game cartridges. These games defined the generation (of mostly boys) who were five to twelve years old between 1972 and 1983, the year the gaming boom went bust, the market saturated with hundreds of bland lookalike products.[47]

That might have ended the craze and set the stage for the video game to become a site of nostalgia for these boys when they grew to manhood a generation later (as was the pattern with other, earlier forms of commercialized nostalgia). But the video game was quickly revived by the Japanese Nintendo Entertainment System (NES) in 1985, with greatly improved graphics, and Nintendo sold $3.4 billion worth of consoles and cartridges by 1990. This began an uninterrupted pulse of periodic innovation in the industry. What made the new video game particularly distinct was that it was popular not only with children: these toys continued to draw consumers into their teens and even young adulthood (often those same males who had played Atari a few years earlier). To be sure, games remained gentle and even cute in the late 1980s, appealing to children with *Super Mario Brothers* and *Sonic the Hedgehog*, while sports and strategy games were popular with older youth.[48] But subtly the video game was transformed as it "grew up" with boys, offering not only more sophisticated graphics and challenging play but also more fast-paced violence, such as with *Street Fighter II* (1991) and *Mortal Kombat* (1992). [49] The video-game industry not only offered consumers continuous novelty but succeeded in holding onto them after they had discarded other toys. In 2013, the Entertainment Software Association claimed the mean age of their consumers was thirty-five and of players, thirty.[50] Of course, these games have become more sophisticated since the 1970s, appealing to older gamers who may still also hold onto their "heritage" games from the 1970s.[51] It seems that a "digital generation" has emerged since the mid-1970s that rather neatly separates the boomers (who matured with TV) from the Gen-Xers and today's youth, who grew up with video games and recently the Internet.[52]

Part of this generational difference also manifests in a divergent sense of the past, especially for men. Digital popular culture did not lead to a time-defined nostalgia as did TV, recorded popular music, cars identified by annual model changes, or other markers of previous generations. It is no surprise that collectors of 1970s video games also own their descendants. Fewer are lost in the 1970s than are lost in the 1950s and 1960s because the video-gaming hobby begun in the 1970s has no age "expiration date" and thus was not associated primarily with childhood memory, and thus a source of nostalgia, but carried on through life. The nostalgic male video gamer does not need to cling to the ephemera of his particular childhood to take refuge from the whirl of contemporary fast capitalism (as might the boomer). He embraces both the past and present by never abandoning his childhood.

Despite these recent generational shifts across the communities of "decade collectors," from those fascinated with the aluminum Christmas trees of the 1950s and the lava lamps from the 1960s to the platform shoes of the 1970s and video games from the 1980s, there remains a common populist appeal. This longing for the consumer goods of the past is more than a fashionable rejection of taste hierarchies (that once produced "refined" collectors of antiques) or even an embrace of cynical, if playful, camp; it reflects a "dedifferentiation" of culture, an acceptance of a welter of styles in art and architecture that reflects the fragmentation of life today. As Susan Stewart notes, the kitsch collector of recent consumer culture has turned the "deep time and narrow space of the antique" into the "narrow time and deep space of the popular." The goal, she says, is the ironic display of an "overmateriality," a celebration of superficiality with an effort to find meaning in these goods, a meaning other than that they once had been trendy and thus are witnesses to the "speed of fashion."[53]

Still, collecting a particular decade gives people a chance to relive their childhood from the perspective of their thirties, forties, and later. It also provides them a way of saying something about themselves and how they personally relate to a wider, complex world, at least as proud members of the 1950s, 1960s, or 1970s generations. As we have seen, this creates community even as it breaks up society. It may be perfectly harmless, but we may still wonder if we couldn't do better with our memories. Let's look next at the sights and sounds of commercialized nostalgia in retro TV and old-time records and radio, to see if we can't come up with answers.

4

Leaving It to Beaver and Retro TV

Modern *merchandising* offers us a ready return to our childhoods, but modern *media* provides us with more—a long list of TV programs that mark off the years, time capsules of fashion, speech, events, and values from another era—available throughout the day and night with a click of the remote. Television and now the Internet offer nearly instantaneous access to any ephemeral sound and sight bite generated in the accelerating wake of fast capitalism. In the summer of 2014, the oldest surviving retro channel, TV Land, offered a twenty-four-hour smorgasbord of nostalgia: an hour of the sentimental 1960s serial *Andy Griffith* at nine in the morning, followed by multiple episodes of *Gunsmoke*, *Bonanza*, and still another western, *Walker, Texas Ranger*. The evening lineup changed daily, featuring a wide range of sitcoms, sometimes including four episodes in a row, from *I Love Lucy* of the early 1950s through *King of Queens*, which ran from 1998 to 2007.

Why would anyone really want to watch two or more successive episodes of an old series like *Gunsmoke*? They aren't certified "classics," like the old movies ranked by the number of stars on the cable information screens. They are not even particularly representative of what was on television when they first appeared. Missing from this and other nostalgia networks are *The Ed Sullivan Show*, *The Dina Shore Chevy Hour*, and other music variety shows that were featured in primetime during the "Golden Age" of TV, say, the 1959–1960 season. Gone too are the dramatic series identified by their corporate sponsors—General Electric, Westinghouse, Kraft, DuPont, Alcoa/Goodyear, and Armstrong/U.S. Steel. Many viewers today, of course, are far too young to remember these relics from Hollywood's past, but the young still love Lucille Ball, and many have seen James Arness shoot it out on *Gunsmoke*, and these shows are a half-century old or more.

Of course, nostalgia for the flickering image on the screen extends far beyond TV Land. The Mid-Atlantic Nostalgia Convention is typical of a broad range of weekend gatherings, generally held in hotels. These shows feature camp movies from the 1950s; old-time film and TV stars (usually sitting at tables signing autographs for a fee); learned presentations from articulate, if "amateur," experts on old TV and radio programs; and, inevitably, a ballroom filled with exhibitors selling a wide variety of memorabilia, DVD recordings of horror and sci-fi movies, and toys related to old movies and TV and radio shows. In 2011, I visited this convention, that year being held in a Baltimore suburb. The crowd included clusters of older devotees of old-time radio. One of them (a distinguished seventy-eight-year-old) gave a spirited talk to a crowd of sixty about his introduction to *Buck Rogers* on radio in 1940 when he was six years old. For him, it all began when his dad gave him a portable radio ("his passport to the world"). The famous late-afternoon sci-fi adventure offered him a dream space of boyhood liberation. A classic in modern nostalgia.

Nevertheless, this gathering included a surprising proportion of men (mostly) in their thirties and forties, Gen-Xers who were too young to have seen *Lucy* or *The Lone Ranger* when they first appeared on TV. A man in his thirties exhibited a large assortment of books that he had published on retro TV and movies. Comfortable in the world of past media fantasy, he went so far as to avoid all modern news and, for that matter, contemporary TV and movies. He told me that he got hooked on pop-culture nostalgia in the 1980s as a child, by watching reruns and old movies on TV. He cared little for media from his own youth. Like the others at the convention, he was "out of his time" and happy to live in another.

Despite the eagerness of exhibitors and representatives of collector clubs to tout the charms of their particular enthusiasms, there was a fog of sadness hanging over the crowd. The only original stars from the late 1940s and 1950s left to sign autographs and tell their stories were the child actors. Tony Dow, who played Wally, the Beaver's older brother in the famous sitcom, told me of how he had lost out on residual income, but "that's the way it is," he said in resignation. The enthusiasts for old-time radio programs seemed the most pessimistic. Clubs like Buffalo Old Time Radio had enjoyed a long run (it was founded in 1975), but, when I met the retired auto worker (born in 1939) who was part of the last group of children brought up on radio and who wrote the club's monthly newsletter, he made it clear that the group's days were numbered. In fact, in 2011, another club, the Friends of Old-Time Radio, decided to end holding an annual convention after having met for thirty-six years.[1] After all, although younger listeners are attracted to the radio detective, comedy, and cowboy shows of the 1940s and early 1950s (on Internet and satellite radio, for example), most of those who grew up with these programs are in their twilight years.[2] If old-time radio is in decline, nostalgia for vintage visual media is hardly so. The television industry, in fact, has a big stake in perpetuating it.

TV AND MEDIA OF MEMORY

Television has shaped modern memory in unique ways. It has a distinct history of delivering packages of corporate-produced entertainment to the home, predominantly in scheduled series of stories with repeated characters and settings. It is the quintessential media of memory because from the beginning it was riddled with repetition, and its viewers were conditioned to expect and even desire recurrence.[3] Taking a still longer view, TV can be understood as a culmination of a half-century-long revolution in how people experienced and modeled intimacy. It largely replaced the novel and magazine story as the dreamscape of fantasy relationships. TV built on what films from the first decade of the twentieth century and radio serials from 1928 through the early 1950s did. Young people identify with the people around them, and in the age of mass media—movie, radio, and TV—celebrities and their stories tended to replace the personalities and tales of parents and other relatives, workplace elders, and the clergy. A longing for intimacy was also the driving force in the attraction to the celebrity. While we might think of the "star" as an elevated being, akin to a celestial object, what raised the star was that individuals in the audience identified with them personally. Since early in the history of films, the star has been the object of fanatical adulation but also intimate familiarity, through the visual and, later, vocal cues that made her or him into a "personality."[4] Repetition and familiarity created fans.

This is what the movie serials that appeared as early as 1913 did. These thrillers featured the same characters in predictable roles and situations, especially the "cliffhanger" teasers at the end of each brief episode.[5] But even for stars who played in conventional stand-alone movies, their often repeated roles and relationships in stories told audiences who they were and how they would behave, and this familiarity made fans feel as if these actors were "friends," even possessions (akin to a doll or toy). Joe Penner on 1930s radio was famous simply for saying "wanna buy a duck?" no matter the occasion. Edward G. Robinson became the stocky tough guy, and Katherine Hepburn, the wisecracking self-assured leading lady—even though both were able to transcend these stereotypes. Nevertheless, mass media relied on repetition of representative roles—much as popular music required repeated tropes—simply because this gave audiences a sense of comfort, possession, and predictability.

The technology of radio helped create the recognizable, comfortable, and thus personal and intimate celebrity. President

Franklin Roosevelt adapted this informality to his "fireside chats," abandoning the incendiary meeting-hall speech for the intimacy of a personal "chat" with millions of listeners in their living rooms. An even more powerful precedent for the intimate celebrity was the invention of the radio sitcom. Drawing on the appeal of comic strips from the turn of the twentieth century, radio "sitcoms" offered familiar, usually friendly, voices attached to predictable characters set in formulaic "situations" that they stumbled through in each episode. Beginning in 1928 and through the thirties and forties, Americans ritualistically tuned in to hear *Amos 'n' Andy*. There was comfort in anticipating the troubles that the African American characters (in reality played by white actors) would get into. And the stars and stories of weekly radio westerns, police dramas, and science-fiction shows had a similar appeal in predictability, and they drew people away from adult conversation and hobbies, children's play, and other uses of scarce American leisure time.[6]

But all of this merely anticipated TV, the quintessential medium of personal identity, repetition, and ultimately nostalgia. And TV dominated the scene quickly. In 1950, only 8.1 percent of American homes had a TV, but by 1960, nearly 90 percent of households possessed one (or more), and the box was watched five hours per day on average. By contrast, between 1946 and 1953, movie audiences had shrunk in half. While network radio shows continued until 1961, the radio networks also developed broadcast TV and seamlessly moved popular radio programs to network TV.[7]

Viewers may "possess" the sounds and sights of TV for only that moment, but when repeated in serials these televisual images became the equivalents of other consumed objects. Even more, TV shows were associated with youth and early memory, producing in many viewers an urge to return to them later in life. These shows served as a substitute for personal memories because they were embraced so personally: people saw themselves and their situations in the characters and stories. Nostalgia is often evoked with "bites," not narrative totalities: obvious examples are the opening theme songs, repeated expressions ("To the Moon, Alice!" said by Ralph Kramden on *The Honeymooners*), and familiar story lines, which are so formulaic that specific details of any show seldom are (and need not be) remembered.

The commercial advantages of the TV series, when first shown and even more so in reruns, may seem obvious now, but the power of this package was not evident to early TV programmers. Historians of TV stress how early network brass expected TV to offer *unique live* programming—news, sports, but also real-time plays, documentaries, and musical variety shows.[8] The box with the tubes was supposed to be a domestic site of a nationally shared, contemporaneous culture and an opportunity regularly to see and hear what hitherto had been available only in New York or occasionally via touring companies of artists—and then at high prices.

But TV only occasionally became a "window" on the world (as in broadcasting national crises), much less a domestic catapult to high culture. Instead, TV perpetuated a pattern of familiarity established by network radio. TV became a site of repetition at many levels—week-to-week reappearances of the same characters and stories in new serials, often daily aired reruns seen shortly after the originals, and reruns offered years, even decades later in syndication and cable TV. Moreover, TV became a filter (much was excluded that appeared in other media—movies, magazines, newspapers, pulp), and what resurfaced in reruns was equally a distorted image of the past, even of TV history. For example, nostalgia TV offers lots of Lucy, but not Chester Riley of the working-class sitcom *The Life of Riley* or the ethnic family comedy *The Goldbergs*; there are revivals of now-defunct formats like westerns, but not of variety shows. All this raises several questions: What from the past moves through the filter of time and why? What do these nostalgic choices say about our time? Who and what types of people are attracted to which programs? TV nostalgia adds a layer of complexity to our thinking about consumed memory. Let's see how.

THE WHERE AND WHY OF RERUN TV

Early TV was centered in New York City, in the Eastern time zone, where most viewers lived. Vaudeville-influenced shows included

Milton Berle's burlesque (1947–1956), the *New York Daily News* gossip columnist Ed Sullivan's variety show (1948–1971), and Red Skelton's comedy (1951–1971). The dominant networks, NBC and CBS, featured live dramas (*Philco Television Playhouse*, e.g.), "intellectually sophisticated" quiz shows (*Twenty Questions* and *What's My Line*), and even live spectaculars, including Mary Martin's role in *Peter Pan* (1955). As late as 1955, 87 percent of network shows were still live. There was a certain mystique about the immediacy of live programming, and the networks knew that they could profit handsomely from selling primetime slots to national advertisers of name-brand products.[9]

Challenging this vision was the idea of recorded and thus repeatable programming. In part, the recorded show grew out of the needs of local stations without the resources to do much live broadcasting to fill viewing time and deliver audiences to local advertisers outside the primetime of network programming. Moreover, to accommodate the convenience of viewers in western time zones (as an 8 pm live show in New York would air live in Los Angeles at 5 pm, too early for the ratings that primetime brought), the networks needed a way of repeating a program in the West later in the evening than when it was first broadcast in the East. In the 1930s and 1940s, these issues had concerned radio, which found solutions similar to what the TV business would later adapt for the screen. Local radio stations substituted live broadcasts with electric transcription discs, phonograph records that ran at 33 1/3 RPM (anticipating the long-playing record). Despite radio's initial aura of simultaneity and immediacy, American audiences had been acclimatized to the idea of repeated, nonlive programs more than a generation before radio, by phonograph records and the mass-produced film reel. Radio transcription discs allowed local stations to air syndicated programming outside the control of the networks. By the late 1940s, even the radio networks used transcriptions of live programs on the East Coast to be heard later in western time zones.[10]

It was inevitable that local TV stations would follow suit, substituting radio's transcription records with syndicated films (old movies and cartoons). Movie companies sold their archived films from the 1930s and 1940s to local TV stations for the "late show" or afternoon movie slot. This introduced a new generation (and many of their elders) to the "golden age" of Hollywood, and it later produced nostalgia for movies seen first not in theaters but at home on TV. Theatrical shorts like *Our Gang* (rechristened on TV as *The Little Rascals*) and *The Three Stooges* were handy weekday afternoon and Saturday fillers that attracted local advertisers, and old Popeye and Woody Woodpecker cartoons became standard after-school fare for boomers in the 1950s and 1960s.

In late 1951, Lucille Ball and Desi Arnaz abandoned the conventional practice of live TV programming in New York to film episodes of *I Love Lucy* in Hollywood. Soon independent ("off network") telefilm companies produced series like *Highway Patrol* and *I Led Three Lives* for syndication to local stations. Ziv, UTP, MCA, and Screen Gems became a major part of programming and soon thereafter distributors of reruns. The networks also produced their own telefilms, with sitcoms like *Our Miss Brooks* (1952–1956), *My Little Margie* (1952–1955), and *The George Burns and Gracie Allen Show* (1950–1958). An early telefilm for CBS (1951) was the TV version of *Amos 'n' Andy*, now featuring black actors. It ran for two seasons before ending partly because of protests against its racial stereotypes. Still the series continued in reruns into the 1960s (and according to the staff at the Museum of TV and Radio in Hollywood in 2006, it was "by far" the most popular TV show requested by patrons). From 1955, many TV series that were first shown weekly were rerun as "strips" of episodes shown each weekday, usually in the late afternoon and early evening before primetime. As for live network broadcasts, the kinescope film (and from 1956 the videotape) recorded a live program in New York to be shown later in western time zones.[11] Beginning in 1958, the networks broadcast summer reruns, realizing that viewers would not object. Meanwhile the demand for off-network syndication grew, and new independent channels like WGN of Chicago ran old episodes of *I Love Lucy*, *Steve Allen*, and *Perry Mason* during primetime.[12]

The tilt toward the recorded and repeated and against the live and unique made TV very different than first intended. While TV brought the here and now (in "breaking" news and big-time sports) and occasionally the best and brightest (less often artists and thinkers than pop celebrities), it increasingly introduced into the living room the comforting familiarity of characters and situations modeled after radio sitcoms and other series. As we shall see, it was these programs, deeply embedded in childhood memory, that returned in later life as nostalgia.

Television transformed what it meant to be a child emerging from the fog of infancy into the world of powerful first experiences. Instead of the impressionable recollections of *public* festivals, parades, or religious rituals, experienced by generations of children before the twentieth century, modern kids recall TV shows viewed in the *privacy* of the home but shared by millions of other children at the same time. To appreciate this better, we need to consider further the TV series and how it shaped memory.

TV GENRE AND THE MAKING OF MEMORY

Over the first generation of TV, programming shifted from live to highly stylized, formulaic serial programming. In a survey of primetime TV in 1959–1960, midway through that first generation, live variety shows still had a strong presence, appealing mostly to a middle-aged audience who had grown up with radio variety and comedy-skit shows (Jack Benny or Doris Day, for example). However, fifteen years later, in the 1974–1975 season, when this audience had aged beyond the advertiser's demographic target, all that was left on the weekly schedule was the comedy of Carol Burnett and a couple of made-for-TV movie listings. Almost none of these shows has resurfaced as nostalgia TV (with the exception of Lawrence Welk, whose conservative variety show aired from 1951 to 1981 on network and syndicated TV and survives on PBS stations).[13] Nostalgia TV is grounded in the recollections of those who were children when they first saw them (in first showings or reruns), and what they saw and liked were not variety shows but series programs with familiar characters and plots.

If variety has disappeared down the memory hole, so for the most part has early entertainment for children. This might seem curious until we consider kids' fare in the 1950s and even 1960s: Miss Frances's *Ding Dong School* consisted mostly of a matronly educator reading stories to toddlers and young children, and *Howdy Doody*, a mainstay of boomer childhood from 1947 to 1960, featured marionettes, a troop of costumed adults (Buffalo Bob, Princess Summerfall Winterspring, and the mute Clarabell the Clown), and a live audience of kids in the "Peanut Gallery." These programs were not only crude (often available today only in low-definition kinescope); they were also too slow and patronizing to appeal to modern children. More importantly, I think, they don't attract older adults, who are nostalgic for their childhoods but *not for childish programs*. What thirty-year-old adult today would watch reruns of *Mr. Rogers*? Cherished memory resides in shows originally designed primarily for adults but viewed by children, for whom these programs provided a transition into the "wider world." It is retro sitcoms, cop shows, and, to a lesser extent, westerns and family drama series that stir memories. Let's briefly consider these genres to see why they attracted us back then . . . and often do today. Because this is a history and because I am interested in origins, I will focus on older programs, but I will try to extend my view beyond boomers and Gen-Xers.

The most common form of nostalgia TV is the sitcom, a genre with significant variations over time; these changes mark TV eras and to some extent create distinct nostalgic/taste cohorts today. The early sitcoms depended on a few well-defined and never-changing characters, often in pairs of contrasting personalities—Ethel versus her stingy and too-old husband Fred in *Lucy*—and simple, largely domestic settings—the modest confines of Lucy and Desi's apartment. What animated the episodes were the "situations," consisting of a crisis, often with a complication (drawing on the classic theatrical form of the comedy of errors), additional confusion, and ultimate solution to or alleviation of the problem. Often the audience knows that the situation "will backfire on the characters." But the chaos is contained, and everything is resolved before the final commercial.[14] There are few surprises, and much of the fun is in anticipating what is said and done. But the sitcom also subtly refers to the wider world. As the media historian David

Marc notes, "The genre comments on American society microscopically, portraying the effects of culture on a family, extended family, vocational group or other microcosmic social unit."[15]

Of course, there were different types of sitcoms. Perhaps the most prominent and influential in the 1950s and early 1960s were "domestic sitcoms" like *Father Knows Best* (1954–1960), *Donna Reed* (1958–1966), *My Three Sons* (1960–1972), and, of course, *Leave It to Beaver* (1957–1963). These series played on the relationships between parents and children. Typical was the cast of *Father Knows Best*—Jim and Margaret Anderson and their children, Betty, an older teen, Bud, about fifteen, and Kathy, the baby of the family, about nine. The stories were mostly built around the foibles, immaturity, and life lessons of the kids: Betty's overbearing confidence and snobbery, Bud's lack of direction and masculine pride, and Kathy's anxieties about being the baby of the family.[16]

The hold of these family shows on the memory of viewers, of course, varied. But the author Susan Cheever's recollections of her fascination with *Father Knows Best* suggests how this "fantasy" might have worked in children maturing during the 1950s (she was born in 1943). For her, the Andersons ideally mirrored her family: "the siblings squabble and the parents have disagreements," but unlike real life, "all this is somehow magically resolved by the end of the half-hour-long show." The show projected a happy family for Susan that may have smoothed over the edges of her own less-than-perfect one: "My father was sarcastic, and my mother sometimes left the dinner table in tears."[17]

The ambiguity that so many children may have felt toward their fathers may explain why domestic sitcoms featured not moms but dads (some, like *My Three Sons*, included no female leads) and thus were "therapeutic."[18] There was a definite bias: while middle-class nonethnic fathers usually "knew best," but that was not true of working-class dads like Chester Riley in *The Life of Riley* (1949–1950, 1953–1958). Riley was a befuddled airplane-plant worker whose wife and his teen kids regularly bested him with their common sense and composure while Riley's emotional immaturity and stupidity got him in trouble (announced with his trademark "What a revoltin' development this is!").[19]

Though most of this string of domestic comedies had ended by 1966, variations would reappear in the following decades (culminating perhaps with *The Cosby Show* in the 1980s). However, the 1960s were dominated by oddly escapist fare, with sitcoms that ignored the decade's generational tension and cultural and political clashes. One form of this escapism was the sitcoms that made fun of the contrast between rural and urban values. This was an old comedic theme in American popular culture.[20] This risk-free theme became ratings gold for the TV comedy writer Paul Henning with *The Beverly Hillbillies*, which aired for nine years (1962–1971). A seemingly endless stream of "situations" were drawn out of the absurdity of the hillbilly Clampett family, who had fortuitously struck it rich in oil on their farm and who then encountered Hollywood pretense and greed after they moved to Beverly Hills while holding onto their folksy ways. In a decade of profound social and cultural change, during which country life was disappearing and generational and social divisions were on the rise, this old-time formula would be successfully repeated in knockoff rural comedies by Henning: *Petticoat Junction* (1963–1970) and *Green Acres* (1965–1971). There was also *The Andy Griffith Show* (1960–1968), set in the Southern small town of Mayberry, featuring the gentle humor of Sheriff Andy Taylor, his cute son, his bumbling deputy, and a cast of colorful characters (none of whom were African American despite the fact that the show was set in the South and aired during the middle of the civil rights movement).[21]

The escapism of these shows went even further in a series of sitcoms that were based on a magical/fantasy "situation," though one set oddly in the context of ordinary American middle-class life. Included in this group were stories of a suburban man with a talking horse (*Mr. Ed*, 1961–1966), men married to witches (*Bewitched*, 1964–1972; *I Dream of Jeannie*, 1965–1970), "normal" families of "monsters," (*The Munsters*, 1964–1966; *The Addams Family*, 1964–1966), and even *The Flying Nun* (1967–1970). As the controversial war in Vietnam heated up, network TV offered absurdly unrealistic military sitcoms (*McHale's Navy*, 1962–1966; *Hogan's Heroes*, 1965–1971).[22] Many of these silly shows appear on nostalgia TV today.

Nevertheless, most of these escapist sitcoms were cancelled by the beginning of the 1970s, when the networks concluded that folksy and fantasy sitcoms would not attract the new generation of youth that ad agencies conventionally favored. This led to more "realistic" sitcoms, especially *All in the Family* (1971–1979), featuring Archie Bunker, the archetypical "social conservative," overreacting blindly to the challenges of feminism, civil rights, secularity, and the cosmopolitanism of the 1960s in endless encounters with his liberal son-in-law Michael. *All in the Family* often reached fifty million households each week, enabling its creator, Norman Lear, to spin off variations with the liberated middle-aged *Maude* (1972–1978), a black variation on Archie's family in *Sanford and Son* (1972–1977), a comedy about an upwardly mobile black couple, *The Jeffersons* (1975–1985), and another featuring poor black folk in the Chicago "projects," *Good Times* (1974–1979).[23]

Lear's success was matched by MTM, a production company launched by Mary Tyler Moore and her husband Grant Tinker in 1969. Moore's company produced a less politically charged but no less sharp break from the domestic and escapist sitcoms of the 1950s and 1960s. Beginning with *Mary Tyler Moore* (1970–1977), MTM productions specialized in postfamily (or perhaps, better, pseudofamily) sitcoms built around the interaction of members of intimate work or social groups. Gone or minimized was humor based on the "cute" child and fantasy. MTM's spinoffs and variations on this format included *Bob Newhart*, featuring a central-city Chicago psychologist and his schoolteacher wife. This, like other MTM shows (*Rhoda*, *WKRP in Cincinnati*, *Lou Grant*) did not dwell on race or countercultural themes but drew on other social changes of the 1970s—the rise of childless couples and single adults. Even more characteristic of its age was *M*A*S*H* (1972–1983), the well-known medical/military sitcom, which began as a veiled anti-Vietnam war comedy set in the historically distant and thus less controversial venue of the Korean War.[24]

These comedic takes on the cultural and social wars that broke out in the 1960s were doable in the 1970s (when those conflicts had abated), but the basic structures of the traditional sitcom remained: in the end, they were about families—nuclear, extended, or workgroup—in which weekly clashes were resolved without anyone changing. Moreover, we shouldn't forget that the 1970s continued to produce escapist sitcoms, as in the nostalgic fare that harked back to the 1950s (recall chapter 3). Most notable was *Happy Days* (1974–1984), set in the prototypical working-class city of Milwaukee, and the spinoff *Laverne and Shirley* (1976–1983).

While early reruns provided older viewers with nostalgic memories from the end of the 1960s, younger audiences found in these retro shows a past that was as real as the present: it was their "present" as seen on TV, and it inevitably became part of their "television heritage" when they grew up. The novelist Jill McCorkle recalls her encounter with *The Andy Griffith Show* in afternoon reruns when she was ten in 1968. By then the show had nearly run its course, but she recalls her nostalgia for the Southern small-town life of Mayberry (which she knew only on TV, of course), and years later she felt homesick when hearing the theme songs of this and other shows of her childhood. "Something clicks in my brain and I am thinking it should be Saturday night and my dad should be alive and out in the yard with the dwindling coals where he had earlier grilled T-bones. My hair should smell like Prell and I would be feeling slightly depressed that I have to go to Sunday school in the morning."[25]

This particular form of TV "heritage" was repeated in the conservative 1980s with the return of fifties-style family comedies, albeit with different looks: *Family Ties* (1982–1989) presented lovable conflicts between ex-hippie parents and Reagan-era conservative children, and *Diff'rent Strokes* (1978–1986) featured white parents and adopted black children. But the most successful was *The Cosby Show* (1984–1992). Bill Cosby's Dr. Heathcliff Huxtable was a resurrection of Robert Young's Jim Anderson for the 1980s. Black and obviously cooler than Anderson, Huxtable was still a middle-class professional and the voice of maturity, while the kids did a modern version of the Anderson offspring of the 1950s, cute and confused, each playing their age and gender role. *Cosby* reached a nostalgic older audience as well as a more hip younger one, leading the TV ratings for four years (1985–1989). Perhaps ending the era was the inevitable retro sitcom *The Wonder Years* (1988–1993), narrated by an adult Kevin Arnold looking back with fondness and bemusement on his 1960s childhood. This traditional family sitcom had to be set in the haze of sugar-coated memory; it hardly conformed to the real world of fractured families of the late twentieth century.[26]

A sharper break in sitcom history seems to have occurred at the end of the 1980s with an abandonment of the family theme for a spate of sitcoms that mocked the old formula and took the MTM idea of the nonfamily family in new directions. These included *Married with Children* (1987–1997). The humor in that show consisted in turning the family sitcom upside down. The father, Al Bundy, not only didn't know best; he was not even the loveable working-class goof. The dysfunctional family became a major genre of the sitcom in the 1990s and 2000s in shows like *Family Guy, That '70s Show, Two and a Half Men*, and the long-lasting cartoon *The Simpsons*. Though there are many variations of the upside-down family comedy, each has role reversals—where the kids are the adults. As common is where the "family acts as a peer group, rather than a hierarchy," everyone is obsessed with their own desires and foibles, and nobody plays the parent.[27]

While the new family sitcoms of the 1990s and early 2000s were usually a cynical challenge to traditional domestic age and sex roles (a trend that continues into the second decade of the twentieth century), there was also a shift in peer-group sitcoms. The "classic" expression of this new type of peer-group sitcom is *Friends* (1994–2004), consisting of near-thirty-year-old New Yorkers, three men and three women, who, instead of settling down in marriage as their parents and grandparents had done, act like siblings in the old family sitcoms, teasing yet supporting one another through their challenges in love and life mostly without the support or interference of parents. In many ways, *Friends* was a comedic take on the protracted singledom of many Americans in their twenties, who, when the show aired, were sharing apartments rather than raising families.[28]

Sitcoms are at the heart of nostalgia TV. They reflected their times (even if through rose-colored lenses) and reminded people of varying ages of those times and of their childhoods living through them. Far more than other formats, the sitcom does what TV is "supposed" to do: it "distracts you as you watch it. It doesn't hold your attention, it eases it," as the TV critic Lee Siegel notes.[29] Along with its variety and time-tied specificity, the sitcom offers comfort and familiarity, in reruns an ideal form of nostalgia.

The second most common TV genre in reruns is the western. With roots deep in American pulp fiction, movies, and radio, the western formula long predates TV. Westerns reached especially an adult male audience across social classes who were attracted to a nostalgic "return" to the simplicity, excitement, and virtue of an age before cities, factories, and offices. At a time when most American men rode in sedans and station wagons, not on horses, and strove to get through a day of office paperwork or factory production lines rather than fighting Indians or outlaws, the western filled hours of leisure time with male fantasy. By 1959, there were twenty-eight Westerns on primetime TV.[30]

Most popular was *Gunsmoke* (1955–1975), topping the ratings between 1957 and 1961 and remaining near the peak for years thereafter. *Gunsmoke* went well beyond the duel between Marshall Dillon and the weekly bad guy, incorporating sophisticated story lines and morally ambiguous characters.[31] Other westerns included *The Life and Legend of Wyatt Earp* (1955–1961), another sheriff of a frontier town, and *Have Gun Will Travel* (1957–1963) featured Paladin, a hired but cultured gunman. The western came in many varieties: *Cheyenne* (1955–1963) offered the adventures of a former army scout; *Rawhide* told stories of cattlemen driving their herds to market. *Wagon Train* (1957–1965) and *The Virginian* (1962–1971) featured weathered western patriarchs. Most primetime Westerns met adult tastes (though kids watched most of them, too). Among the more familiar today through reruns is *Bonanza* (1959–1973), built around a patriarchal widowed rancher, his adult three sons, and the vicissitudes of character and relationships.[32]

Another formulaic genre was the crime show, beginning with the documentary-style police procedural *Dragnet* (1951–1959), produced by Jack Webb, which he reprised between 1967 and 1970, along with the spinoff *Adam-12* (1968–1975). Webb combined repetition ("My name is Friday"; "I carry a badge") with a realistic narrative that sounded like a police report. Other cop shows followed the original *Dragnet*, including *Highway Patrol* (1955–1959), starring Broderick Crawford, a beefy version of the lean Webb, whose trademark was his barking "ten-four!" on his police radio. Later crime shows, including *77 Sunset Strip* (1958–1964) and its sequel, *Hawaii Eye* (1959–1963), traded up to exotic locations and sophisticated heroes but oddly do not seem to have generated the nostalgia audience Webb's products attract.

But probably the most popular crime shows from vintage TV are *Perry Mason* (1957–1966) and *Murder, She Wrote* (1984–1996), both highly stylized whodunits. *Mason* shared much with the sitcom: the appealing, entirely predictable, leads—Perry, the calm, rational lawyer, who weekly defended an innocent person from a murder charge with the able assistance of his "confidential secretary" Della Street and debonair private investigator Paul Drake. Mason defended the wrongly accused and inevitably uncovered the clues, usually forcing the real murderer into a courtroom confession.[33] Following the long tradition of the improbable middle-aged female crime solver, *Murder, She Wrote* featured the mystery writer Jessica Fletcher, from peaceful Cabot Cove, Maine, who somehow weekly found herself in the middle of a murder case, often gently combating patronizing police detectives to unmask in the end the "surprise" criminal.

For all their variations, these crime shows still offered the predictable in character and situation. As Horace Newcomb writes, each program presents the "inevitable movement from crime to capture, the pattern of events, clues, false leads, etc., a game that the audience plays along with." Combating acts of passion and selfishness, the hero ultimately restores order.[34] Once again the fondly recalled characters and predictable "situations" made for successful retro TV.

From the beginning, TV was built on the recorded and repetitious. Despite innovation in sitcoms and the near disappearance of the western, the 1970s also began an era of nostalgia for TV in the golden age of its infancy.[35] Inevitably the three networks took the opportunity to air multipart anniversary documentaries of their contributions to TV "heritage." Though touted as retrospectives, they neither chronicled the history of programming nor studied the origins and development of the network or TV medium, instead offering a series of clips designed to evoke warm memories of past shows. Produced at a time when broadcast networks and the variety show still prevailed, these anniversary shows offered something for everyone, from young to old.

The first, a week-long tribute to fifty years of NBC aired in 1976, began not with the origins of the first network in 1926 (radio) but with a mélange of clips from 1950s NBC TV icons (*Dragnet*'s Jack Webb, variety-show stars Dinah Shore and Tennessee Ernie Ford, and the pioneer *Tonight Show* host Jack Paar) to establish the idea that the 1950s represented the "Golden Age of TV." The five nights of memories were an almost random mix of featured TV genres, with appearances by everyone from the ancient radio crooner Rudy Vallee to the then cutting-edge pop singer David Bowie. As Dean Martin says early in the first episode, "No matter how old you are, your favorite is going to come along." Clips from shows were unidentified for a few seconds, probably to give viewers a chance to recall and play the game of "name the star" in their living rooms. And instead of presenting a parade of shows from oldest to newest, the clips consisted of a back and forth between old and new (a bit of the Mills Brothers of 1950 followed by the Rolling Stones of 1968). The producers stressed not difference or conflict between different artists or genres but similarities (pairing, for example, the image of the classical orchestra conductor Arturo Toscanini of the 1930s with the white-bread big-band leader Lawrence Welk).[36]

The other networks, CBS and ABC, inevitably followed with their own nostalgic specials: ABC's was a lovefest of present and former celebrities like Fred MacMurray, whom ABC made great (and vice versa). And, like the NBC series, there was no attempt to identify TV generations, presenting instead an image of one big happy family. And, to make the harmonious theme complete, the ABC series included gestures like the rock music host Dick Clark introducing the old-fashioned Lennon Sisters on Lawrence Welk's show.[37]

CBS's version was similar, but with more showmanship: veteran stars focused on a single genre, and each night's show featured what was viewed that day of the week on CBS during the "Golden Age." Saturday night was (as Carol Burnett sang in the opener to the final episode), "When CBS Ruled the West." The CBS special offered a bit more history and even explained the famous quiz-show scandal of 1957 (where the producer fed answers to a popular contestant, Mark van Doren). But there is no effort to identify a TV generation (the "greatest generation" or boomers, e.g.). This was still the age of the broadcast, when producers tried to reach everyone's nostalgia, a time when many families watched a single set in the living room. This would change by the 1980s.[38]

It is no wonder that the aged leader of CBS, William Paley, inaugurated in November 1976 the Museum of Broadcasting in New York City on the fiftieth anniversary of network radio but featured the TV "heritage" of its formative decade in the 1950s. As the media historian Derek Kompare notes, 1950s TV became in the 1970s a "cultural touchstone, instantly signifying particular times," not a distant epoch but a time in living memory, providing comfort to many distressed by the upheavals of the 1960s. This "heritage" fostered "the subsequent development of the cultures of retro and nostalgia that pervaded the last quarter of the century."[39] Still, nostalgic TV would enter its modern age only later, as audiences fragmented and attention spans decreased in the age of cable and the ultrafast sound bite.

MODERN NOSTALGIA TV AND CABLE

Broadcast TV had long dominated the screen. Because cable TV was pay TV, from the late 1940s it had been relegated to markets where broadcast reception was poor or nonexistent. However, in the 1980s, cable companies won customers long accustomed to "free" ad-financed broadcast TV with the promise that cable reception was better than antenna, at least in some cases was ad-free, and, more importantly, that cable offered many more channels than local broadcast stations provided. Reduced regulation and new satellite technology made nationwide cable possible. Beginning with Home Box Office (HBO) in 1972, a spate of new cable

networks emerged. Pioneer efforts included the national transmission of Ted Turner's superstation, WTBS, in 1976 and the
Chicago-based Tribune Company's WGN in 1978, followed by ESPN
and Nickelodeon in 1979, BET and TLC in 1980, MTV in 1981, Lifetime in 1984, and Fox in 1986. Turner launched other cable channels (especially CNN in 1980, the Cartoon Channel in 1992, and
Turner Classic Movies in 1994). By 1991, 61 percent of homes were
linked to cable, despite cable subscription fees and advertising.[40]

In the early 1980s, innovative cable networks expected to find
niche audiences for *new programming* that focused on high or specialized cultures and tastes that broadcast networks inevitably
neglected. This was the hope of the Learning Channel, the Discovery Channel, Arts and Entertainment (A&E), and others. Instead,
cable quickly found that fresh documentaries, concerts, and plays
were prohibitively expensive, given the small audiences that a
cable channel could draw. Instead, they discovered that niche programming of popular shows (many of which were cheap reruns)
was far more cost effective and profitable. For example, A&E ran
reruns of off-network syndicated shows like *Quincy*, *Columbo*, and
Remington Steele. Bravo abandoned its "film and arts" format in
the 1980s for youth-oriented programming and made its mark in
"reality TV" with the fashion program *Queer Eye for the Straight
Guy* in 2003.[41]

After thirty years of cable evolution, several conclusions can
be drawn. (1) The narrowcast channels that were profitable were
news, sports, and children's channels, not specialized arts networks. (2) The proliferation of channels meant that programmers
focused on attracting narrow age, gender, ethnic, and religious
cohorts designed for specialized ad markets. (3) Cable television
ended up looking a lot more like the old TV than once expected,
but with hundreds of channels and with many more hours to fill.
This meant a lot of reruns. (4) Out of this came a "new" type of
format, channels playing "classic" TV all the time.

The consolidation of media reinforced these trends. In the
1990s, Fox created a series of new cable channels (Fox Family, Fox
Sports, Fox Movie Channel, and especially Fox News) in combination with an empire of local stations. In an effort to challenge Fox,

Ted Turner merged in 1995 with Time Warner, creating an empire of broadcast networks, movie studios, and cable networks. This led to a 2006 corporate shakeup that excluded Ted Turner himself.[42] In the late 1990s, other consolidations followed the vertical integrations of Fox and Turner. These included Viacom's purchase of Paramount and CBS, NBC's partnership with Microsoft and purchase of Universal, and Disney's acquisition of ABC. More consolidations followed, with, for example, Comcast's purchase of NBCUniversal shares in 2009. The result was six multimedia corporations in control of both broadcast and cable TV as well as most movie and TV archives. Networks became content providers with access to a vast array of old films and TV shows.[43]

Cable meant more—but not necessarily more diverse—TV. The logic of the business required cheap (and thus often old) programs as well as niche advertising and audiences. With dozens of channels, the old logic of trying to "broadly cast" to a large share of a "general"—preferably eighteen-to-forty-nine-year-old—audience gave way to the logic of reaching "purer" audiences, specialized "demos" (demographic groups) to whom specialized advertisers pedaled their wares. These audiences included children (Nickelodeon), working women (WE), male sports fans (ESPN), youth (MTV, VH-1, and E!), conservative religious audiences (Christian Broadcasting and, later, the Family Channel), males in their late teens and twenties (Spike), and, yes, eventually aging baby boomers and others nostalgic for their youth (Nick at Nite, TV Land, etc.). With so much choice and viewers' armed with remotes, the best way to create channel loyalty was to immerse viewers in blocks of similar programming. All this was part of a broader process, the breaking up of America into ever narrower taste cultures—and the decline of family viewing (with multiple TVs per household) and the programming that had dominated the network era.[44]

Distinguishing themselves from others and winning a distinct "demo" required cable channels to adopt a new way of branding programs in their schedules. Each channel used promos, as Joseph Turow notes, to cue "viewers to read and understand it in particular ways." This branding of mostly cheap programs began with MTV in the early 1980s, when it created a cable channel featuring rock music videos. Nickelodeon pioneered a number of branding devices to win a children's audience: specially designed logos and bumpers (program promotions).[45] The idea was to create a kind of media community based not on specific programs but on the channel and its presumed appeal to a target audience. Nickelodeon used focus groups of children to evaluate its lineup of kids' programs and network promotions. Its promotions were designed to make viewers into a "nation," encouraging youngsters to identify with "Nick" as a channel made for them (not parents and educators, as was PBS's kids' programming). Nickelodeon claimed in effect to "empower" its viewers with programs that met their needs and desires.[46]

By 1985, this strategy would be applied to nostalgic viewers with promos that assured them that they were not watching dated TV but instead their TV "heritage." The business and technological imperatives of cable assured age marketing of cheap, ready-to-hand reruns. This led cable channels to devote themselves wholly or in part to the TV "heritages" of different age groups.

This shift was anticipated by a new wave of nostalgic specials that contrasted sharply with the all-inclusive network retrospectives of a decade earlier. While Disney and other specials continued to appeal to a broad audience,[47] by the late 1980s boomers were entering their forties, and, as the largest age cohort, TV and movie producers were ready to tap into their fond memories with "homecoming" specials based on the characters of *their* favorite old TV shows.

Still the Beaver (1983) picked up the lives of the Cleavers (minus the father Ward—Hugh Beaumont—who had recently died). Deftly written, the story brought back the two brothers— the Beaver, now a father with two boys of his own but struggling with a failing marriage, along with Wally, a successful local lawyer, married but still without children. The story played on the contrasts (and parallels) between the brothers as kids and as adults. The story ends happily as the Beaver learns how to be a good father, and he and Wally learn to be friends. And June says over Ward's grave, "You would be so proud of your boys. They turned out just the way you thought they would."[48] And boomers would be proud too that the fantasy family of their TV childhoods had a happy ending.

More curious was the 1989 reunion of the Smothers Brothers Comedy Hour, a variety show that was cancelled by CBS in 1969, despite high ratings, because of the brothers' vocal opposition to the Vietnam War. Two decades later, all had been forgiven, and boomers, who recalled with fondness the (in fact) rather gentle radicalism of the show, were expected to watch and remember the fun of the 1960s. And inevitably, PBS, following the popular trend in a neverending effort to find an audience, offered in 1991 a six-hour series on "Making Sense of the Sixties," with plenty of footage flattering to sixties sexual and political rebels.[49]

Repeatedly, producers fished in the same river of niche nostalgia, appealing to often narrow cohorts of viewers. In the late 1990s, there was a number of movies based rather uncreatively on TV series from the 1970s (*The Brady Bunch* and *Charlie's Angels*) trying to appeal to older Gen-Xers who had been subteens when these shows came out. And then in November 2001, reunion TV specials featuring footage of Carol Burnett and Lucille Ball were followed in the spring of 2002 by specials (with diminishing ratings) recalling *The Cosby Show*, *M*A*S*H*, *The Mary Tyler Moore Show*, *Laverne and Shirley*, and other long-gone programs. More followed in 2004.[50] There were, of course, numerous efforts of PBS to make documentaries out of the history of commercial TV programming (for example, The *Pioneers of Television* series beginning in 2010), though this series was much more about factoids and sentiment than a serious recounting of that history.[51]

Given all this, it is no surprise that in the new world of narrowcast cable there was ample room for channels dedicated to rerun TV. This category rose from Viacom. An early cable player and spinoff company from CBS in 1971, Viacom controlled key network "evergreen" programs, once broadcast on the networks (*I Love Lucy*, *Andy Griffith*, etc.), and had been a major syndicator of rerun TV programs even before cable. Viacom had acquired key cable networks, including MTV and VH-1, which had pioneered video music, and the fledgling Nickelodeon, for daytime kids' programming. Understanding the power of age-linked TV channels, it isn't surprising that Viacom spread from narrowcasting children and youth programs to marketing nostalgia for the oldsters. The first dedicated block of nostalgia shows was aired on Nickelodeon in July 1985 in the evening, presumably to discourage parents whose kids had been watching Nickelodeon until bedtime from changing the station. What Nickelodeon offered were the sitcoms of mom's and dad's own childhoods. Dubbed Nick at Nite, early fare included *Green Acres*, *Bewitched*, and *The Donna Reed Show*, programs from the 1960s and early 1970s that young parents in 1985 would have recalled from their earliest memories through their early teens. Frequently, the lineup changed (a process familiar to any regular TV viewer), and Viacom producers tried to make sure that everything shown, as one official noted, was what "our TV-generation audience grew up with." Before running a series, Nick at Nite used focus groups to test the appeal of proposed shows. These shows were not simply run half hour by half hour and interlaced with commercials; they were packaged as "classic TV," with catchy, whimsical promotions for many of the shows (similar to the strategy for daytime Nickelodeon). For example, in 1990, one promo stated, "You've gained ten pounds. There's a hole in the ozone. Your dog has worms. Donna Reed can help," openly acknowledging the escapist motive of viewers, but this rather bleak statement was presented in merely mock seriousness, by overenthusiastic announcers and overlaid with pastel-colored images of 1950s space-age kitsch. Again, the 1950s represented the nostalgic even though most Nick at Nite shows had actually been produced later.[52]

Early on, Nick at Nite recognized the possibilities of branding its reruns as nostalgia for older audiences and as camp to reach younger viewers who might find ancient shows amusingly corny. Cable channels often have used "marathons" of sequential episodes of a sitcom to make a day's viewing an event or to bring an audience in for hours to compete against a high-viewership event (like the Superbowl, for the millions of viewers uninterested in football). Other ways of dressing up reruns include the "hosted program," as in the trivia-filled introductions to the films shown on Turner Classic Movies; another is the revivals of gag hosts for

"B" horror films on Friday or Saturday nights. The intentionally obnoxious Gilbert Gottfried for the USA channel's *Up All Night* played this role in the 1990s. More recently, this same gimmick has reappeared on the retro channel Me-TV on Saturday nights with the character Svengoolie (Rich Koz), who wears face paint and a top hat while telling corny jokes and making fun of the werewolf or Dracula movie being aired. In 2012, Me-TV hyped its varied twenty-four-hour lineup of sitcoms and crime shows with the tagline "Me likes it," an exuberant statement of unreflective pleasure in old TV as a right of personal choice.[53]

The clear purpose was to repackage old TV, not just to air cheap entertainment fillers; it was to create audiovisual time capsules, but also with a dash of irony, whimsy, affection, and the promise of fulfilled longing. Scott Webb, the vice president of Nick at Nite in 1990, claimed to base programming on two driving ideas: serving the "TV generation—everyone who grew up on television" and creating the idea of "TV Land"—a place where viewers feel that they are part of a "common family. . . . We probably know more about the characters and places of TV Land than we know about the history of America or our own extended families."[54]

This "commitment" to those who grew up with TV and longed for a "family" experience in watching old shows was not confined to the first "TV generation." Nick at Nite gradually shifted from programs linked to the (late) boomer childhoods of the 1960s to appeal to a younger group who grew up in the 1970s. In 1992, Nick's parent Viacom acquired MTM's 1970s adult workplace sitcoms (*Mary Tyler Moore* and *Bob Newhart*) to reach this younger group and also scheduled the more naive family sitcoms from the 1970s (*Happy Days*, *The Brady Bunch*, and *The Partridge Family*). In the first decade of the twenty-first century, Nick at Nite shifted again to 1980s (and some 1990s) programming for new Gen-X parents. These shows included *Cheers*, *Cosby*, *The Facts of Life*, *Three's Company*, *Family Ties*, *Full House*, and *Roseanne*.[55]

This trend created a "demo" gap: boomers and their fixation on earlier shows were left out. Viacom solved this by launching TV Land in 1996. TV Land reverted back to boomer nostalgia (without abandoning younger viewers) under the moniker of "Classic TV" and the promise to preserve "our television heritage."[56] The 1996–1997 lineup included the occasional rerun of old variety shows (*Sonny and Cher* and even *Ed Sullivan*), but these soon disappeared. The wide range of sitcoms and dramas included the ancient western *Gunsmoke*, the silly sitcom *The Munsters*, the once provocative *All in the Family*, and the barfly family of *Cheers*. In 2000 and 2001, TV Land added action and drama with *The A-Team*, *Barney Miller*, *Charlie's Angels*, *77 Sunset Strip*, (briefly) the satirical *Get Smart*, and especially *Dragnet* and *Adam -12*. By 2007, the age gap between the two sister stations was enormous (a mean of twenty-three years of age for Nick at Nite, with an obvious share of teens and kids, and fifty-five for TV Land).[57]

Viacom recognized the need for a distinction between pitching to parents of young kids on Nick at Nite and to an older audience of "heritage TV" on TV Land, but there was clearly no long-lasting loyalty to boomers. TV Land's president Larry Jones made this clear in 2006 when he noted that "With the boomers there's an opportunity we identified, and now our focus is on viewers in their forties, but in ten years, we'll still be targeting the forties; we will not follow the boomers. It's the life stage we want." This point of view was reflected in TV Land's introduction of "reality" shows, including *The Big 4-0* (2008–2009), about the life-changing transition to the forties; *High School Reunion* (2006), featuring a high-school class from 1986; and *She's Got the Look* (2008–2010), a search for a female model over thirty-five. As Jones observed, "a show [like *The Big 4-0*] that resonates with forty-year-olds will still generate more dollars than if it's *The Big 6-0*."[58] In 2007, TV Land shifted programming to viewers just entering their forties with *Murphy Brown*, *Third Rock from the Sun*, and even the Gen-X medical sitcom *Scrubs*, for late primetime viewers. The point, of course, was to attract a "demo" with age-segmented nostalgia, and, following the old logic, viewers over the age of fifty were not valued, at least during primetime.[59]

Thus, like Nick at Nite before it, TV Land tried to disassociate itself from an aging demo. In 2012, TV Land began an effort to spruce up its increasingly dowdy image with a new logo and the slogan "Laugh More," even though western dramas—*Gunsmoke* and *Bonanza*—still filled the channel's weekday afternoons. TV Land added more recent sitcoms from the 1990s and later (*Everybody Loves Raymond*, *The King of Queens*, and *That '70s Show*).[60] Yet, despite this attempt to reach the under-fifty-year-old crowd, TV Land in 2012 still offered many of the same range of reruns as a decade before (including *Lucy* in the morning), and most of its advertising was obviously directed toward viewers over fifty (from companies offering help with disability claims and supplements to Medicare to sellers of powered wheelchairs, catheters, and even burial insurance). It seems that there was still gold in the "Golden Years" crowd. After all, in 2012, boomers were projected to hold 70 percent of disposable income over the next five years, and at seventy-eight million, they still constituted a large portion of the U.S. population.[61]

Inevitably there were others who tried to tap into the nostalgia TV market, especially of those well beyond forty. One was Nostalgia TV, subsequently called Good Life TV and then American Life TV. It went so far as to relabel itself "Your Baby Boomer TV" in 2005. However, in 2007, the channel reached only eleven million American homes.[62] Another small network is Retro TV, launched in 2005 as the RTN channel, one of four digital networks owned by Luken Communications. RTN adopted the TV Land model of 24/7 reruns of shows from the 1950s to early 1990s (though by 2012 it specialized in dramas, mostly westerns and crime shows, rather than the sitcoms of TV Land).[63]

Perhaps the most successful is Me-TV ("Memorable Entertainment" Television), owned by Weigel Broadcasting and distributed by Metro-Goldwyn-Mayer. Like TV Land, Me-TV has access to telefilm archives, including CBS Television Distribution, Twentieth Century Television, and other companies. Originating in 2005 and growing out of a local Chicago station that had specialized in classic TV shows, Me-TV's programming was taken national by its owner John Weigel in November 2010 with a standard schedule available to local stations via satellite. By early 2012, Me-TV reached 45 percent of American homes. With about one hundred series to choose from, Weigel's network embraced the boomers with programming that extends from the 1950s to the 1980s with weekday blocks of both vintage sitcoms (from *Mary Tyler Moore* and *The Beverly Hillbillies* to the inevitable *I Love Lucy* and *The Honeymooners*) as well as dramas (from *Gunsmoke* to *Perry Mason* and *The Twilight Zone*). In 2011, most of its viewers were in the fifty-to-sixty-four-year range—and the channel was determined to hold that demo. Neal Sabin, the vice president of Me, claimed that the network has received more than twelve thousand letters from viewers, imploring it not to adopt the strategy of the Viacom nostalgia networks: "please don't change, please don't get younger—don't start showing things from the '90s. . . . Our niche is truly classic television, and that's where we plan on staying."[64]

Similar to Me is Antenna TV, a product of the media giant Tribune Broadcasting, which was launched in August 2010 from a base of seventeen Tribune-owned stations. It followed the same strategy as Me and TV Land, with block scheduling by genre and decade to lead niche audiences through hours of viewing. For example, in the summer of 2012, weekday afternoons on Antenna TV included double doses of *McHale's Navy*, *Hazel*, *Dennis the Menace*, and *Leave It to Beaver*, all from the late 1950s and early 1960s; it featured crime shows during the late afternoon and evening (*Adam-12*, for example), and the vintage *Alfred Hitchcock Presents* at 11 pm. Like Me-TV, Antenna can draw on its link to a large library of four thousand films and 270 TV series owned by its partner Sony Pictures Entertainment as well as access to NBC Universal Television Distribution (shared with Me).[65]

From the mid-1990s, a wide range of other cable channels used inexpensive retro series (often shown in five-day "strips") to win young as well as older viewers to their formats. In 2014, TV One and Centric targeted African American audiences with numerous airings of *Cosby*, *The A-Team*, and other programs with black stars. In 2012, family-friendly channels like Hallmark and GMC (originally the Gospel Music Channel and since 2013 UP TV) offered sentimental historical series like *The Waltons* and *Little House on the Prairie*. HUB copied Nickelodeon by airing sitcoms from the 1980s (for parents) after a daytime schedule of kids' stuff. Women-oriented channels (WE TV and Oxygen) featured blocks of *Frasier* and *Roseanne*; young-adult channel Reelz ran 1990s sitcoms (like

Becker, Spin City, and *Cheers*).[66] All this amounted to another form of consumed nostalgia in an era of fast capitalism: a daily opportunity to return to a childhood that for all Americans—from the boomers through the Gen-Xers and on even to the millennials—was so largely lived in front of the TV set.

THOUGHTS ON WHY

I began this chapter wondering why people today would spend so much time watching old, but surely not the "best," TV. Many have offered ideas that may help us understand. The most common theory was advanced more than thirty years ago by Fred Davis in *Yearning for Yesterday*. We watch old shows for the "contrast or, more accurately the way we *make* them contrast—with the events, moods, and dispositions of our present circumstances." The attraction comes from a sense of loss that for Davis emerged from the stresses of the 1960s and was manifested in the 1970s nostalgia for the 1950s. Davis found this especially true of boomers whose identification with 1950s TV (and much else) created a kind of generational bonding.[67] This analysis is easily transferred to later generations who, fifteen to twenty years after their childhood viewing, rediscover, as part of a general disenchantment with the present, "their" old shows on Nick at Nite. By 2014, this led to a spate of nostalgia shows for the 1990s, even the 2000s. The speeding up of social and cultural change seems to create age cohorts that identify with particular pasts, deemed superior to the present when seen through the distorting lens of old TV shows and childhood memory. However, this argument may focus too narrowly on "historical crises" and generational identity to explain viewer attraction to rerun TV. It ignores how changes in modern media and marketing make retro appealing.

According to Frederic Jameson and others, nostalgia TV shows (like much other retro) are substitutes for a "real past" (events, social and cultural institutions, even personal relationships). This results from the simple fact that we spend more time in front of the screen than we do engaged in "reality." Modern media has not only become a substitute for relationships, but, because memorable bites of media can be and are cut, recirculated, recontextualized, and even intensified thanks to the technology of recording, editing, and replaying, TV can become "hyperreal." The result is a mediated memory detached from events and artificially constructed. Thus the real past is replaced by a series of media stereotypes of the past. The fifties of memory becomes a series of seemingly random images—Lucy wrapping chocolates on an assembly line or stomping grapes into wine.[68] This argument gives weight to the enormous impact of TV and other forms of modern consumption on our psyches and memories. The power of mediated sight and sound has been radically expanded since Jameson's writing (1991) with cable and Internet downloading. Still, does this postmodern critique explain how viewers actually consume retro media, or does retro necessarily lead to its passive consumption, as Jameson assumes?

Another, more positive take on retro media comes from a younger generation of commentators: Paul Grainge, for example, argues that the prevalence of nostalgia TV reflects the availability of reruns and the need of so many channels to fill time slots rather than some pathological need of aging viewers to recover a lost innocence or the inexorable power of the simulacra or the hyperreal media. Of course, it isn't just a matter of supply (many if not most people won't just watch whatever is cheap and available to cable channels). The pastiche of sound and sight bites of retro programs and their promotions may have displaced other forms of experience, but this can be understood in a positive way as a modern aesthetic. Grainge explains:

> Rather than suggesting an amnesiac culture based on sanitized or hyperrealized memory, I would argue that the proliferation of nostalgic modes, markets, genres, and styles may instead reflect a new kind of engagement with the past. . . . Retro America need not describe a culture in crisis, but may rather suggest a moment distinguished by its re-evaluation and re-presentation of the forms, contexts, and values of the past.

In other words, the availability of reruns and digital technology of cable has produced a new way of relating to the past—not necessarily a crisis or a loss of "historicity" in a postmodern illusion. The modern technology of cable TV and the remote (as well as YouTube and other downloadable features of the Internet) give us a multimedia past that we choose for aesthetic as well as psychological reasons.[69]

I don't see why a synthesis of views is not possible. Nostalgia TV attracts different audiences for different reasons, and some shows reach more of one age (gender, sex, class, or other sociocultural category) than another—or, at least, that is what the cable channel owners hope. Thus first, repeatedly we see generational longings for an idealized past (memories of TV when viewers were between six and twelve) and, with this, efforts by cable channel programmers to target successive cohorts as they reach about forty years in age and become the newly nostalgic, longing for a "simpler" time. In effect, these groups are seeking an escape from the fast capitalism of today in a frozen focus on a few faces from the rapidly passing parade of their commercialized childhoods. Viewers reinterpret that TV experience in an often illusory and nearly always negative contrast with the present—thus the popularity of the many retro shows that feature "inspiration" (*The Waltons*) or naive sexuality and family life (*Three's Company* and *Leave It to Beaver*) as an antidote to the cynicism and the flippant vulgarity of the present. Second, these longings are expressed through a childhood of TV watching, which is at most a distorted mirror of the real-life experiences and historic events of that childhood. Thus, because of reruns, this nostalgia is not confined to the generation of first viewers but can be part of any generation of viewers (who become nostalgic for small-town America, for example, by seeing Andy of Mayberry on afterschool reruns).[70] Finally, nostalgia TV can often become a playful reinterpretation of the past or simply a first-time or renewed encounter with the "foreign territory" of the past. Why shouldn't youth today get a kick out of the pratfalls of Dick van Dyke from the 1960s? All of this can be part of the channel surfer's ahistorical and many-sided TV culture; it meets diverse "needs" or simply whims because of the sheer ease of access. It may reflect a growing toleration, even embrace, of endless change, especially among younger consumers.

Retro TV, like other forms of "reconsumption," need not be an escape from the present and future, or an inauthentic read of the past, or a cocooning into some comfortable identity. Old TV can be experienced in many ways: reruns can led us to new understandings of the past that correct and enrich memory because we bring to our viewing a perspective that differs from our memory of what we saw as children. Rerun TV can tell us how the world and we have changed (and not just negatively).[71]

Still, classic TV, like so much of consumed nostalgia, turns on the simple appeal of predictability and on our longing to recover our childhoods, which seem to be inescapably defined by those bits of consumer culture that we possess and that possess us. And, since the first generation was brought up on TV in the 1950s, despite and even because of TV's constantly changing palette of programs that divides us into different taste cultures, TV has shaped the psyches of almost all of us.

5

Give Me That
Old-Time Radio

One of the successes of the Public Broadcasting System has been its doo-wop specials, aired out of Pittsburgh in 1999 for WQED and then used nationally by local PBS stations to raise funds for public TV. Cosponsored with Rhino Records, a pioneer in publishing retro rock, and hosted by Jerry Butler, a one-time crooner ("For Your Precious Love"), the "Doo Wop 50: Five Decades of Vocal Group Harmony" celebrated a subspecialty of 1950s and early-1960s rock. Doo-wop vocal groups emerged from the streets and hallways of Harlem and other urban spaces, featuring high tenor lead voices belting out love songs, with verbal "nonsense" harmonies and a prominent bass in the background.[1]

The "Doo Wop 50" show was pure nostalgia, as mostly plump, grey-haired or bald crooners in purple or gold tuxes sang their signature songs, hits from forty years before. The performers looked pretty much like the mostly white crowd, except that many on stage were black—The Del-Vikings ("Come, Go with Me"), the Five Satins ("In the Still of the Night"), the Penguins ("Earth Angel"), the Marcels ("Blue Moon"), and the Platters ("The Great Pretender"). But, of course, the real purpose of the show was to persuade viewers to pledge money for local public TV. The performance was interrupted for long "pledge breaks with the offer of "gifts" of doo-wop CDs for anyone giving one hundred dollars. In mini-interviews, the performers recalled those simple days of fun and romance when, as one put it, instead of fighting on the streets, they used their singing groups to compete for girls. Since 1970, from almost the beginning of the perpetually cash-strapped PBS network of TV stations, special pop concerts have been mainstays of fundraising. They still are. My PBS station replayed Elvis's 1973 Hawaii concert in September 2013; over the years, according to PBS, this concert has been seen by one billion people. But the "Doo Wop 50" show was exceptional for its time, raising twenty-six million dollars for public stations. Two sequels followed, along with a series of rock revivals produced by T. J. Lubinsky featuring Motown, disco, soul, and country rock.

In a way this has always struck me as odd: I suppose I have always assumed that PBS is supposed to provide public-interest documentaries like *Frontline* and serious drama like *Masterpiece Theatre* (now just *Masterpiece*) to viewers seeking an alternative to reality TV and raunchy sitcoms. Yet even though these specials may have annoyed PBS purists, the one cold fact is that PBS viewers are older than those of most other stations (with 37 percent over fifty-five), and by 1999 that meant that a large group of the PBS audience fondly remembered the happy and melodious sounds of doo-wop, associating it with their childhoods and youth, with memories of firsts, especially first loves.[2]

Public TV was not the only way that rock music was classed up as nostalgia. Powerful enthusiasts who wanted to turn the pop music of their youths (and the source of their fortunes) into "heritage" created rock museums. The Rock and Roll Hall of Fame Foundation was launched in 1983 by the creator of a major rock label, Ahmet Ertegün of Atlantic Records, along with the editor of *Rolling Stone*, Jann Wenner. This led to the construction of a rock museum in

Cleveland (which outbid other certainly more musically significant cities for the honor, including Memphis and Detroit). The legendary architect I. M. Pei designed a striking building of geometric and cantilevered forms in glass, anchored by a tower and located on the shores of Lake Erie. It is a grand and glorious site for remembering rock and roll. The first major exhibit at the Rock and Roll Hall of Fame featured the psychedelic era, 1965 through 1969, reflecting, perhaps, the musical biases of the directors. That was followed by displays of Elvis and later hip-hop, indicating a desire to be more inclusive. The foundation annually inducts celebrated rockers into the Hall of Fame, beginning in 1986 with Chuck Berry and Elvis, obviously, but also including "early influence" performers like the country singer Jimmy Rogers and even the rock impresario Alan Freed. By 2014, there had been 304 inductees, mostly performers from the 1950s, 1960s, and 1970s, but, in the past few years, gradually acknowledging more recent trends in hip-hop, punk, and rap, groups such as the Beastie Boys and the Stooges have also been inducted. There is a display, for instance, called "Rapper's Delight," which exhibits clothing worn by Ice-T and the Sugar Hill Gang. The current array of permanent displays at the Hall of Fame also reflects the broad narrative of rock "heritage": this includes a precursor's section with homage to country, blues, and gospel as well as large displays of Elvis memorabilia (rings, watches, and military cards). Other pioneer rockers are grouped by city of origin: Memphis, Liverpool, and Detroit. Also included are special tributes to the Beatles and to Jimi Hendrix. In the "Legends of Rock" exhibit, figures from the 1960s and early 1970s like Michael Jackson, the Allman Brothers, Stevie Nicks, the Supremes, and the Beach Boys are featured, along with their clothes, instruments, and other trappings. There is even room for Frank Beard from the Texas band ZZ Top (including his bearded drums). This apparent generational bias didn't seem to bother a mother of about forty with her teenage son, whom I met at the "Pink Floyd Wall," when I was visiting the museum in 2014. Though very knowledgeable about the groups and trends of the rock of her own youth (the 1980s), when asked whether she listened to those musicians any longer, she admitted, "not much." Instead, when I queried why she was interested in the rock music of the 1970s and earlier, she looked surprised and said simply, "Well it's classic rock, the beginning of it all."[3]

The Cleveland site is hardly the only tribute to rock history. Paul Allen, a founder of Microsoft, built the Experience Music Project (too hip to be called a museum) in Seattle. But there is also Detroit's Motown Historical Museum and Memphis's Smithsonian Rock 'n' Soul Museum, each city claiming its rock heritage. Some exhibits border on the religious by featuring "relics" like Bob Marley's dreadlocks and the ashes of Alan Freed, both at the Rock and Roll Hall of Fame and Museum.

In the fourth grade, when I first heard Elvis sing "Hound Dog" on my older sister's little white cola-stained plastic radio, I couldn't have imagined that almost forty years later this loud, repetitive, and, frankly, rather crudely simple music would have been given such an honored place in our culture. The "inferiority" of Elvis Presley's smash "cover" hit "Hound Dog" in 1956 was obvious to my untrained ear—I was precociously familiar with popular classical music from my father's collection of Copland and Rossini on 45 RPMs and felt a little superior toward my sister's taste. But, today, I enjoy listening to early rock on Sirius/XM satellite radio's channel 5. I like even more channel 6, devoted to the sixties, and even occasionally channel 7 for the seventies, though, not surprisingly, given my age rarely do I turn to channels 8 or 9 for subsequent decades. Although I never collected rock 45s (but rather classical LPs), just being young during the years when Elvis was the King and Frankie Lymon and the Teenagers had their fifteen minutes of fame made ephemeral commercial tunes on the radio part of my memory and—despite my youthful disdain—a nostalgic memory.

ROOTS OF RETRO: RESEARCH, RECORDS, RADIO, AND TIN PAN ALLEY

For a long time psychologists, neurologists, and students of advertising have told us how music fosters memory. Tunes from a distant personal past mitigate the effects of Alzheimer's disease, familiar songs increase recall of ads, and popular music from childhood sparks recollections of personal events long forgotten by the elderly. One among many similar studies showed how even people in their late sixties recall songs from their youth and express strong emotional feelings toward these tunes even though they could provide fewer associated autobiographical details than could younger listeners. The key to the intensity of the memory was the emotional response to the song.[4]

But even more basically, pleasure in music depends upon its repetitive quality, which creates the ability to anticipate what will come next in a composition, based on recalling what has already been heard in that arrangement and in one's musical memory. Reiteration is necessary in music because, unlike prose or a painting, music flows in time rather than unfolds in space, and thus it is repetition and familiarity that give it structure and meaning. We understand and appreciate music in our culture by drawing on the information stored in the brain's long-term memory about the "musical lexicon" of our culture, which leads us to expect certain patterns upon hearing even an unfamiliar piece of music. This results in the common ability to know and often sing along with a song from its beginning. Thus, "from infancy to old age, we are able to recognize a familiar tune; we associate many moments of our lives with particular songs or other music."[5]

Since the earliest days of commercial radio in the 1920s, the advertising industry has understood the power of the jingle and the borrowed tune in selling America's name-brand goods; along the way, the makers of popular music and commercials have often become the same people.[6] In recent years, the academic study of the impact of music on winning the attention and memory of consumers has become a cottage industry.[7] And there are gender differences: Morris Holbrook and Robert Schindler found a strong nostalgia among females for songs popular in their late teens and early twenties; men had stronger positive memories of cars from their youth.[8]

These studies are not surprising. They only confirm what music people have known for over a century. From the beginning of recorded music in the 1890s, manufacturers understood the appeal of songs that consumers associated with their youth. An ad for Thomas Edison phonographs of 1899 made an often-repeated point—that the phonograph record makes "permanent the otherwise fleeting pleasure" of sound. An ad of 1904 appealed to the elderly with Edison's recordings of "marches, ballads, and arias that stirred you in the old days."[9]

Certainly, the coming of recorded music in the 1890s made it far easier to recover the songs of youth. The key innovation was the exact repeatability of music on records (something that never can happen with live music even when it is performed by the same musicians). Historians tell us that music based on oral traditions, such as the music of the Middle Ages, was seldom performed for more than one or two generations. With the coming of records, however, not only were the "classics" preserved, but ephemeral "hits" survived as "oldies," the music of each generation's youth played years later in life. Romantic memories of falling in love or just being free and having fun were linked with a favorite tune that would be recalled unchanged throughout life, thanks to the recording. Once again, the ephemeral consumer good, in this case the "hit" song, like novelty toys, annual model changes in cars, and so much else in the modern age of fast capitalism, created the possibility of modern nostalgia.[10]

The phonograph record was essential in this process. As important was a nearly simultaneous development: the emergence in the 1890s of Tin Pan Alley—the commercialized song industry, which created the modern "hit" tune that was ephemeral and thus associated with a particular time. An unintended effect of these hits was that later they became the "music of a generation" in nostalgia. The popular song has created a unique lexicon of musical memory: Short and familiar, easy to sing and play, and topical, sentimental, or romantic, the modern tune has its roots in the mass-manufactured, fleeting products of the sheet-music industry. These printed songs were performed in vaudeville but were also sold to amateurs for singing around a home piano. These tunes were easily adapted to the record player when it appeared for home use in the mid-1890s, and then to radio in 1920, and to sound motion pictures from 1927. So ubiquitous was this music that it became the backdrop to almost everyone's lives. These songs were distinct from the regional, historically deep tunes of folk music. They were relatively short, without the common practice in folk songs of adding a long series of verses, and commonly had choruses that were melodious, catchy, and easy to remember. Tin Pan Alley songs were distributed nationally for a short period and thus were associated with a particular time (personal and historical), creating, in the long run, ideal markers of individual memory shared by Americans everywhere. In this way, these popular tunes were, like the parade of toys, dolls, and cars that emerged with modern consumer culture, hooks on which to hang recollections of the past. A brief account of the history of Tin Pan Alley will make this clear.

Named for a block on Twenty-Eighth Street between Sixth Avenue and Broadway in Manhattan, where American popular-music publishing was first centered (before moving north to Forty-Ninth Street), Tin Pan Alley eventually referred to a wide variety of mass-produced popular tunes regardless of where they were published. It dominated commercial music from about 1890 to 1955. Although sentimental love songs were common on the Alley, the music appealed to all age groups. While popular songs had been written and published long before Tin Pan Alley (often as a side business by local printers or music stores), only in the 1890s did professional songwriters produce tunes on demand for publishers. This was part of the revolution in mass commodification: the centralized production of goods for the national (and even international) market. For makers of candy bars and cigarettes, this meant promoting daily purchases of the same product; for publishers of sheet music, success required producing "hits," a variety of tunes that attracted mass sales by becoming fashionable. Essential to the "hit" business was that these tunes were soon replaced with new ones, an excellent example of the modern disposable consumer economy. Because "hits" were hard to predict and because the tunes had to be so accessible that they were inevitably simple and "turned over" quickly, there had to be a continuous flow of a large number of songs.[11]

Tin Pan Alley became a veritable song factory (much like the manufacturing of pulp fiction at the same time). There tunes and words were produced by the likes of Irving Berlin, a man who never learned to read or write music and could hardly play the piano but who had a knack for tapping out a melody on the keys and for writing lyrics that captured a fleeting popular mood and the emotions of a mass American audience. Publishers like M. Witmark and Sons were excellent salespeople (even if they often had little knowledge of music) and understood popular taste. Their job was to find the hit that separated the rare tune from the mass of ephemeral, and often unprofitable, ditties cranked out daily by the industry. Alley publishers hired "pluggers" to perform songs in music stores, beer halls, and even streetcars; some cozied up to vaudeville singers to get them to sing and thus promote their songs.[12] Vaudeville, a national string of music halls across the country (introduced by Tony Pastor in New York in 1866), was where Americans came to hear the latest hits.[13] These efforts produced relatively few mega hits (perhaps a hundred songs sold a million copies in the first decade of the twentieth century). But that was the goal. And thus many of these tunes became "standards" (beginning in the 1890s with tunes like "The Band Played On" and "A Bicycle Built for Two"), sustained in part by nostalgia.[14]

All this encouraged a homogenized American taste in music, even though publishers had to appeal to particular taste cultures as well (divided by ethnicity and class, especially). This led to an amazing variety of mass-produced music—everything from opera arias and hymns to college fight songs and ethnic comedy, little of which entered the American nostalgia banks.[15] Early record makers appealed to the tastes of the rich who could afford them (Victor's Red Seal records, e.g.). The elite favored an emerging canon of "classical" music heard in concert and especially opera halls. Still, the bread and butter of the industry was recording the music of Tin Pan Alley (Victor's Black Label, e.g.) that later became the "oldies."[16]

Greatly magnifying the impact of Tin Pan Alley was the fortuitous arrival in the 1890s of the acoustic phonograph.[17] And Tin Pan Alley's array of tunes fit closely with the record format—roughly two or three minutes long. Music had once been a community experience with families singing on Sunday evenings from sheet music, gathered around a piano. However, recordings of professional, even celebrity, musicians, played on the phonograph, changed that. Recordings made music a private experience, often integrated into routine life as background sound. And they set the stage for modern musical memory.

Records hugely magnified the influence of the commercial hit. More than the publishers' sheet music, the recording offered small intense packages of words and sound that were even more accessible to a mass audience than sheet music because it required no skill in singing or piano playing. The ephemeral and centrally produced "hit" song was delivered to a home audience, which required the consumer only to be aware of current fashion, have access and money to patronize a record store, and the ability to operate the phonograph. And, inevitably, the record was played often, creating an unheard-of familiarity, filling a moment of time with a tune. This may have meant that songs were relatively quickly abandoned to be replaced by another novel hit as consumers grew tired of them, but it also meant that the saturation of a particular moment with this or that melody made it later an emotional gateway to memory.

Radio further accelerated this dynamic. With the coming of NBC in 1926, the radio industry could transmit live programs nationally across a network of broadcast stations. By the 1930s, radios were in most American living rooms, and music was mainly featured in commercial programming. Tin Pan Alley songsmiths survived by shifting to this new medium and relying on royalties for income. During the Depression, most music was heard on the radio, both because it was free after initial purchase (while records remained pricey) and was even simpler to use: no more changing records every couple of minutes.[18] With this shift, the Alley became ever more wed to the imperative of winning over the broadest possible audience. This produced the modern parade of hits, rising and falling within two or three months. The result: a small number of tunes were heard over a shorter time, filling a few weeks or months with identifiable music.[19]

Phonograph records regained some of their past glory with the development of the long-playing (LP) record by Columbia in 1948. Running about twenty minutes per side at thirty-three revolutions

per minute (RPM) in microgroove vinyl, this was a vast improve-
ment over the traditional 78 RPM disc, which played for three or
four minutes. LPs made it practical to record whole movements
of symphonies or musicals, for example, on a single side. This no
doubt deepened the music culture of Americans, especially with
the coming of high-fidelity and stereophonic records and phonograph equipment after 1957. But in the short run, the introduction
of the 45 RPM record in 1949, which held a single song per side, like
the old 78s, but was smaller, more convenient, and rugged, had a
greater impact on popular listening. This led to cheap recordings
(often costing under half a dollar), especially the familiar recording of mass-produced tunes sung by celebrity crooners. And so the
hits kept on flowing, heard to the point of boredom but burrowing
their way into listeners' memories.[20]

A REVOLUTION IN POP:
ORIGINS OF MODERN RETRO

Struggles within the popular music industry in the 1940s, along
with generational changes, led to the demise of Tin Pan Alley and
the birth of rock and, later, the modern "oldie." The American
Society of Composers, Authors, and Publishers (ASCAP) boycot-
ted broadcasters briefly in 1941, demanding higher royalties for
playing their songs. Likewise, the musicians' union struck record
companies (August 1942–October 1943) for higher earnings.[21]
These events unintentionally resulted in a shift from the established music of ASCAP (at that time big bands especially) to musicians linked to the broadcaster-affiliated BMI, who mostly performed vocal and "alternative" music. The musicians' action also
favored vocalists who could continue to record during the strike.
One result was the decline of the big bands and the introduction
of music beyond the conventional world of the Tin Pan Alley songsmiths. This included niche music from the south (country) and
from African American performers (especially rhythm and blues),
the hybrid of which became a leading precursor of rock and roll.
These events set the stage for the nearly total substitution of live

broadcast music for the recorded song and for the eclipse of Tin Pan Alley and the rise of rock.[22]

That shift in music finally came in the early 1950s with the swing from movies and radio to TV. The decline of the film musical and the end of network radio variety shows led to the rise of the radio disc jockey. Tin Pan Alley publishers lost control over the music market to record companies and local radio stations, and they no longer controlled the process of deciding what was heard by American listeners. The rise of television also meant a transformation in pop music's audiences, as adults abandoned radio (except for news, talk, weather, and light music mostly listened to on car radios). Teenagers in effect became radio's (and the recording industry's) primary market. Cheap radios, especially in equally cheap used cars and in portable transistor units, offered youth an entertainment site away from the family home and dad's control over the TV dial.[23]

Music appealing to the young was not new to the 1950s. Love songs directed at those in the courting phase of life was Tin Pan Alley's lifeblood. But the music industry sought an adult market, and, far from fostering age differences or conflicts, it appealed to the generic listener. Though shifts in fashion repeatedly pitted the old against the new (as in the introduction of ragtime, jazz, blues, and swing), until the 1950s novelty was identified with the fashionable and daring, not just with the youngest group of listeners. In 1937, bobbysoxer girls may have mobbed the bespectacled clarinetist Benny Goodman ("The King of Swing") and, in 1942, screamed for the youthful vocalist from the Dorsey Band, Frank Sinatra. Still, this was only a blip on the musical radar. Grownups listened to the middle-aged Paul Whiteman and his relatively sophisticated variety show. And, as we saw in the chapter on retro TV, the adult music variety show continued into the early 1970s, often featuring the oldies of middle-aged people.[24] Yet by the mid-1950s the songs that sold the most records and were heard the most on radio (and eventually seen in movies) were sung by the young for the still younger. That music was, of course, rock and roll, and its identification with successive waves of youth later created the ideal form of consumed nostalgia in oldies rock radio.

What made this music distinct was obvious to all at the time: it was primarily vocal rather than instrumental, it downplayed wind instruments (especially brass) and emphasized guitars, and it adopted a heavier beat. The musical style and content of lyrics was a long way from Tin Pan Alley, be it the sentimental ballad "After the Ball" of 1892 or the novelty tune "How Much Is That Doggie in the Window?" of 1953. As pop-music historians document, rock and roll was mostly a composite of two musical forms largely ignored by Alley publishers—white working-class country (hillbilly) music (popularized by Buddy Holly and Jerry Lee Lewis) and black rhythm and blues (identified with Chuck Berry, Little Richard, and Ruth Brown). Because of their wild, raw, and sometimes sensual qualities, hillbilly music and rhythm and blues gained the attention of youth in the early 1950s. Embracing the tastes and topics of the working class and minorities had long been (and still is) a form of rebellion among the offspring of the respectable white middle class. Yet the abandonment of the gentle and sentimental tunes of Doris Day ("Secret Love") and Eddie Fisher ("Oh My Papa") in the early 1950s for the jumping beat of Bill Haley and the Comets' "Rock Around the Clock" (1954) was revolutionary. And the fact that the first rock songs attracted almost exclusively teens was clear to everyone: variety show MCs (Ed Sullivan, Steve Allen, and Milton Berle) booked rockers to attract kids to their otherwise oldster lineup of performers, and preachers and old-guard radio managers railed against rockers and ceremonially destroyed their records as a threat to the morals of the young.[25]

The powerful combination of youth-oriented 45s turned out weekly by the record companies and Top 40 radio playing the two-minute tunes of rockers led to the demise of Tin Pan Alley—pushing the logic of fast capitalism to extremes. A new marketing strategy emerged: record companies paid radio announcers to play their discs (what later became known as payola). By 1956, almost all the Top 40 was rock and for the kids.[26]

Rock music was a break, but it also accelerated trends evident in Tin Pan Alley from its earliest days: rock tunes were even simpler, more repetitive, and shorter than their predecessors. Brevity (songs were often only two minutes long or even less) accommodated the fast-paced programming of Top 40 radio and fitted on the 45 RPM record. To attract listeners, rock led to "catchy hooks taking precedence over longer melodies." And the rock list turned over even faster than did the "hit parade" on the radio during the Tin Pan Alley era. These hits worked their way into the memories of listeners (especially the young) quickly and often permanently.[27]

All this coincided with the rise of the disc jockey or "deejay," the live radio announcer who introduced and at first selected records to be played on scheduled programs. Perhaps inevitably, with the decline of network radio and big bands and the migration of performers like Bing Crosby and Nat King Cole to TV (as the proportion of American homes with television sets grew from 9 to 50 percent in the first three years of the 1950s), radio station owners scrambled to find audiences and advertising dollars. The solution was obvious, at least to the radio entrepreneur Todd Storz from Omaha. Beginning in 1953, he created a Midwestern empire of all-hits radio stations. He modeled his innovation on the jukebox, which offered a continuously changing but small range of tunes at a time. Just as TV programmers realized that viewers wanted the familiar and thus embraced the repetitive sitcom and drama series, radio stations discovered that listeners wanted to hear their favorite tune over and over, exactly the same, and cared not a bit that the music wasn't live. This led to the era of the deejay.[28]

Of course, the central role of the record-playing radio announcer wasn't new to the 1950s. In 1933, Al Jarvis hosted a program of records from Los Angeles, but, given the prejudice against "canned" music at the time, he created the illusion of broadcasting live from a ballroom. Only in 1941 was the, at first derisive, term "disc jockey" invented by *Variety*. Despite the efforts of the musicians' unions to raise their earnings from record companies and deprive radio stations of new records to play during their strikes in the 1940s, by the decade's end canned music made DJs into celebrities (some, like Arthur Godfrey, Dave Garroway, Mike Wallace, and Hugh Downs, later migrated to TV fame).[29]

But the big change was the emergence of DJs who appealed directly to the new listener: an emerging audience of youth, many African American, but also rebellious whites eager to embrace the "hip" counterculture of new music. In 1948, Memphis's WDIA station reached a predominantly Southern black audience with the African American DJ Nat Williams. The next year, he was joined by the R&B performer B. B. King. At the same time, white DJs, like Hunter Hancock at Los Angeles's KFVD, featured R&B records appealing to a youth audience. Perhaps most celebrated of these early DJs was Alan Freed, a white radio announcer with a background in classical music but who in the spring of 1951 accepted an offer from a Cleveland record shop to host an R&B radio show. He gradually developed a distinct style, especially when he moved to WINS in New York in 1954. He talked and hooted over the records, attempting to sound stereotypically black. His show quickly became a cult, attracting youth but repelling their elders (from Todd Storz to the music arranger Mitch Miller). Freed's over-the-top style got him into trouble, leading to his firing from WINS when a riot followed one of his concerts in 1958, and he was exiled from the industry when he refused to sign a statement that he never accepted payola in 1960. He died in 1965 but today has a coveted corner in the Rock and Roll Hall of Fame and Museum devoted to his memory.[30]

Other DJs followed, like Robert Weston Smith, better known as Wolfman Jack. This Brooklyn-born (in 1938) white man was an early enthusiast for R&B and the black DJs who played it. When twenty-four, Smith, while spinning records at a Louisiana country station, developed his distinct "Wolfman" style, including a raspy voice interrupted with howling. His patter imitated black hipster DJs, making many listeners think that he was African American. In 1963, Smith got his big break with XERF in Ciudad Acuña, Mexico, on the Texas border, a station that blasted fifty thousand watts of radio throughout the South and Midwest. In 1966, he shifted to XERB, just south of the California border, for which he taped a daily show that was sent north with 250,000 watts of power. Though the Mexican government banned this and other "border blasters" in 1971, Wolfman found new opportunities in syndication (including Armed Forces Radio, where he had a show from 1970 to 1986). He even edited old XERB tapes for broadcast in up to two thousand stations (some are still available on the Internet).

He worked mostly out of Los Angeles, where he appeared in 1973 in *American Graffiti* and many TV shows, including as an announcer for NBC's *Midnight Special* (1972–1981).[31]

Less demonstrative was the DJ Bruce Morrow (Cousin Brucie), though he also was loud, fast-talking, and ever so hip. Born in 1935, he was twenty-four when he got famous at WINS, a Top 40 station in New York City. Like so many other regional DJs, he made Top 40 radio into an "a clubhouse, a semi-private hideaway for kids who saw themselves as different from their parents," as he described his show in an interview. Morrow led a somewhat peripatetic life, bouncing from stations in Miami back to New York at WABC in 1961, the most powerful station in the East, just in time to catch the boomer wave and soon thereafter to exploit the popularity of the Beatles and other British rockers. But, as a man about ten years older than his listeners when he started, he could talk sympathetically with his call-in teen audience about their lives, dreams, and struggles. In 1964, his show captured an amazing 25 percent of the New York radio audience.[32]

But the raucous style and independence of the DJs of the 1950s and early 1960s soon faded when station owners reined in their patter and radio managers began to use survey data to pare down the playlist to as few as thirty records at a time. And, from 1970, electronic devices allowed stations to program ads and playlists days in advance, reducing the need for DJs. No longer were they the kids' friend, freewheeling storytellers, or wild characters.[33] Cousin Brucie continued on WABC but was increasingly constrained not only by program managers but by changes in music, with the introduction of album-oriented rock. And so in 1977 he finally left broadcasting to run a successful empire of radio stations. Morrow's kids had grown up, and the new generation was not his, but, as we will see, he enjoyed a comeback when his kids got nostalgic.[34]

The firm linkage of rock with the young led to the later return of the once young to the music of their youth. This confirms what we have seen throughout this book. Rock and roll was not a passing fad but rather a musical form with many distinct expressions. Thus, it became a succession of "fads" (much in the way that Tin

Pan Alley did), each of which gained lifelong loyalty from those "brought up" (as teens) on it. Of course, nothing is as clean and clearly cut as that. Let me illustrate with some episodes from this history of how the ephemeral became traditional.

FIRST REVIVAL OF RETRO ROCK

Given how fast rock came and went, it shouldn't be surprising that the term "oldies" dates from as early as 1957, when the New York DJ Alan Fredericks played the not-so-old rock hits from 1954 to 1956. In 1959, the Los Angeles DJ Art Laboe released a compilation album, *Oldies but Goodies*, featuring popular rock and doo-wop songs of the fifties. But the idea of "oldies" as a longing for a retro style of music and with it a past youth and its memories matured at the end of the 1960s. Following on the heels of the turbulent 1960s, it isn't surprising that the 1950s icon Elvis Presley would attract large crowds of the middle-aged middle class for a performance in Las Vegas in 1969. That same year, Sha Na Na wowed crowds of nostalgiacs with their leather jackets and pompadour hairdos (presumably in imitation of 1950s white working-class teen greasers). Although the group began as a glee club of Columbia University students, some of whose members later became professors and physicians, Sha Na Na became famous for their campy song-and-dance program of classic fifties-style rock and roll numbers. Oddly, Sha Na Na seemed to parody the greaser look, and the group offered satirical versions of 1950s songs rather than a true revival, appealing in part to an audience that was putting on the 1950s.[35]

Throughout the 1970s, long-eclipsed rock groups found new audiences for their old hits in free park and ticketed performing-hall concerts. For example, Chubby Checker and the Five Satins played in July 1973 in Central Park (sponsored by the oldies station WCBS) mostly to a curious teenage crowd, and WNEW sponsored an annual free Central Park concert featuring groups like Jefferson Airplane and the Beach Boys. But a paying crowd mostly in their forties and even fifties heard Frankie Valli and the Four Seasons, the Four Tops, and Jay and the Americans in December 1972 in New York City. And even the bubblegum tunes of Neil Sedaka ("Happy Birthday Sweet Sixteen") drew crowds of the long-ago-sixteen-year-olds to Avery Fischer Hall in November 1978.[36]

Drawing on this nostalgic trend, Richard Nader organized a number of 1950s Rock and Roll Revivals, beginning in 1969 at Madison Square Garden with a program that included Sha Na Na, Chuck Berry, and Bill Haley but also the Platters (a black doo-wop group) and the Shirelles (a female vocal ensemble). Nader followed up with twenty-five more Madison Square Garden oldies shows in the next decade, eventually taking oldie revues to eighty cities and college campuses. In 1973, he produced a documentary film based on his concerts, *Let the Good Times Roll*. That year he told a *New York Times* reporter that his audiences "came not to cheer for the old hit makers, but their own memories and associations. . . . They were getting back into the irresponsibility, the carefreeness, the fun they had before they got married," Nader claimed. "They were crawling into the womb at Madison Square Garden."[37]

While the 1950s revival consisted mostly of reunions of old bands playing familiar hits, the punk movement of the mid-1970s seriously embraced the old style, though with new music. Punk groups were opposed to the musical complexity and "pretentious-ness" of late-1960s and early-1970s rock. The Ramones and the Sex Pistols, for example, harked back to the simplicity and adolescent working-class rebelliousness of early rock and roll and acted out a cult of destruction on the stage and in their publicity (the Sex Pistols flamboyantly rejecting their nomination to membership in the Rock and Roll Hall of Fame in 1996).[38] Others followed with the retro sounds of rockabilly, soul, and even a country/punk blend (cowpunk). Nostalgia for traditional rock and roll even affected the Beatles ("Back in the U.S.S.R.," e.g.), and the quintessential late-1960s bands the Doors and the Byrds followed suit by returning to country and blues sounds in 1969. Credence Clearwater Revival revived a variation on old-time country and western music.[39]

While nostalgia sold in the 1970s, many of the old acts resented the crowd's insistence on their old songs. At a Nader oldies concert in 1971, Rick Nelson was booed for his long hair and daring to sing new material rather than his oldie "Hello, Mary Lou." In response, an irate Nelson wrote "Garden Party" (1972), with the refrain "you can't please everyone, so you've got to please yourself" and the bitter line "if memories are all I sing, I'd rather drive a truck."[40]

But there was "gold" in the shift from the Top 40 to oldies. DJ Gus Gossert introduced a retro playlist in 1970 on New York's WCBS-FM; WNBC offered oldies on weekends by 1972. And Cousin Brucie got back in the game. Despite his departure from the Top 40 in 1977, he returned five years later to WCBS, this time peddling not the current hits but oldies. By 1985, Morrow hosted the popular *Saturday Night Dance Party*, which was syndicated as *Cruisin' America*. Aiding his return in 1987 were appearances in rock nostalgia films (*Dirty Dancing*, set in 1962), an autobiography, and a PBS documentary, *Shake, Rattle, and Roll*, in 1988. Morrow continued on WCBS playing the oldies until 2005, when the station changed its format, leading Brucie to sign with Sirius XM Satellite radio for a series of programs on its 1960s station that in 2014 aired on the weekends.[41]

The Wolfman also saw a revival in the 1980s, hosting up to 150 concerts and car shows and races a year and playing mostly oldies. He hawked oldie rock record collections in extended "infomercials." And after his death in 1995, a number of tapes from Wolfman Jack's shows were released by off-brand labels. Wolfman and Brucie were not alone in rejoining the generation that brought them fame and fortune. Black DJs like Jacko Henderson (whose career in Philadelphia dated back to 1953 but was broadcast in many American cities) returned in the 1980s and 1990s with oldies shows on radio.[42]

DOO-WOP: FROM TEEN POP
TO MIDDLE-AGED OBSESSION

At the core of the oldies circuit was doo-wop, a subset of rock that prevailed from about 1955 to 1958, with a brief revival in 1961, the year when the term doo-wop seems to have been introduced by Gus Gossert. Unlike the country and R&B styles of rock and, later, Motown, doo-wop produced few celebrity performers but consisted of a large group of ensembles who made records mostly for small companies. Many doo-wop groups were "one-hit wonders," if that, and quickly broke up and were forgotten. Despite doo-wop's cursory treatment in "official" histories of rock and roll (dominated by writers who matured in the 1960s and who often favored the rock of that decade), doo-wop's impact in nostalgia radio and concerts is actually greater than it was during its first run: only 15.4 percent of *Billboard*'s number-one hits between 1955 and 1963 were doo-wop songs, but surveys by WCBS in the 1990s found 30 percent of the station's oldies' Top 500 lists were doo-wop tunes. Doo-wop artists still draw big crowds at nostalgia venues, places like the American Music Theater in Lancaster, Pennsylvania. These concerts, the endless CD collections, oldies radio stations, and even amateur Internet radio streams have produced powerful outlets for doo-wop nostalgia. According to John Runowicz's authoritative *Forever Doo Wop* (2010), doo-wop music offers a "kind of sonic portal to a past self—often a much younger self. . . . Fifties-centric nostalgia consumption set the standard against which the hawking of the goods of subsequent eras would be measured."[43]

Doo-wop has distant roots in the vocal harmonizing of the black barbershop quartets of the 1890s. Influential also were jazz-age vocal groups like the Ink Spots and the Mills Brothers, who used high tenor leads and deep bass backing vocals. Black gospel quartets shaped doo-wop with rhythmic motifs that underscored the lead singer's melodies. And, especially in the "jump" (as opposed to ballad) form of doo-wop, the beat and often the dancing of rhythm and blues groups from the early 1950s were also influential. But doo-wop was also a special product of a distinct culture of 1950s American inner cities: groups of friends worked up their tunes on the street, in community centers, and school gyms. Early ensembles were mostly formed by African Americans from New York City but also Los Angeles and Chicago. The genre also included ethnic Italian groups from Staten Island and Brooklyn (the Elegants and the Capris) and the Pittsburgh-based Skyliners.[44]

In the 1960s, doo-wop was soon upstaged by Motown vocalists and the British Beatles, Rolling Stones, and Dave Clark Five. Most of the groups folded, and many of their singers took "regular jobs" after tours of duty in the military. The lead singer for the Cadillacs, Earl Carroll, found a day job as a grade-school janitor while singing on the weekends. But gradually an oldies circuit emerged, sparked by DJ and record-store interest. As early as 1961, specialty record shops in New York especially (Times Square Records, e.g.) featured vocal harmony from the 1950s, giving patrons a sense of the stylistic particularity of doo-wop performers. Beginning in 1969, Gus Gossert of WPIX-FM of New York promoted doo-wop records. For decades, Don Reed presided over doo-wop concerts, and there were a number of magazines and newsletters devoted to the cause starting in the 1970s.[45]

Thirty years after the first revival, oldies shows continue to attract the same, but now aging, crowd, often former "urban-dwelling white males who seemed to pine for the lost neighborhood street of their youth." Sometimes of Italian or Jewish background, many fans were part of the suburban flight of the past half-century. Often they were brought up in working-class families in the 1950s and resented the look and manner of the sixties counterculture, whom they identified with an unpatriotic privileged college-going middle class. For them, doo-wop was a badge of honor and identity no matter how suburban and middle-class they may have become.[46]

ELVIS GOES LAS VEGAS AND IS ENSHRINED AT GRACELAND

The most famous figure in retro rock is of course Elvis. As seemingly countless histories of rock point out, Elvis Presley combined the music and style of his native white South with borrowings from black rhythm and blues, creating a popular style for a generation coming of age in the mid-1950s. He was exposed to both types of music as a child in Tupelo, Mississippi, and as a teen in Memphis, Tennessee. As Karol Ann Marling notes, Presley was as much an "old-time hillbilly" as a "cool cat." And he was influenced by gospel music, as were so many others who got rich on rock. But he was hardly the founder of rock: Bill Haley's rhythmic country-music band began during World War II in Pennsylvania (replacing the "Cowboys" with the "Comets" in 1952).[47] Instead, Elvis offered a unique sound that produced both ballads (influenced by the crooners of his day) and hard-hitting covers of "race" music (like "Hound Dog").

Presley's signing with the publicist Colonel Tom Parker in August 1955 and contract with the mainstream publisher RCA set the stage for an amazing run outside the South. Nationally, his music, manner, looks, and youth (in contrast with the chubby and aging Bill Haley) appealed to a new generation of kids. In 1956, he appeared in rapid succession on network TV shows, including the bellwether *Ed Sullivan Show*, along with a dizzying array of concerts and movies. In the process, he attracted increasingly younger, often screaming crowds. As a child in 1957, I heard, from over a mile away, the eerie birdlike screeching of thousands of fans as Elvis performed in my hometown's stadium in Spokane. By the spring of 1957, Elvis had bought the hilltop Graceland "mansion" just above a shopping mall in suburban Memphis. This five-bedroom house was nostalgically fashioned with columns, looking like a scaled-down version of Tara from *Gone with the Wind*. Presley filled it with TV sets, garish white furniture, and loud carpets; in the 1960s, he added the Jungle Room, with a seven-foot throne and chairs in pseudo-Hawaiian style (recalling some of his favorite movies).[48]

But, in March 1958, Elvis was drafted into the U.S. army. The photo of his extravagant pompadour being unceremoniously clipped into a buzz cut by an army barber appeared in *Life*. When I saw it, I couldn't help feeling sorry for him, losing his dignity that way. He was sent to West Germany, returning in March 1960 with the rank of sergeant, ready to resume his recording, concert, and movie career. The "Elvis films" have been almost universally panned as repetitive quickie musicals, often thinly disguised stories of Elvis's own rags-to-riches story, but they made a lot of money for the Colonel and Elvis. Despite being eclipsed by the Beatles in the mid-1960s, Elvis made a "comeback" special for TV in 1968 after eight years off the stage, and he signed on in Las Vegas for a lengthy string of shows in 1969. A successful tour followed in 1970, along with a spate of new hits ("Suspicious Minds," "In the Ghetto," etc.). But, like so many first-generation rock stars, he mostly sang his old hits before sold-out venues. He drew ecstatic crowds with dramatic poses and his increasingly wild costumes of jumpsuits draped in pearls and ropes of gold, with ever broader belts and higher collars. His extravagance echoed the pianist Liberace's gaudy grandeur but also harked back to the self-indulgent display of the "Cadillac cowboys" of the earlier country scene.[49]

Elvis was already a nostalgic figure by the time of his comeback. He played no longer to kids but to kids grown up and resentful of the usurpation of the Beatles and the Rolling Stones.[50] And despite his spiral into drugs and the pitiful (and much mocked) image of a bloated Elvis bursting out of his jumpsuit, Elvis became a folk hero in August 1977 after his mysterious early death at the age of forty-two. He had become a symbol of the aspirations and resentments of a generation, most of whom were a few years older than the boomers and had origins in the white working class. Shortly before Elvis's death I recall visiting the apartment of a widow then in her early thirties whose husband had been a truck driver and had recently been killed in a road accident. She was moonlighting from her office job by typing my dissertation. Hanging over her sofa was a velvet painting of Elvis, which she said reminded her of her dead husband, a strangely religious displacement. Later that summer when Elvis died, I was taking an evening walk in Madison, Wisconsin, home of the University of Wisconsin and dozens of antiwar and leftwing protests, when I saw a parade of about forty women chanting and carrying signs and flashlights "demonstration style," declaring their undying loyalty to the dead King. They all seemed to be wearing those rhinestone-framed glasses that I immediately identified with the conservative white working class, and they were walking from the working-class side of town toward University Avenue, the venue of student demonstrations. They seemed to be saying, "now it's our turn to have a protest march and for you kids of the sixties to hear our story."

Elvis-studies scholars may debate over whether the cult of the King is a "religion," but there is no doubt that his story, music, image, and belongings soon after his death reached cult status. An obvious explanation is the incessant promotion of Elvis's memory by Priscilla Presley, the ex-wife whom Elvis's father let control the estate. She not only turned Graceland into a shrine but, until 2005, along with their daughter Lisa, managed Elvis Presley Enterprises (EPE), controlling the Presley image down to the smallest detail. And local people have cherished his memory and made money by turning the mall opposite Graceland into a tourist trap; others transformed the shack in Tupelo where he was born into a landmark and state park, including a chapel, garden, and museum. But the key to his memory is his multiple meanings: rebel, teen idol, a romantic movie star, Las Vegas headliner, loyal American who served his country, a rags-to-riches hero who never forgot where he came from. Yes, he was a troubled man who succumbed to drugs, attempted to cope with the abuse of ungrateful hangers-on and hateful detractors, and who left this world (or not) mysteriously in the prime of life. And some even have seen him as "an androgynous image, a heroic subject that was neither completely male nor female."[51]

Still, the predominate feature of Elvis nostalgia is one side of this very complex man. For many who go to Graceland or collect Elvis memorabilia, he is not the man that "helped break down some of the barriers of race and class in post–World War II America," as revealed in his music and style (Elvis had plenty of black fans). Instead, as Erica Doss notes, devotees hold "an image of Elvis that corresponds to their own racial and class prejudices. In their eyes, Elvis is the perfect symbol of a mostly middle-class white American getting what it feels it deserves: money, fame, a mansion in Memphis." And this is the image that has been cultivated by EPE. Certainly part of the cult of Elvis is a reaction to those snotty boomers who laughed at the "comeback" Elvis who dressed like a clown and pitifully paraded in front of middle-aged women grasping for a chance to touch him. The Elvis crowd in 1957 had been rebellious working-class kids who, according to a survey in 1957, got lower grades than fans of goodie-goodie Pat Boone or of Perry Como. And most were female. Members of this crowd twenty years later would still be loyal to Elvis, seeing themselves as a persecuted minority defending their hero against the "sniggering stereotypes about an obese pill-addicted Elvis." To counter the "media," fan-club members claimed to be "taking care of Elvis" in their devotion, setting the record straight. This may explain the curious velvet paintings of the sad, suffering Elvis with a tear-streaked face (prohibited by EPE since 1995). And Elvis fans are not above attacking EPE, especially Priscilla, for altering the beloved Graceland, for tirelessly suing anyone using the Elvis image without paying EPE, but mostly for never loving Elvis and Graceland the way they do.[52]

Elvis has been materialized for nostalgia in so many different ways: from 1956, EPE has existed to exploit the Elvis image, licensing Elvis-branded clothes, lipstick, charm bracelets, display buttons, and even school supplies. There have been Elvis fan clubs since 1954. And of course there are his records. Much about Elvis fandom is in collecting these things; a few devotees even display them in basement rooms as if in a chapel where they can retreat to watch his movies, listen to his records, or just look at his picture. "For such fans, Elvis Rooms are creative means to help them cope with the difficulties and needs in their lives, refuges where they experience the depth of their feelings for Elvis privately, on their own terms."[53]

And many make pilgrimages to the 4,500-square-foot Graceland, the site not only of Elvis's life but of his death. Devotees come to Graceland for a candlelight vigil and procession to Elvis's grave on the anniversary of his death. Though the house is small (by today's celebrity standards) and visitors see only some of the ground-floor rooms (from behind a velvet rope), up to 750,000 visitors visit Graceland annually. The Elvis channel on satellite radio is located at Graceland and regularly promotes it along with its touching stories about the King.[54] Then there are the Elvis "tribute artists" who dress and look as much like the sainted Elvis as possible. And, perhaps inevitably, there was the "Elvis Lives" crowd, convinced that Elvis never died but that he faked his death to become free of the burdens of fame. Elvis is an incarnated world of memory, and if he can no longer be touched, the places where he lived and the things that he owned can be. Most of all, his voice can be heard anytime, anywhere.[55]

BOOMER OLDIES AND BEYOND

Just as Graceland was being turned into a shrine in the early 1980s and as doo-wop concerts were hitting their stride, the oldies radio

stations were reaching their peak. However, by the 1980s the pioneering rock and roll of Haley, Bo Diddley, the Platters, and, of
course, Elvis were also giving way to a new generation of nostalgiacs, the boomers and their 1960s rock. There was a lot of "old" to
choose from.

Radio stations that had once catered to the fourteen-to-twenty-
four-year-old set with the Top 40 began to follow WCBS of New
York and KRTH of Los Angeles by cultivating an older audience.
Many of these newly christened "gold" stations were AM, the radio
signal that could not compete for sound quality with FM in playing stereo albums that featured complex instrumentation. AM
stations lost most of their ad revenue in the 1970s and 1980s to
FM radio and were forced to shift to news and talk. Still, these
stations could still play the old unsophisticated 45s from the 1950s
and early 1960s, with their mostly straightforward singing backed
by small ensembles of guitars, drums, and piano.

Meanwhile, some FM stations that had cultivated the more
"cultured" and complex rock of the later 1960s and 1970s continued to feature this music, newly christened as "classic rock," in
the 1980s. By 1986, there were four oldies stations in Los Angeles
and three in Phoenix. The number of "golden oldies" stations grew
from 317 in 1985 to 596 in 1988, even though stations switched
formats frequently. The Satellite Music Network, based in Dallas,
which included more than six hundred affiliate stations nationwide in 1986, introduced the "Heart & Soul" format, featuring
Motown artists. Still others offered the "Music of Your Life" formula of melodic hits from the 1940s through the early 1960s for
a still older group of the musically disenfranchised. At the same
time, other stations adopted a mix of old and new. In 1986, for
example, New York's WNEW's playlist featured about 60 percent
oldies; Dallas's KTXQ played "gold" 40 percent of the time, offering
in the morning groups of ten tunes from a given year for nostalgic
listeners. Stephen Holden of the *New York Times* complained that
these stations provided listeners no sense of time or place because
they played the softer ballads from both the past and present (Bar-
bra Streisand, Billy Joel, Elton John, the Carpenters, and Barry
Manilow; "Angie" by the Rolling Stones but not "Satisfaction").
And the DJs, he claimed, sounded like airline stewards.[56]

Radio stations mostly went "gold" in the mid-1980s because boomers were aging but their tastes in music were not changing. They constituted the largest and increasingly an affluent generation. And what they wanted was the music of their youth. Of course, this cohort might have experienced a "maturing" of taste, perhaps a shift from pop to sophisticated vocals or even classical music—as certainly the promoters of "serious" music believed would occur in the 1970s, when numerous cities established performing-arts centers and built symphony orchestras and opera companies. Instead, former hippies (or at least pot-smoking college students) who turned into yuppie bankers and other professionals stuck to the Beatles, the Supremes, and Fleetwood Mac. And this new wave of oldie lovers had money to spend on big-ticket items and more diverse items than did teenagers, all good news to stations seeking advertising revenue. Not only listeners but the DJs too had aged (they were no longer expected to retire at thirty or so). Cousin Brucie was still on the radio at seventy-nine in 2014. And oldie stations added news, weather, sports, and even traffic reports to their programming (all of interest to older listeners commuting to or from jobs).[57]

Just in time to pick up on boomer nostalgia, Time-Life Music in early 1986 launched "The Rock 'n' Roll Era (1954–64)," its first record series devoted to rock, complete with nostalgic commentary and photos. A new series, "Classic Rock (1964–69)," followed. Another effort to pick up on boomer nostalgia was the mid-1980s uptick of advertisements featuring 1960s rock tunes (despite their licensing cost of up to $200,000)—recall Chuck Berry's redo of "No Particular Place to Go" to sell Volkswagens.[58]

All was not gold for vintage music stations, however. Reaching and keeping the valued demo (twenty-five to forty-four) has proven difficult for oldies radio. Nostalgic music formats came and went. In 1993, only 7.5 percent of American stations were pure oldies (country stations dominated with 26.4 percent).[59] Inevitably, in the 1990s oldies radio finally shifted from the rock of the 1950s, 1960s, and early 1970s to the oldies of the 1980s—just as Nick at Nite moved their programming up a half-generation in the 1990s. Like retro TV, popular music continued to divide generations, as it has since the passing of Tin Pan Alley.

By 1990, groups and solo artists, largely from the 1970s, such as the Eagles, Boz Scaggs, Pink Floyd, and the Marshall Tucker Band, were returning to the stage on the nostalgia circuit as audiences who were teens in the 1970s reached their thirties. And into the twenty-first century, old bands regularly (and, to many, relentlessly and boringly) returned to the stage in reunion concerts: Chicago, the Little River Band, Santana, and Steely Dan offered, as one rather bitter critic complained, "that musty smell of nostalgia, fouling the air and dulling common senses as veterans of The Great Rock 'n' Roll Wars of the 1960s and '70s again suit up and trudge down the concert trail to play in The Great Rock 'n' Roll Swindle 2000." Often commentators observed that bands from the 1960s and 1970s like the Grateful Dead, Fleetwood Mac, the Eagles, Bruce Springsteen & the E Street Band, and Crosby, Stills, Nash & Young far outdrew the crowds gathered to hear 1980s groups like the Go-Gos. One of the obvious explanations is that younger Americans lacked the social bonding experience that reinforced the nostalgic memories of their parents' generation. Their elders shared memories of listening to the same rock hits on Cousin Brucie's radio program and sometimes attending massive rock concerts or festivals. The kids growing up in the 1980s and later experienced far more cultural fragmentation—more diverse musical genres, eventually delivered through the Internet. This may mean less (or less shared) nostalgia for their songs. Time will tell.[60]

There is some evidence that there is a breakdown of cohort consumer nostalgia in music (as seen elsewhere in this volume). Clearly, taste in old music doesn't segment neatly by age. The ephemeral nature of rock music and styles leads to special bonds between particular bands and particular cohorts who were young when they were popular. However, rock has persevered for the last sixty years, with no end in sight. This has meant that older listeners, especially from younger boomer and early Gen-X rockers (fixated on the 1960s and 1970s) have not entirely rejected the rock that came after "their songs" (as did many of older Elvis and doo-wop fanatics). While their parents, who had grown up with big bands and Tin Pan Alley melodies, rejected Elvis, some boomers and Gen-Xers have tried to use their love of rock and pop music to build bridges to their young offspring. This is evident in the curious phenomenon of multigenerational groups visiting the Rock and Roll Hall of Fame and Museum. Sometimes parents took the kids to their oldies' concerts.[61]

There is anecdotal evidence and a Pew survey in 2009 suggesting that some of the old generational schisms of the past have softened. Nostalgia, once again, did not have to be for one's actual personal experience. The journalist Fred Setterberg reported how cruising teens in the early eighties on the San Leandro Strip bordering Oakland, California, upheld the old hot-rod traditions by "debating the relative merits of Little Richard and Chuck Berry—an argument steeped in false recollection, since most of the Strip regulars were not then old enough to clearly remember the Beatles, never mind the actual beginnings of rock 'n' roll."[62] Though Gen-Xers (as we have seen) sometimes have resented boomer cultural dominance and presumption, and no more so than against early boomer disdain for rock after the Beatles and Motown, many Gen-Xers and their children have learned to love the 1960s through the ubiquity of this music on the radio and movies. As was the case with retro TV, old music can be experienced as "original" and essential to those who weren't even born when the music was first heard. Young people think of the Beatles or Bob Dylan as young men, just as their elders do, because they saw them in videos looking as they did decades ago. Both age groups experienced these celebrities through the media, and this is repeatable and thus doesn't age. Moreover, rock music has increasingly become a mixed bag as old acts return, styles are blended, and old sounds revived.[63] While doubtless rare, the young have indulged in "time-warp tribes" forming or listening to bands that try to reproduce not only the sound but the costuming of old styles—think of the long-lasting appeal of the Grateful Dead and their cross-generational fans who for decades showed up at concerts in tie-dyed shirts and cutoffs, practicing a quasi-hippie communalism in memory of the 1960s.[64]

A more concrete sign of cross-generational music is the curious return of vinyl LPs in recent years, especially to those too young to remember them new in the stores (they disappeared along with cassette tapes in 1991).[65] Journalists note with surprise that young people show any fascination with this antique technology in the era of the digital download. They explain it by the appeal of the "ceremony" of removing the disc from its jacket, placing it on a turntable, and setting the needle in the groove. Unlike the MP3 digital sound, the vinyl recording requires effort and thus produces anticipation, and it offers 144 square inches of cover art and "liner notes," which are truncated in the much smaller CD jacket and absent altogether from the digital download. The fascination with obsolete music players fits well with nostalgia for the music of the 1980s and before. Even the imperfections of the pops and scratches make the vinyl record seem more "natural." And some listeners believe that the direct reproduction of the analog sound wave (rather than reconstruction of the waveform from a "sample" of waves, albeit at 44,000 samples per second on a CD) makes for a "purer" sound. That was certainly the view of a sixteen-year-old boy who I met at the Rock Hall of Fame "gift shop" in May 2014; he was excited to buy a vinyl recording of the ancient rock group Frankie Valli and the Four Seasons and proud to have updated his dad's old stereo phonograph with a new cartridge.

But this blending of generations only has gone so far. By 2000, oldies stations were changing: a 1997 federal law accelerated a long-developing trend, the concentration of radio into the hands of a few companies, especially Clear Channel and Infinity. These giants abandoned the earliest rock on their oldies stations for pop from the Beatles on into the 1980s. And in 2005, the pioneer of oldies stations, New York's WCBS, dropped the oldies format for "Jack," an eclectic blend of tunes from the past four decades. Stations have often hired companies to conduct listener surveys to identify oldies favorites. Selected oldies fans (mostly males in their forties) evaluate tunes after hearing short segments, leading inevitably to predictable, limited playlists. But when markets are so segmented that a station can succeed in a big market with as little as a 4 percent share, the retro-rock station will survive, at least, for a few more years. And the Jack formula failed at WCBS: the station quickly lost half of its audience (the older ones), and, after public protests, in 2007 it returned to its oldies playlist.[66]

To the noted pop-culture critic Simon Reynolds, "retro consciousness . . . seems most chronically prevalent in music. That may well be because it somehow feels especially *wrong* there. Pop ought to be all about the present tense, surely. It is still considered the domain of the young, and young people aren't supposed to be nostalgic." But, as we have seen, music on the radio and elsewhere has become increasingly directed not to the young but to the once young, (and perhaps to the young who wish that they had been young when the "classics" first were heard). And, as Reynolds acknowledges, the "very topicality, this date-stamped quality [of modern pop music] is what causes it to become quickly dated and then, after a decent interval, so potently epoch-evoking, so *reliveable*." And because modern pop music is shaped by the past, "old songs don't lose value with the passing of time." For all of its frantic search for innovation, rock music really is governed by "bipolar rhythms of surge and slowdown, mania and nostalgia."[67]

As we have seen, the first of these "slowdowns" took place in the early 1970s with nostalgia for the musical styles of the 1950s. The appeal of oldies comes in part from the fact that we have so readily at hand archived media that extends far beyond radio and records (including CDs, MP3s, and YouTube videos). This means that today nothing is really old because we can get tunes no matter when they were recorded exactly as they were first recorded. In fact, Reynolds's lament is not that pop music divides generations but that it relies today so heavily on old forms of pop, leading to a seemingly endless cycle of revivals. Pop music, especially since the turn in the 1950s toward youth, has nostalgia built in. Rock's obsession with youth created a time-marked deck of sounds, each with distinct musical styles and artists that were embraced by narrow cohorts of the young or once young. To be sure, the old generational wars of the 1950s and 1960s have abated, with some "adult" appreciation of the avant-garde; even more, younger listeners have embraced retro. But this may mean that the old suffocates the new. If Reynolds is right, rock/pop may today be a spent force. New rock "is a museum piece. . . . It's been done. The rebellion's over." But, we must add, the bands play on, and especially the old tunes.[68]

6

Dilemmas of Heritage in an Era of Consumed Nostalgia

Many of us have visited heritage sites, places like Old Sturbridge Village, Greenfield Village, Colonial Williamsburg, or many of the "living museums," historic houses, factories, and battlefields restored to "take us back" to another time and place. We may have been dragged there by a well-meaning parent or school group or gone voluntarily, even enthusiastically, to witness authentic worlds of our or other people's ancestors. One appeal is certainly "nostalgia." But what do these visitors to heritage sites really have in common with collectors of childhood toys, cars, and kitsch or consumers of nostalgia TV and popular music? At first glance, we might say "little." After all, these places are supposed to be about encounters with worlds long gone, not our own youthful memories. Even more, they seem to challenge our association of nostalgia and consumer culture, often very consciously. Heritage sites are mostly supported by decidedly noncommercial philanthropists seeking to leave behind a cultural legacy, not build a business, or by dedicated academics and public-service-oriented nonprofit groups. These places insist that we step out of our modern worlds of fast-paced work and ephemeral goods and into realms of long-forgotten skills and folk knowledge, of simpler times, but often also of refined tastes and materials. And heritage sites often have a pedantic, even defensive, aura about them: they are places that you "should" see, places that will "challenge" you (or your children). They offer the authentic past, not fantasy. They are not amusement parks or malls; they are there to enlighten the adult and teach the child; their job is to uplift. To recall a lost Victorian expression, they offer "rational recreation" rather than mere "fun" (and in the eyes of heritage purists, the "phony"). Yet does this distinction really hold up when we look closer? And, in so far as it is true, is it possible for the "improving" and "authentic" to survive in a modern world that expects entertainment, the fantastic, and the "pixie dust" of personal childhood memory?

Let me begin with a report on a visit in July 2011 that I took to Old World Wisconsin (OWW), a relatively little-known heritage site composed of a cluster of fully functioning farms, moved from their original settings, to represent Wisconsin's ethnic diversity to the mostly suburban families who visit the site. Buildings were rescued from their original sites scattered across the state, faithfully representing German, Norwegian, Finnish, Danish, and Polish homesteads. The site even includes a church and schoolhouse representing a long abandoned rural African American settlement in southwest Wisconsin. OWW was pioneered by the Wisconsin architect Richard Perrin, who has long been engaged in the study of ethnic farm and other structures.[1] Intent on saving the ethnic diversity of farm buildings, Perrin won the support of the State Historical Society of Wisconsin for the arduous task of moving every board and brick from these structures to the site near Eagle, Wisconsin. Opened in 1976, OWW officials soon saw the need for interpretation and social history, not just historic buildings set in farm yards. By the early 1990s, there were up to 110 interpreters on staff.[2]

Located on six hundred acres of wooded land in the glaciated Kettle Moraine some thirty-seven miles south of Milwaukee and

forty-six miles north of Chicago, Old World Wisconsin is not particularly easy to get to; it is miles from the freeway and down a
country road, a place out of time. My day-long visit was greatly
enhanced by my two-hour chat over coffee with Marty Perkins,
curator of research, whose roots at OWW date back to 1974. Then
he was a graduate student in urban studies and part of the construction crew for a Wisconsin Bicentennial–funded project that
led to the founding of OWW. Two years later, he was offered a
research job and in 1983 became manager of the interpretation
staff at the site. Perkins is part of a small cadre of career professionals in heritage. They even have national groups: the American
Association of State and Local History and the Association for Living History, Farm, and Agricultural Museums, the latter of which
is divided into nine North American regions.[3] These professionals are a committed group, steeped in the study of rural society,
technology, and material culture. Old World Wisconsin is a prime
example of their achievements, hopes, and challenges.

Perkins told me how OWW has changed over the years: First,
viewed as a collection of buildings that otherwise would disappear, the site was a classic open-air museum. Soon, though, OWW
staff began to focus on the families that lived and worked in these
unusual structures. The appeal was to ethnicity and to offer visitors with family ties to Polish, German, Finnish, and the other
immigrant groups that once owned these farms an opportunity to
recall being brought up in rural Wisconsin and share their memories with their mostly suburban children and grandchildren. A
steady patronage of school kids is guaranteed by the inclusion of
field trips to historical sites in state curricular guidelines (producing busloads of fourth graders on weekdays, especially in spring).
And a large share of annual visitors are from the ranks of members
of the OWW Foundation, a private support and fundraising group
of enthusiasts, some with personal roots in rural life. But by the
late 1980s, Perkins noted, OWW began to scale back its outreach to
ethnic communities. It still offered special holiday events for small
groups of Polish or German-Americans, but Perkins admitted that
over time visitors with strong ethnic identities have dwindled as
activists aged and died.

Programs shifted to contemporary appeals, some of which were perhaps only loosely related to the collection and its original mission. I was impressed with the range and creativity of the activities offered throughout the year at OWW, such as vintage baseball games played in 1880s uniforms and with 1880s rules (no gloves, batters hitting balls caught on one bounce are out). The day camps and field trips for kids offer all the wholesome hands-on activities that you might expect (cow milking, butter churning, etc.) while giving kids a way to connect to the past. And classes in traditional skills (blacksmithing, favored by men; spinning, by women) continually draw a small but enthusiastic clientele. And then there is the corn labyrinth, a winding path cut through a corn field, which enchants small children and their indulgent parents, even if a labyrinth has no historical roots and thus irritates some OWW staff, volunteers, and old patrons. This is but one example of the conflict between sticklers for documented authenticity, devoted to the original mission of the site, and a more pragmatic, increasingly market-oriented staff.

Perkins talked of the difficulty appealing to the memory of visitors. In the mid-1990s, staff tried a "remember when" day with displays in OCC barns, schoolrooms, and kitchens, designed to evoke the memories of older visitors, but few of the elderly responded when asked by staff. This veteran of classic heritage research and programming recognized the need to appeal to a younger audience, one with no recollection of farm life, ethnic or otherwise. Maintaining public patronage may require compromising education with entertainment. He listed the many plans to improve rest areas for picnics and refreshment, the efforts to survey audiences to maximize "peak" and "flow" experiences, and, of course, the efforts to increase interactive activities and theme tours. Finally, rather than appealing to the memories of the old (in tow with younger family members), OWW, like others, has begun to focus on the imaginations and needs of young children (who seem to "lead" their elders at the site). OWW is surely trying to adapt.

Leaving Mr. Perkins, I hopped a ride on a "tram" driven by a retired elementary school teacher and went straight to Crossroads Village, a reconstruction of the "typical" buildings of a rural hamlet serving a late-nineteenth-century farm area. There, and at the various farms along the roads bisecting the site, I met many interpreters and the sadly very few visitors there this particular Thursday in July. Although there were only about twenty-five costumed staff members scattered throughout the site that day, they certainly appeared devoted and knowledgeable. A woman in her late twenties (on staff for six years) played the role of innkeeper from the 1880s, answering thoughtful questions about the foods and their preparation from a small group of middle-aged parents and their kids. She told me that she had got into heritage as a child of five when her family joined groups that reenacted events from the French and Indian War across the country. From this experience she identified with reenactors who strove for the authentic against those who saw the activity as a form of play. Her admiration for the tenacity and skill of those early settlers and disdain for suburbanites wed to their cars was shared by a couple I met at the inn who owned an online company making "Simple Country Playthings."

There was something very out of time about OWW. The Crossroads Village's cluster of buildings (inn, general store, church, blacksmith's shop, etc.) seemed anything but an imitation of Disney's Main Street USA: everything was spread out, dusty, and really very "unintense." At one of the farms I met a middle-aged lady with a thirteen-year-old daughter who regularly went to such sites and had never visited Disneyland. Hardly typical tourists. The interpreters were a smattering of retired schoolteachers, small-business people, and young former history majors devoted to reliving a bygone age in all of its specificity. They relished describing German half-timber farmhouses and how Prussian Germans had tomatoes in their square-patch gardens but Pomeranian Germans didn't. Despite the pride of the staff, the need to reach out to a larger, even different, crowd was obvious, especially when I heard that the gate had in recent years declined by half: only about seventy-five thousand paying annual visitors—not much more than a single Green Bay Packers game. And when later that day I visited with some lifelong Wisconsinites from Green Bay, I was surprised to learn they had never even heard of Old World Wisconsin.

All this might suggest that those few trying to preserve the memory of lost communities have nothing in common with the many who are nostalgic for their childhood consumer cultures. Yet the two value systems inevitably meet. Both emerged about the same time (the late 1920s and 1930s) and both took off in the 1970s. Heritage sites had links with older forms of nostalgia— longings for preserving or rediscovering ethnic and belief communities—but, like today's collectors of cars, toys, kitsch, and popular media entertainment, heritage nostalgia evokes memory through the *goods* of lived lives—not the monuments and other symbols of ideas, institutions, and iconic individuals of past regimes.

To be sure, heritage nostalgia is very different from the consumed nostalgia that grew up with it. It has claims of seriousness and usually requires the patronage of wealthy individuals, private foundations, and often government subsidies to survive. Heritage means the collection of the things of work and family, rarely of play and individual obsession. It takes us back to a time before the "frivolity" of modern fads and fantasy, when young and old all had to chip in and work together with ingenuity and perseverance. Heritage is also more challenging to access: it requires not personal recollections sparked by objects from personal life but learning about the tools, spaces, tribulations, and simple joys of people long gone. The task of heritage is to imagine a world before our era of packaged pleasures, not to recover the ephemera of our personal consumer cultures. This requires a willingness to step out of the world of consumption to identify with the daily lives of people with whom we share little.

But this leads to a dilemma: For almost all of us it is hard to abandon the perceptions shaped by consumer culture—its ever more sensuous spectacles and its promise of entertainment whatever the setting. Thus for those who would try to take us back to the unfamiliar worlds of the long past, there was and is the constant dilemma of choosing between an often didactic authenticity and an appealing but distorting showering of the heritage scene with the pixie dust of romance and "Disneyfication." The result is a continual problem of heritage people: how to reach and sustain audiences without abandoning "authenticity." I left Old World

Wisconsin with an admiration for the staff and visitors but also with a sense that, given declining attendance and the inevitable disappearance of heritage enthusiasts, the tensions between purists and compromisers would grow. The inevitable question: Just how and how much to adapt?

SOME SITES OF HERITAGE

Let's look at some of the most notable attempts at creating sites of heritage to set the stage for exploring these vexing challenges. In many ways, the common quest for lost or disappearing communities began in 1891, when Artur Hazelius began the reconstruction of Swedish village and farm buildings at Skansen near Stockholm. This open-air "living" museum, complete with costumed craftspeople, farmers, dancers, and musicians, became the model for heritage sites throughout Europe and the United States. Romantics with the support of philanthropists sought to recover a lost community of artisans and peasants. Yet, even before that, as early as 1876, a romance for fast-disappearing village folk and material culture was displayed in the tableaux vivant of Swedish folklife exhibited at the Philadelphia Centennial Exhibition. The Essex Institute of Salem, Massachusetts, seeking to lend an air of authenticity to the mid-seventeenth-century house of John Ward that they restored in 1909, introduced costumed reenactors to interact with visitors in hopes of transporting them to another age in ways that mere artifacts could not.[4]

During the 1920s, concern about America's vanishing material culture inspired two of America's best-known tycoons, John D. Rockefeller Jr. and Henry Ford, to spend lavishly on restoration and recovery. The Rev. W. A. R. Goodwin, an Episcopalian priest of Bruton Parish Church in Williamsburg, sought financial aid from the automobile manufacturer Henry Ford before turning to Rockefeller, the son of Standard Oil's founder, in 1924, to restore Williamsburg, then a sleepy, down-at-the heels village, to its glory 150 years before when it had been the colonial capital of Virginia. From 1926 until his death in 1960, John D. Rockefeller Jr. devoted much of his energy and wealth to purchasing and restoring some 146 structures dating from colonial times (as well as demolishing about seven hundred pesky modern buildings, especially those primarily occupied by blacks). While the public magazine, courthouse, and George Wythe's home had survived, only the foundations of the capitol and governor's palace remained, and these buildings had to be rebuilt from surviving plans. Colonial Williamsburg (CW) was opened in 1934, attracting affluent local southwestern Virginians, greeted by young hostesses, many from elite Tidewater families in period costumes. Within two years, CW opened craft shops that offered reproductions of colonial furnishings. And as early as November 1937, *House and Garden* devoted thirty pages to CW and its influence on architecture, gardening, and decoration, especially with the revival of colonial styles in fine American homes. Segregated white crowds admitted to CW grew to 210,824 in 1941. Rockefeller proudly claimed that his restoration was to "free [CW] entirely from alien or inharmonious surroundings" as well as to preserve "the beauty and charm of the old buildings of the city and its historic significance."[5]

Thanks to deft publicity and the site's ties to Washington (the State Department made CW a regular venue for visiting foreign dignitaries and international-affairs conferences), by the end of the 1960s, CW was attracting a million visitors per year. Some of the about four hundred costumed interpreters spoke in the "first person" as if they actually lived in the eighteenth century and performed skits and staged encounters with visitors; others worked as skilled craftspeople demonstrating more than twenty historic trades. Behind this cast were the "suits and skirts," the managers and scholars who trained the interpreters and planned programs.[6]

As Colonial Williamsburg became a major tourist site in the 1950s, the inevitable critics found much to fault. In 1958, the famed cultural historian Daniel Boorstin questioned the authenticity of a restoration (especially with complete reconstructions of key buildings) that made the past look better than it ever actually had been. In 1963, the architecture critic Ada Louise Huxtable called Colonial Williamsburg "a dangerous bore" because it created an "unforgivable fuzziness between the values of the real and the imitation in the popular mind." She complained: "It has been a very short distance down the yellow brick road of fantasy from Williamsburg to Disneyland." In 1966, the historian David Lowenthal complained that "Williamsburg has the flavor of a well-kept contemporary suburb."[7] Sensitive to this criticism, an official guidebook (1972) opens with the question of authenticity: Would the site be recognizable to a "printer's widow or slave" from eighteenth-century Williamsburg? The answer: a "qualified yes," even though the authentic buildings and grounds were admittedly "tidier" and "better painted" and missing "horses and riding chairs" and livestock. But moderns would not "tolerate" the messiness of the "real" site.[8]

However, in the 1970s, with a flat and even decreasing gate and visitor tastes shying away from an over-the-top patriotism, Colonial Williamsburg went through a change of approach and leadership. Carlisle Humelsine arrived in 1977 with a cadre of scholars who were intent on shifting from the patriotic glorification of famous residents (like Patrick Henry and Jefferson) to stress the lives of common people and especially to address the fact that half of Colonial Williamsburg's population had been black slaves. Humelsine opened a reproduction of the slave quarters at CW's Carter's Grove plantation in 1989 (purchased in 1963) and attempted to increase greatly the number of African American interpreters.[9]

Colin Campbell, the director of CW, wrote in 2001: "We adhere to one over-arching principle: authenticity"—not only by striving for painstaking historical accuracy (as in abandoning papermaking because it wasn't done in eighteenth-century Williamsburg) but also by shifting from triumphalist stories of the Founding Fathers to the theme of "Becoming Americans" and the struggle to be both equal and free as "part of an effort to make connections with choices we face now."[10] But this emphasis on the "bottom up" and relevant history had to coexist with a need to market the site to a still essentially middle-class and often conservative but also fun-seeking audience. By the 1990s, CW was losing that audience. In 1996, Susan Stuntz, CW's marketing director, admitted, "We are competing with Disney and Six Flags. . . . And with considerably fewer marketing dollars." The Colonial Williamsburg Foundation realized that admissions had fallen from 1.2 million in 1989 to about 900,000 in 1996 and invested in a spate of TV and magazine ads (*Martha Stewart Living, People,* and *Better Homes and Gardens*) to reach the middle-class mothers who often made their family's vacation decisions.[11] In 2001, CW began a hundred-million-dollar "makeover" by expanding the Williamsburg Woodlands Hotel and Suites and Williamsburg Lodge (the latter with a new thirty-thousand-square-foot conference center) as well as the renovation of the Williamsburg Inn by enlarging rooms for high-end guests. This was, of course, a continuation of the decades-long program of appealing to discerning affluent customers via reproductions of period furniture, fabrics, and china. All this meant that CW reached multiple markets, but it was also sending mixed messages during a time of shrinking audiences.[12]

This multipronged effort to reach an audience led to continuous waves of criticism. After a prolonged study of the site, the anthropologists Eric Gable and Richard Handler concluded that CW "transforms public history into private memory by collapsing the distance between the reconstructed past (the museum's history lesson) and the visitor's touristic or familial experience on the site." Academic historians disdained CW staff as "vulgarizers who have borrowed so much from Disney" that they have turned CW into a theme park.[13]

About the same time as John D. Rockefeller became enamored with restoring Colonial Williamsburg, Henry Ford was infected by a very different sort of heritage bug—the gathering of an idiosyncratic mix of the homes and possessions of Ford's historical heroes, vestiges of American material culture on the eve of industrialization, and examples of the technological revolutions of the late nineteenth and early twentieth century. The collection was very much an expression of Ford's own identity as a transitional figure—born on a Michigan farm in 1864 to become America's most famous industrialist in the first half of the twentieth century. In his fifties and sixties, Ford became an avid collector of craft and farm tools as well as buildings from a then vanishing pioneer world of rugged individualists. He also gathered the machines and inventions that made the modern world of mass production, transportation, and communication. Famous for his disparagement of academic history's obsession with documents and politics (recall his comment in 1916 that "history is more or less bunk"), he nevertheless relished the material and practical worlds of the recent past.

Beginning his collection in 1920, Ford was determined to preserve the iconic settings and objects that he felt shaped the contemporary world. Ford had a passion for authenticity, gathering as much as he could from the American history that he valued: the Waterford General Store, "Abe Lincoln" (Logan County) Courthouse, Scotch Settlement School, and Martha-Mary Chapel, buildings that were set in an artificial Greenfield Village opened in 1933. Most characteristic are Ford's collection of the homes and offices of his American predecessors and heroes: Edison, Luther Burbank, H. J. Heinz, Robert Frost, Charles Steinmetz, Noah Webster, W. H. McGuffey, and George Washington Carver. Characteristically, he even salvaged his own birthplace, built in 1860 near Dearborn. As in CW, but set in the nineteenth century, Ford's Greenfield Village offered visitors the opportunity to watch weavers, potters, printers, blacksmiths, and farmers who explained their trades in their shops and fields as they went about their work. Greenfield also featured ingenious machines (for example, an up-and-down-type sawmill from 1855) that celebrated the industrious and inventive origins of modern capitalism.[14]

Nearby, Ford built a large structure housing the Henry Ford Museum. The center portion of its facade was a scaled-down replica of Philadelphia's Independence Hall, which led to the Mechanical Arts Hall (featuring tools of farm and factory), a replica of a street of early American shops, and the American Decorative Arts Gallery.[15] Ford's exhibits shared much with the celebratory tone of American World's Fairs, from 1876 in Philadelphia down to 1939 in New York. Like them, it largely ignored the stresses and conflicts of the era of individualistic craft production and culture (in Greenfield Village) and the anonymity of industrial production and urban life (at the museum).[16]

Ford's main objective was to preserve the memory of heroes and iconic events in all their authenticity. In fact, Ford insisted that one of the greatest events of industrial history be reenacted by the heroic inventor himself even before the museum opened: On October 21, 1929, a bevy of notables, including the American humorist Will Rogers, Nobel laureate Marie Curie, airplane pioneer Orville Wright, and one hundred or so others sat with Henry Ford in a darkened Dearborn Hall while the frail eighty-three-year-old Thomas Alva Edison turned on the incandescent lamp, just as he had done exactly fifty years before. This bit of romantic reenactment was shared by millions via radio broadcast. This painstaking reconstruction of Edison's achievement, along with the reconstruction of his Menlo Park laboratory located at Greenfield Village, and the single-minded quest for authenticity became a hallmark of heritage, the goal of emotional identification with the past. The fetishistic quest to recapture the precise event with all of its exact objects is similar to the goal of many of collectors of cars and toys, a longing less for the meaning and impact of the past than an effort to overcome the pastness of the past through a personal encounter with the authentic objects that inhabited a moment in time gone by.[17] By 1980, forty-one million persons had passed through Ford's museum and village, peaking at 1.5–1.7 million annually in the 1970s. During their first ten years, Ford supported rapid, if rather unplanned, expansion. However, after Ford's death in 1947, the exhibits grew familiar and unimaginative. Many criticized the disorganized display of old machines in the museum and the lack of coherence in the village, where an English cottage was included among the American buildings. Gaps in the collection were obvious, especially given the clash between the bucolic Greenfield Village and the mostly modern industrial artifacts of the museum.[18]

Just as at Colonial Williamsburg in the 1970s, museum trustees (still controlled by the Ford family) began a sixteen-million-dollar renovation, hoping to make the Henry Ford (THF)—the corporate name for the Henry Ford complex—competitive with other Michigan-area recreational sites. Changes included comforts that appealed to the middle-class family tourist, including the construction of a new restaurant, a Disney-like railroad around Greenfield Village, and even a restored 1913 carousel.

But the complex had little to offer the affluent "Martha Stewart" crowd that reveled in colonial-era reproductions of fine china and linens. Instead THF focused on its modern industrial displays at the Henry Ford Museum. In June 1979, the Mechanical Arts Hall was rechristened the Hall of Technology, with $2.4 million spent to help visitors make sense of the cluster of machines and tools. A far more innovative change came in 1987, with a new display, "The Automobile in American Life," which stressed not just a line of historic vehicles (with the most recent first) but also tableaux demonstrating how the car had shaped American life and consumer culture. This included a 1946 roadside diner, a 1940s Texaco service station, a 1950s drive-in movie, a 1960 Holiday Inn guest room, a 1932 Ford as a hotrod, and a vintage McDonald's single arch, under which was a 1956 Chevrolet.[19]

THF tried to reach modern audiences by showing how technology has shaped modern life, sometimes through nostalgic appeals to familiar scenes of consumer culture. This became even more obvious with the opening of the 1992 exhibit "Made in America," a dramatic redo of the earlier display of industrial innovation. It began with a celebration of American consumer goods, with a vast array of American products—including a toilet, bike frame, and even a kitchen sink looping overhead on a conveyor, familiar icons of the comforts brought by industry. The exhibit began in the present with flashy displays of consumer goods and ended with the origins of the Industrial Revolution in the rear of the building. This extraordinary display of steam engines and dynamos offered little modern interpretation. Ford's original message of the march of technological and capitalist progress from its roots in nineteenth-century hard work, craft ingenuity, and heroic invention was subdued by a distinctly "presentist" perspective emphasizing the "relatable" technologies and consumer goods.[20]

Of course, THF retained much of Henry Ford's nostalgia for the world of his rural and small-town boyhood at Greenfield and his love of the machines and products of early-twentieth-century industrialization. The problem was that today's audience was born long after the romantic fascination that the boy Henry had with blacksmithing and waterwheels and even after these objects and their heroic associations had disappeared from children's litera-ture. It is hardly surprising that the museum has had to downplay Ford's theme of the heroic inventor and technological progress now that the golden age of Detroit's assembly-line production (1913 to the 1970s) has been eclipsed by the shift of factories to the southern states and overseas—and from workers to robots. The most obvious change has been a subtle shift to the personal per-spective of the visitor rather than the viewpoint of people from the heroic past. In a 2007 paper, Kerstin Brandt finds that the "Made in America" exhibit offered not "the subject position of workers engaged in labor struggles or even just routine activity on the shop floor" but instead that "THF visitors-as-consumers become his-torical actors. Numerous displays trace the development of con-sumer culture from household goods and furniture to entertain-ment." This change seems to reflect a shift from the dominance of the conventional museum curator to a very different type of leader. An example is Scott Mallwitz, THF's "experience designer," with a background working for Coca-Cola, Walt Disney Attrac-tions, Lego, and Time-Warner, who wrote in 2004 of the need for "emphasis on personal engagement, memory, and theatrical immersion" at THF and other heritage sites.[21]

Since a redesign project begun in 2007, the Henry Ford Museum has undergone changes that qualify Brandt's analysis.[22] The main objective was to simplify the array of displays, especially at the entrance to meet changing audience preferences, but there was also a deemphasis on consumerist presentism with the elimina-tion of the conveyor of modern goods at the entrance of the "Made in America" manufacturing exhibit, which now features the Model T and offers visitors the opportunity to help reassemble a disas-sembled "T." In the "Driving America" exhibit, curators reversed the order of the display of historic cars (now beginning with the oldest, a steam car and Ford's quadricycle of 1896), each vehicle accompanied with a description of its social and economic con-text, giving an effective twentieth-century U.S. history lesson through a parade of cars.

But Ford's early stress on material goods and technology has been further reduced by the replacement of an exhibit of robotics and other modern machinery with the "With Liberty and Justice for All" exhibit, featuring the artifacts and history of American social and political struggles from the Revolutionary War and Civil War to the civil rights movement (with a center place given to the bus that Rosa Parks desegregated). Floor staff repeatedly told me during my 2014 visit that the goal of the museum was the story of American innovation and ideas (in all its forms) and how this heritage may affect our future—once again an attempt to shift from Ford's obsession with and celebration of machines and heroic invention. Moreover, the theme of consumerist nostalgia (albeit with social-historical contexts) pervades the "Your Place in Time" exhibit. Displays of the media, appliances, and toys identify a succession of generations of twentieth-century Americans (including a nickelodeon from the 1900s and a typical teen's bedroom from the 1980s).

There were many imitations of Colonial Williamsburg and the Henry Ford and their efforts to balance material and experiential authenticity with contemporary audience appeal. Yet although CW and THF tried at least at the beginning to preserve and hark back to iconic eras of American history and "greatness," other more recent heritage sites often strive for a more modest goal— the preservation of the spaces, sounds, and sites of the everyday past. They mostly are biased toward life before, often immediately before, industrialization. Many were doubtless motivated, as were the founders of Skansen, by a desire to recall simpler times and to "teach" those who never knew anything but commercialized mechanical work what it was like to live, work, and play in a "world that we have lost." Part nostalgic, part didactic, these sites often appealed to regional identities and ethnic ties that, like the folkways of preindustrial life, were vanishing (or gone) when these open-air and living museums first opened. These heritage sites usually downplayed conflict and often the hardships of these long-past times, presenting picture-postcard replicas of idealized village or farm life, reminding many, perhaps unfairly, of movie sets: painstakingly researched and historically authentic spaces filled with artifacts that visitors could walk through and encounter live reenactors engaged in their make-believe tasks. There were many of these places, but here I will focus mainly on Old Sturbridge Village.

Located in rural central Massachusetts, Old Sturbridge Village dates from the 1930s. Like so many others, it has its origins in the enthusiasms of the wealthy, in this case, the brothers Albert B. and Joel Chaney Wells, whose collection of early nineteenth-century tools and household goods was made possible by their father's profits from the American Optical Company. Albert developed an obsession for work tools and iron artifacts (latches and handles), and Joel specialized in clocks and paperweights—first from England and later from nineteenth-century America. Albert Wells's collection became so vast that he formed the Wells Historical Museum in 1935 to house it. Two years later, his son George Burnham Wells went much further when he bought 240 acres near Sturbridge, Massachusetts, in order to recreate a rural village as it might have looked between 1790 and 1840, when the early American republic was on the eve of industrialization. George hired the architect Arthur Shurcliff to design a town square presumably from this period. Old Sturbridge Village (OSV) was centered on a sawmill (powered by waterwheels in the Quinebaug River), a village tavern, general store, and other buildings moved from various New England sites to the imaginary Sturbridge Village. It officially opened in 1946 under the leadership of George's wife Ruth Wells. In 1954, a Quaker Meeting House was moved to one end of the town green, followed in 1957 by the Salem Towne House, which was sited at the other end. In the 1960s other buildings were resettled on the green, including a schoolhouse, pottery shop, and bake house. Later still, a carding mill that once prepared fiber for spinning into yarn was moved from Maine to Sturbridge.[23]

Though originally intended to house the eccentric collections of the Wells brothers, the site expanded to feature a wide assortment of objects (guns, glasswork, and lamps, especially). Moreover, like other living-history museums, from the beginning OSV also featured craftspeople employing period tools and skills to spin yarn, make pots, and fashion iron and tin goods. And, by the end of the twentieth century numerous programs were offered to attract everyone from gardeners, cooks, and musicians fascinated by period skills and materials to parents of precocious young children attracted to its "children's museum" with appropriate hands-on activities (playing school, dressing up in period clothing, and playing vintage games).[24] But a major appeal of the site has always been its romantic sentimental appearance: A 1969 pamphlet for visitors declares that Sturbridge offers an

> idyllic picture of a region blessed by nature with a fine coast-line, broad rivers, rushing streams, still abundant forests . . . [before] European immigration that was almost to engulf it a few years later. . . . In our sometimes groping for a way out of today's dilemmas, this view of New England in the early nineteenth century appeals to our sense of serenity and order. These New Englanders lived in a quieter, more secure world than ours, but both their clear-eyed view of their own society and its needs and their vision for the future of America remind us that the bond is closer than we think.

The author admits "their very virtues had a darker side"; they were steadfast but "also provincial, suspicious of foreigners and new ideas." But this only humanized them. The abiding impression was fixed by photos of "Whittieresque winter scenes" of the meeting house and green. In another brief account of the village (1965), the curator Charles Van Ravenswaay writes that modern people see "the Village as a kind of ancestral home where, in contrast to their restless and mobile everyday lives, they can put down personal roots and feel a kinship to the past."[25] This seems to be nostalgia not for a remembered childhood but for grandma's framed Currier and Ives or the sentimental writings of John Greenleaf Whittier.

Numerous other heritage sites have long offered variations on these sites, each with a promise to take visitors back to a lost time in full authenticity and sensuality: At Plimoth Plantation, restored in 1957 close to the original site, the date was always 1627. At Gettysburg, the site of a famous Civil War battle, officials bowed to visitor and advocacy group's demands for authenticity and have progressively restored the battlegrounds and their environs to the way they looked in July 1863, removing buildings and roads that "spoiled" the visage of the "original" battlefield. The quest of Gettysburg battle enthusiasts was often less for historical context or broad significance of the battle than for the experience of returning to the immediacy and detail of an accurately imagined past. This was especially true for those thousands who annually reenact the battle in historically precise costumes and equipment.[26] This quest for "originality" extends far and wide, from the restoration of the rural museum complex at Cooperstown, New York, to the Calico Ghost Town (a silver mining camp rebuilt by the restaurateur and amusement-park entrepreneur Walter Knott).[27]

But these sites of heritage memory have had a difficult time surviving in an increasingly commercial age. Despite adaptations made since the 1970s to accommodate the "fun morality" or to appeal more personally to crowds, attendance at these sites has decreased substantially since the 1990s. Explaining this may help us understand the place of heritage nostalgia in our story.

THE DECLINE OF HERITAGE NOSTALGIA AND THE ATTEMPTS TO REVIVE IT

Popular interest in heritage tourism has never been large. Support for the founding of Colonial Williamsburg, Greenfield Village, and their offspring came mostly came from the wealthy—in fact, eccentric—few. But by the mid-1970s, the political will to fund local historic projects had grown (witness the expansion of state-supported heritage sites leading up to the bicentennial) in Pennsylvania with the building of heritage sites along the "trail of history" and in Wisconsin with a number of other attractions. Paid admissions peaked at Colonial Williamsburg at nearly 1.3 million in 1975 and at nearly five hundred thousand at Old Sturbridge Village in the 1970s. For a generation of mostly middle-class and white American children, a day or overnight visit to Gettysburg to see the "Electric Map" and tour the July 1863 battlefield was a rite of passage as much as was the obligatory visit to a national park. This was a part of a family bonding ritual—a shared learning across generations about a common past, even occasionally an oldster telling a story to a youngster as an artifact or even recollection of an earlier visit evoked a personal memory. A very similar impetus for heritage appeared in Britain in the 1970s as witnessed, for example, by the open-air museum at Beamish in rural northeastern England near Durham. But heritage sites and their quest for authenticity were always part of a counterculture that was swamped in popularity by sensuously more intense sites, ones more closely linked to the consumer experiences of modern people; they also suffered from a generational shift that reduced the number of Americans willing to engage the past as heritage. By the 1980s kids balked at attempts to impose the foreign past on them, and the adults able or willing to tell the stories that went with the artifacts of these places were passing from the scene. Hopes of opening historical sites in every Pennsylvania county failed, and efforts to make Colonial Williamsburg more "relevant" had produced fluctuating gates in the nine hundred thousands in the 1980s and 1990s.

And after 2000, a sharp decline took place at virtually all heritage sites: paid visitors dropped from 895,000 in 2000 to 709,000 in 2004 at Colonial Williamsburg. In response, in 2003, CW officials announced job cuts to adjust staffing back to mid-1990 levels and slashed one-day ticket prices by more than 15 percent in 2004. An uptick in fundraising helped offset lost ticket sales (for example, in 2002 the Colonial Williamsburg Fund received $46 million despite a slide in the gate).[28] The number of paying visitors rose slightly to 710,450 in 2005 and 745,000 in 2006. But cutbacks continued, and the Carter's Grove plantation was put up for sale in 2006. Worse, in 2008, another decline in admissions (dropping to 707,000) led to new layoffs of staff. And partly because of the recession, ticket sales hit a forty-seven-year low in 2009 of 660,000, accompanied by a drop in payroll from 2,061 to 1,811. This decline continued in 2012.[29]

At Sturbridge Village, visitorship had already dropped 10 percent between 1987 and 1996 to 430,000 a year. A decade later in 2005, the number of visitors plummeted to less than 300,000. In 2003, facing a drop in the village's endowment from $12 to $8.7 million and a million-dollar deficit, the museum laid off employees, froze wages, and cut employee benefits, reducing its operating budget from $13 million to $9 million. Attendance declined further to 221,432 in 2007 (though it rose slightly the next year, and fundraising efforts doubled).[30] The trend at OWW was similar: family visitorship had dropped by about 50 percent in 2010 from a high of 150,000 visitors per year in the late 1990s. And a tornado in July 2010 destroyed a swath of trees at the entrance, setting back plans for the facility.[31]

Explanations of these trends are predictable: competition with Disney and other theme parks, the decline of the traditional family group, and the resistance of kids brought up on Nickelodeon insisting upon their "rights" to fun instead of having to endure an educational pilgrimage. But more subtle is the passing of a generation who knew what a seed drill and an andiron were or cared to know. The transformation of the pleasure crowd forced these sites to adjust—even more than they had before—producing confusing, even contradictory, compromises.

From the 1950s on, Colonial Williamsburg has rejected the claim that it was turning into a "glitzy Las Vegas venue." And its public relations manager, Sophie Hart, reinforced that in 2004, saying: "Our appeal is different. We have a core constituency that wants to come here. They are highly educated family groups that want to study history."[32] But, of course, that "core" was not large enough to pay the bills in a very labor-intensive enterprise; moreover, that committed group frequently objected to any compromises with mere entertainment. An example is the 1996 introduction of riverboat rides on the Quinebaug River that ran through Old Sturbridge Village. Devoted patrons complained both of the motor noise and of the historical inauthenticity of the boat.[33] And a single-minded commitment to authenticity was often costly. In the 1990s, Plimoth Plantation, long the strictest proponent of historical accuracy in everything from the accents of the "first-person" interpreters and thatched-roof cottages to the period clothing (complete with rough underwear), faced a series of financial crises. The loss of uninsured vintage farm animals from a fire, the costs of rebuilding barns, and the failure to raise an endowment left the site deep in debt, forcing layoffs and a 10 percent budget cut in 1998.[34] Clearly, more compromises with entertainment would have to be made, despite original mission statements and the heritage ethos of supporters.

The most common response was to increase crowd opportunities to interact verbally and physically with the sites, especially to appeal to children, the "leading" members of many family groups of tourists. Interpreters at Colonial Williamsburg, for example, were told to ask kids to "help" with chores at historical sites. And, of course, marketing campaigns increasingly featured children laughing and playing in their tri-cornered hats—while reminding parents that young kids stayed free at CW hotels.[35] It might be even surprising that the Henry Ford Museum waited until 2009 to come up with the idea of a weeklong "I want to learn how to build a car" camp for mechanically minded eighth-graders. The week-long day camp included a side trip to the Rock Stars' Cars and Guitars, an exhibit featuring more than twenty cars and fifty guitars from the 1950s, and the camp ended with the building of a Model T.[36] That same year, the Old Sturbridge Village added a hands-on craft center and offered ice skating, sledding, and sleigh rides during the winter months. The museum also expanded its "Dinner in a Country Village" program, which offered lessons in fireplace cooking, and the "Discovery Camps," where children could dress in period clothes and experience life in the 1830s.[37]

More dramatic were efforts at Colonial Williamsburg to expand the use of "first-person" interpreters. CW created dramatic street scenes that offered visitors the illusion of witnessing past events in real time (for example, a seemingly authentic meeting of slaves on the green that was broken up by the authorities). These efforts became more elaborate with the development of the interactive two-day program "Revolutionary City: From Subjects to Citizens," begun in 2006. A series of scenes portraying key events from 1774 to the beginning of the Revolution in 1776 were followed by scenes from the Revolutionary War. This elaborate production was acted out by a troupe of about thirty-six actors on the streets of CW. Actors re-created real events, but the emphasis was placed on conversations that people in Revolutionary-era Williamsburg might have had (a slave pondering the prospect of freedom or townspeople rebelling at high prices) along with reenacting the town's reaction to the Declaration of Independence and Washington's victory at nearby Yorktown. For a time in 2006, a troupe of British actor-interpreters from Past Pleasures (who had performed at the Tower of London) joined the CW performers, roaming the streets while playing the roles of an Anglican priest, escaped convict, and naval officer and sharing a loyalist British perspective with the crowd while making remarks about fashion and travel. In 2011, in a perhaps overly obvious attempt to engage preteens glued to their first cell phones, CW introduced *RevQuest: Save the Revolution!*, a scavenger-hunt game played on a cell phone, which required listeners to follow directions to "Avert the Crisis and Save the Revolution." The game involved visiting several CW sites (an apparent trick to expose the kids to a little history), with clues to find and questions to answer in a booklet.[38]

A more inclusive and varied adaptation might be called "Disneyfication" (though critics had been accusing heritage sites of copying the "feel-good" techniques used at the Disney theme parks since the 1970s). Rather than resist this charge, in 1997 Alberta Sebolt George, Sturbridge's president, sent half of Old Sturbridge Village's managers to "Disney University" seminars to learn "how you move crowds and keep smiles on people's faces." Soon thereafter, costumed "farmers" were entertaining crowds waiting on line the way that Disney uses cartoon characters in their crowds. It became common to copy Disney's success at creating festival-like attractions: these included special July Fourth firework displays at OSV and nightly "closing festivities" at CW and even special holiday decorations and events.[39]

A more daring foray into Disney's marketing land came in the late 1990s when Colonial Williamsburg adopted Disney World's model of destination tourism by joining with other area sites to bring in families for whole vacations. These efforts culminated in 2001 with the formation of Williamsburg Flex, a cooperative business effort that included not only the Jamestown Settlement/Yorktown Victory Center (heritage sites) but also the Williamsburg Hotel and Motel Association, the Williamsburg Conventions and Visitors' Bureau and the theme parks Busch Gardens and Water Country USA. The package, which included tickets and accommodations, offered guests unlimited visits to all the attractions on three- or five-day plans. Even earlier, in 1997, Disney-style advertising accompanied this effort, abandoning "Williamsburg's old history-lesson image" and instead stressing the variety of fun things that families could do around Williamsburg. One print ad with a picture of a preschooler wearing water fins declared: "Wasn't it nice of those colonists to choose a place so close to shopping, theme parks, and great restaurants?" That year CW offered a "Surf, Sun, and Revolutionary Fun" package that combined a visit to the site with fun in the sun at Virginia Beach. Of course, this effort to "synergize," combining the beach, theme park, and heritage site (as well as nearby shopping malls) in a multiple-day family experience, had its detractors. Purists believed such commercialization compromised the educational mission despite the obvious appeal of greater stimulation and variety. Jamie Haines, Plimoth Plantation's marketing vice president, still insisted in 1997 that there should be no accommodation to fakery or convenience: "Nothing from the setting should be changed just so people can get around more easily. . . . We want them to struggle." This, however, was increasingly a minority view.[40]

Although heritage sites learned from Disney's success in attracting family crowds, they also followed another marketing trend—attempting to draw single adults and avant-garde consumers, not an easy task considering their product and "brand." One pretty obvious effort was CW's decision to transform its period Shields Tavern into a coffeehouse. Abandoning the menu and mood of the old tavern, the newly christened Mr. Charlton's Coffeehouse (2005) consciously reached for the allure of Starbucks and other coffeehouse chains, going so far as to offer espressos and lattes along with frozen beverages and desserts such as peanut pie despite their utter lack of historical authenticity. But, of course, what made Mr. Charlton's special was the presumed ambiance and interior decorations, which suggested the eighteenth-century coffeehouses of London and Paris, if not Colonial Williamsburg. "People are trained for the coffeehouse experience. . . . We get people looking for that," noted Joe O'Callahan, a CW official.

An even more elaborate effort to exploit the experiential consumption of the young set is the Spa of Colonial Williamsburg
(opened in 2007). It is, of course, not the massage and beauty spa
of the typical suburban shopping center; rather, it promises "five
centuries of wellness," including representative cures and treatments from the seventeenth to the twenty-first centuries. The
look of heritage is assured with the spa's Georgian Revival–style
brick building reached via a pathway bordered by wisteria and a
formal garden with a fountain. The subtle scent of lavender and
lemongrass drifts through the three-story facility's treatment and
relaxation rooms (featuring an "experiential shower for women"
and a "cold plunge pool for men"). Treatments reached back to
a "cleansing hot stones experience" presumably adopted from
the Powhatan Indians that the Jamestown settlers met in 1607.
From the eighteenth and nineteenth centuries came the Colonial
Herbal Spa Experience and the Root and Herbal Spa Experience
(with claims of African linage). Rounding out the five centuries
of "wellness" is the "Williamsburg Water Cures Spa Experience": a
full-body, dry-brush exfoliation followed by a "hydrotherapy Vichy
shower" (presumably a twentieth-century experience) and the
avant-garde "Skin Rejuvenation Spa Experience with laser treatments and microdermabrasion." Adding to the long-established
commercial partnerships of CW with manufacturers of colonial-
style furnishings, china, and linen (Colonial Williamsburg owned
twenty-four retail stores in the Williamsburg area at the time), CW
copied another recent marketing innovation, the suburban theme
store. Like the mall outlet shops of Disney and Warner Brothers,
CW opened a store promoting the site and selling colonial-themed
goods at the Gaylord National Resort and Convention Center near
Washington, D.C., in 2008.[41]

Of course, Colonial Williamsburg is not likely to introduce a
"Wiley Willie" cartoon mascot for its logo and dress him up on the
CW green or put a waterslide at its entrance; that would overly
compromise the brand and its eighteenth-century associations.
However, the Henry Ford Museum complex has no such limita-
tions, especially in its special exhibits, even though as noted above
the museum retained its core mission of presenting the social and

cultural history of American innovation, even reemphasizing that history in recent years. However, since the opening of the car and "Made in America" exhibits, the museum has been eager to integrate contemporary popular culture into their displays of machines and manufactures. In 2004, the Henry Ford Museum jazzed up its serious image with "Disco: A Decade of Saturday Nights," combining cars, fashion, and music from the late 1970s. Apparently this was to appeal to the memories of forty-five-year-olds who were nostalgic for their teen years, when John Travolta was big. Five years later, the museum presented the New Lego Castle Adventure Exhibit, an imaginary medieval castle made of Lego bricks with an area for kids to build their own. This was a well-tested kid pleaser at the LegoLands in Denmark, England, and the United States but hard to fit into Henry Ford's vision of celebrating American innovation. Reaching out once again to a crowd presumably not interested in steam engines and automobiles, in the summer of 2014 the Henry Ford Museum featured an exhibit provided by the Rock and Roll Hall of Fame and Museum, "Women Who Rock: Vision, Passion, Power," featuring the outlandish costumes of female rockers.[42]

More subtle were the new programs at Old Sturbridge Village and Old World Wisconsin. Nevertheless, they too compromised the goal of historical authenticity by providing a "visitor experience that is both educational and fun," in the words of James Donahue of OSV in 2009. The object was "having a visit to the village be the best experience that it can be," all times of the year, for all members of the family. Donahue was convinced that this approach explained a rise of attendance by more than 7 percent and an uptick in museum membership by 8 percent in 2008. But did "experience" necessarily have anything to do with "heritage"?[43]

Similarly, Old World Wisconsin began to drift toward "experiences" loosely related at best to bygone rural life but very much accommodating changing values and family patterns. After 2002, OWW introduced programs to attract a broader and more diverse audience: children's birthday parties and special events like Midsummer Magic, attracting hundreds of couples in their twenties and thirties for an evening of food and music. In 2006, the museum's children's day camp doubled its program to eight weeks to accommodate the growing numbers of two-income families seeking summer activities for their otherwise undersupervised children. As Alicia Goehring, an official from the Wisconsin Historical Society (of which the OWW is a part), said in 2006, "In general, historical societies and museums have looked at it from an internal point of view. We're breaking away from that and looking at it from the customer's point of view." Peter Arnold, OWW's director at that time, was more specific about the changing perspective: "The idea was, 'Let's educate, recreating the nineteenth century and take them into a time warp'. I'd say now it's 'let's demonstrate what life was like.' The more interactive, hands-on stuff, the more immersed visitors are, the more fun they'll have." And at least short-term gains in attendance encouraged this approach.[44]

From the 1970s, critics of heritage sites in the United States and elsewhere have condemned these places as "merely nostalgic indulgence."[45] But the recent trend is different—a shift not merely away from historical fact and explanation of historical change but toward emotional engagement and sensory intensity. The setting or catalyst may be the past, but that is increasingly incidental. This is harsh and maybe unfair because the intent is certainly to perpetuate these sites of historical memory. However, as noted above, by the 1980s heritage sites were abandoning the old model of the museum curator: "to convey expert information through formal programs. Exhibits were assumed to be authoritative, based on the expertise of the curator/scholar, but they were often inaccessible to the nonexpert," says Barbara Franco in 1994, then the assistant museum director at the Minnesota Historical Society. Franco called for "greater opportunities for self-directed learning experiences that address visitors' emotions as well as their minds." She reported that "cognitive learning objectives are being replaced by affective learning; school tours are supplemented by programs for families and adults." These are all things that heritage sites have tried repeatedly since the 1990s. She called for "historians and curators to share authority for exhibits with educators, designers, community advisory groups, and academic scholars," reducing the role of the former "to serve only as factual experts, or as critics, to pass judgment on the accuracy or completeness of the product." This approach was hardly an embrace of Disney but rather a challenge to older historical models in museums (such as Henry Ford's): the abandonment of the idea of "inevitable progress" and the triumphalism of the winners and the centrality of chronology and timelines. It was a defiant rejection of the notion that historians know best. Instead, Franco embraced a let-the-people-decide approach with a strong emphasis on audience-preference research. These studies found that museum audiences do not share the historian's and curator's way of seeing "time as a continuum." Rather, "the general public seems to lack bridges between historical time . . . and contemporary time (what you have experienced)." Of course, historians might respond that this is a problem that needs to be overcome through education and not merely a different perspective to be accommodated or humored. Still, for Franco, when the past is presented from the "standpoint of common human experiences of family, work, community, and sense of place," when exhibits stress "emotional engagement, active participation, and first-person narratives of real people," displays may succeed in connecting "individual experiences [of audiences] to the experiences of people in the past. . . . Each of these experiences brings historic time into contemporary experience and bridges the gap that separates many visitors from the past." In 1992, the Minnesota Historical Society expanded its displays, drawing on these principles. Instead of emphasizing an "epic narrative" of the state's political history and the recent past (themes that research showed were not as interesting to the public as formerly thought), they focused on native peoples and their ways of life, including "personal stories" that the staff believed touched visitors emotionally. "Research helps explain why empathy and emotion are such effective bridges between past and present."[46] This approach, of course, has been widely adopted across the heritage movement. But to what effect?

I understand the need to abandon the perspective of the chronicle and the fact gatherer. And, as argued in postmodernism, I realize that visitors to heritage sites seek and embrace diverse experiences.[47] The difficulty comes when the contemporary exhibit designer emphasizes the audience's emotions, present-mindedness, and need to be entertained but in doing so abandons the efforts of traditional heritage sites to challenge audiences by drawing them into a past that they never knew or that they had forgotten. The stress on "personal experience" inevitably negates this, offering mostly a romantic memory of modern childhoods. All this seems to confirm a central thesis of this book: the triumph of "consumed nostalgia" and its focus on personal memory and experience, the "relatable" artifact rather than the collective if distant and even strange past of the heritage movement. All this may become clearer as we explore the themed nostalgia of the commercial site—of Disney and its imitators.

7

Pilgrimages, Souvenirs, and Memory at Disney

In informal surveys of my mostly engineering and business students in my history of technology class at Penn State, I found that scarcely 10 percent have *ever* been to the Smithsonian Institution museums (for most, three hours or less from their hometowns). I discovered, however, that only about 20 percent have *never* been to the Walt Disney World theme parks, a fifteen-hour drive or more and, of course, very expensive (compared to the Smithsonian, which offers free admission). No one finds this surprising. After all, Disney is fun and the Smithsonian not obviously so— though rich in the heritage of natural science, aerospace, fine arts, and American history. But there must be something more to this extraordinary preference than that.

Recently, I visited a different theme park, Knott's Berry Farm, which made me think about the relationship between educational/ heritage and amusement/theme parks. The "Farm" is a curious amalgamation of structures: dated pioneer and half-developed "roaring twenties" and Mexican "fiesta" buildings that suggest heritage themes, over which loom the massive steel columns of spiraling rollercoasters. Along with a relatively new kiddie section embossed with *Peanuts* characters, Knott's is pretty typical of the modern theme/amusement park, a curious blend of thrill rides and concentrated simulations of culture. Knott's began in the 1930s as the fruit stand of its founder, Walter Knott, and chicken restaurant run by his wife, Cordelia. In 1940, Walter added a "ghost town" (not so different from other fake "historical" attractions of the era) to draw families with children off the highway. Walter took his ghost town seriously and later attempted to endow it with an aura of authenticity by including pioneering craftspeople at work. Only a few miles up the freeway from the Disney complex in Anaheim, which opened in 1955, Knott's seemed destined to fade, as did many other roadside attractions. Instead, the family added rides and entertainment in the early 1960s and in 1968 fenced in its attractions, Disney fashion, and charged admission. By the 1970s, as the founding father, Walter, turned operations over to some of his children, Knott's Berry Farm joined other amusement parks in building tubular steel coasters appealing to a new generation of thrill seekers. Yet the ghost town remained, though sanitized, and a museum of Western artifacts survives (though hardly a crowd magnet). The site also includes an accurate replica of Independence Hall, a pet project of the conservative patriot Walter in his old age (though some distance from the rides and easy to miss).

Knott certainly saw himself as a custodian of heritage and memory: in the 1950s he personally restored a real ghost town at Calico in southeastern California that later became a county park. But today at Knott's Berry Farm the historical serves as a backdrop for the "iron" thrill rides, like movie sets, evoking memories in older visitors and maintaining a brand that distinguishes Knott's from other thrill parks. Rides and their physicality dominate the scene, and the young, tweens on up, not their elders with memories, dominate the crowds. If there ever was a contest between Knott's vision of pioneer heritage and the mass (especially youth) appeal of thrill rides, it is obvious which won.[1]

But does that mean that theme parks aren't really sites of nostalgia, as opposed to many heritage parks? Certainly, at least, a part of the attraction of Knott's Berry Farm remains its nostalgic pioneer backdrop. Still, after visiting many of both types of parks, and from my research with John Walton for *The Playful Crowd*,[2] I think that theme parks in general are sites of memory, but in ways very different from the nostalgia at heritage sites in the last chapter. Thinking of theme parks as highly commercialized, it is easy to conclude that they appeal to the "lowest common denominator," immediate gratification, and a free-spending crowd of young people with little refinement, experience, or desire for more than an adrenalin rush. But this would miss a lot. Though they are ultra-efficient machines for sucking up cash and frequently exploiting the latest novelty, theme parks nevertheless seem to draw on old, even medieval and ancient, longings; they appeal to what historians have called the carnivalesque or even bacchanal in traditional seasonal festivals: the emotional intensity of periodic excess in color, movement, and activity that drew crowds whose lives were short treadmills of unrelenting routine and physical drudgery.

But theme parks have become more than duplications of those rare bursts of festive extravagance. They are places that can make saturnalia happen every day (at least in warm regions of the South) and are available to anyone who can afford the time and money to get to them (often merely a ride on the freeway or a few hours' flight).

Theme parks and their crowds inevitably bring up associations with another old tradition—the medieval pilgrimage, a destination of wonder that confirmed the beliefs of the faithful (or today the enthusiast) in real time and space. As many have noted, the original Disneyland that opened in 1955 was a blown-up version of Disney's playsets, storybooks, TV shows, and movies, allowing visitors to envelop themselves in Disney fantasy in three dimensions and often on a gigantic scale. This is not so different than the pilgrimage experience to the Vatican or Mecca today and centuries ago. And, like those visitors to holy sites, people visiting Disney return home with souvenirs—remembrances—of the pilgrim experience, miniatures of the gigantic, in a compelling if often futile effort to extend the special feeling of being there through the possession of tokens of remembrance.[3] But in the case of Disney, "pilgrims" return not with a bit of a saint's relic, as did the "superstitious" faithful in the past, but with manufactured relics of Disney characters in bisque or plastic.

So let's look at the theme park, using Disney as an example, a site of commercialized pilgrimage and souvenir collecting. In interesting ways, the theme park and its miniatures has become the quintessential form of consumed nostalgia.

PILGRIMS TO DISNEYLAND

Both heritage and theme sites attracted respectable, middle-class, and often child-centered families, but they diverged in how they tapped into childhood memory. Nostalgia at heritage sites seems to be for past communities grounded in craft, manual skill, and nature, producing cultures that have been difficult to pass from one generation to the next. By contrast, theme-park nostalgia is often evoked in and through fantasy places and characters recalled from childhood films and other media, which, thanks to modern repeatable media technology, is reexperienced across generations.

These divergent nostalgic ideals were middle-class options that emerged and diverged in the first half of the twentieth century. These ideals emerged first from a middle-class rejection of the noise, dirt, and perceived danger of the crowds that had been attracted to the amusement parks and entertainment zones of cities. These places, dating from the late 1890s and accessible through a newly built network of streetcars and buses, had consisted of dazzling collections of thrill rides, spectacles depicting distant travel and disasters, freak shows, and evocative architecture with allusions to the grandeur of European capitals or the exoticism of "oriental" cities. These amusement parks are often associated primarily with Coney Island, in New York City's borough of Brooklyn, but they were in fact located throughout America, in and near cities large and small. However, from the 1920s, these places had increasingly gone downmarket, appealing to working-class and minority youth often too poor to afford cars but still able to travel on cheap subways and trams to increasingly shabby amusement parks.

In shunning these places, a broad middle class sought alternatives that were more refined but still fun. Just as middle-class families fled the cities for the suburbs, they abandoned streetcars and amusement parks for vacation routes available only by private automobiles—and away from crowds of working-class (and eventually minority) youth. Moreover, they sought sites of nostalgia. Nevertheless, middle-class sensibilities were divided in the twentieth century in their distaste for the plebeian pleasure parks and streets. In the 1950s, middle-class American families split (but hardly evenly) between those wishing to find an alternative to the plebeian pleasure crowd in a "grounded" (heritage) versus "fantastic" (themed) nostalgia.

Second and more subtly, there emerged from these alternatives two distinct understandings of nostalgia shaped by divergent understandings of memory and childhood. As often noted in this book, modern nostalgia has "privileged" childhood and personal memory, reducing the value of past "eras" and "collective" memory. Yet recollections of childhood worked very differently in heritage and themed nostalgia. As we have seen, heritage focused on eclipsed communities and traditions; the object was a "return" to the space, materials, and activities of a personal and family life that was no more. In effect, heritage sites like Colonial Williamsburg evolved from places where elites displayed rare and historically significant artifacts to destinations where the lifeways of the past could be relived, often through the child, who was treated an as inheritor of an eclipsed but authentic past. The child's edification made the project "serious" and educational. By contrast, the fantasy/themed nostalgia of Disney and others evoked children's wonder, not edification, and the adult's memory of childhood delight. It was this use of childhood and memory at Disney and similar parks that ultimately explains why themed nostalgia prevailed over heritage.

In our earlier book, Walton and I found that Disney created nostalgia by drawing upon a fantasy culture that emerged from earlier amusement parks, especially those at Coney Island.

Disney's customers shared with Coney an aesthetic of playfulness, and his park attracted customers with highly commercialized, sensuously intense and evocative sights, sounds, and movement quite foreign to the genteel and improving cultural heritage of the late Victorian bourgeoisie (expressed in Skansen) and its successors in the heritage community.

Yet Disney also broke sharply from Coney. Disney introduced a systematic and sophisticated appeal to nostalgia that the middle-class crowd seemed to long for by the 1950s. The amusement parks of the early twentieth century instead featured novelty and the shock of the new. Luna Park and Dreamland at Coney Island changed their exhibits and rides every year. Rides and spectacles were often cheaply constructed, thus subject to fires and rapid deterioration. All this eventually led to a dowdy look because the parks could not afford further innovation. Despite large beach crowds, Coney's Luna Park closed in 1944 and Steeplechase in 1964. (Dreamland burned down in 1911 and was never replaced.) By contrast, Disney was built to last, making possible slower, more deliberate transformations. More to the point, Disney's park was always less about novelty. Disney emphasized the past. People expected it not to change and often complained when it did. Novelty was secondary.

Instead of the "wow" of the new and thrilling, what Disney did in 1955 was to create mockups of his own childhood memories and fantasies (he was born in 1900), which he invited others from his own generation to share with their children and grandchildren. As Karol Ann Marling notes, he conceived of his park (in part) as an extension of the miniature railroad that he built in his own back-yard.[4] He also offered younger adults a nostalgic return to their own childhoods, which had been filled with Disney cartoon images. In so doing, Disney offered a pilgrimage of consumer nostalgia—a destination site where visitors experienced walks or rides through childhood memories of Disney products. They encountered the delight of seeing and engaging with gigantic versions of the child's miniatures, from Sleeping Beauty's Castle to the oversized heads of Disney "cast members" dressed as Mickey Mouse.

Disney and his "imagineers" developed a distinct set of principles and procedures for patrons to relive their Disney memories in a sensation-drenched environment. Far more consistently than the planners of Coney Island amusement parks (where many rides and shows were subcontracted out and conventional), Disney and his company orchestrated a totalizing experience, succinctly analyzed by the longtime Disney imagineer John Hench in 2003: Disney parks were designed to give the visitor a "sense of progressing through a narrative, of living out a story told visually." Through careful planning, using techniques borrowed from motion pictures and animated features, Disney staff created "guided experiences that take place in carefully structured environments, allowing our guests to see, hear, even smell, touch, and taste in new ways." Attractions had to be "magical," hiding (as the old amusement park rides seldom did) all mechanisms and "backstage" processes (machinery, warehouses, delivery trucks, dressing rooms, etc.). Imagineers designed sequences of experiences that offered guests a way to relive "the story through their senses," taking them to "peak moments" and "an enhanced reality, the 'realer than real' thrill that is the signature of the Disney parks." All this brought them back to the Disney delights of childhood.[5]

Buildings and other structures were to evoke moods and memories: sharp-edged pointed forms suggested danger and adventure; rounded forms evoked feelings of fun and reassurance. The heads and faces of costumed Disney characters, Hench observed, were "similar to the proportions of a human baby's head and face," thus drawing on "an instinctual nurturing response to creatures with baby-like proportions and features." Nothing in a visual field should break the "mood," not even restrooms and restaurants, which therefore must be "themed." The uninterrupted flow of crowds and reduction of waiting in line was paramount, so rapid transportation was essential, as were spacious hubs to facilitate the making of choices about what part of the park to visit next. Each "land" has its own character, identified by a symbol or landmark, which the imagineers dubbed "weenies," dominant structures like Sleeping Beauty's Castle, which set the tone of "storybook charm" in Fantasyland. Other weenies like Mark Twain's Steamboat for Adventureland and the Rocket to the Moon for Tomorrowland epitomized these distinct themed zones. And rides like Peter Pan's

Flight were designed to take the visitor into a dramatic section of a movie; in this case, it was the journey to and from Never Never Land. The ride vehicles were to "function like a camera, revealing a story sequentially." And these were the stories often seen years ago in Disney movies, picture books, and toys.[6]

Disney was inventive, but he did not invent the architecture of audience-participation fantasy. These spectacle sites date from the pleasure gardens of the eighteenth-century European aristocracy if not from the Hanging Gardens of Babylon (seventh century BCE).[7] Dreamland and Luna Park dazzled European immigrants in the 1900s with mockups of grand piazzas of ancient European cities while playfully mocking them with a grand tower at one end and a water slide into a central lagoon at the other.

Disney copied Coney's fantasy architecture but abandoned many of the old European references. Instead, he drew on the romantic memory of a new generation, one, like himself, born in the twentieth century and with a distinct American perspective. Disney designed his park to oblige crowds to enter into his personal vision of the past: through a single entry gate and into a fantasy of an American small town circa 1900. Visitors first walked through a romantic replica of a train station and then onto Main Street USA before reaching the "happy" lands of Disney fantasy, adventure, the American frontier, and Disney's own sentimentalized view of tomorrow. In his widely distributed park guides published in the 1960s, Disney observed from his distinctly grandfatherly perspective: "Many of us fondly remember our 'small home town' and its friendly way of life at the turn of the century." But this was a far cry from the social history and authenticity of Greenfield Village. Sensation and mood creation meant the sacrifice of authenticity. For example, as Hench observed, the Market House on Main Street had to be a "vibrant, happy place": staff (or "cast member") costumes had to be colorful, not the gray and white uniforms of reality. Stores were painted in a "happy palette of pinks, reds, yellow-greens, and red-oranges that were popular for interior and exterior paintwork at the time." But the colors were intensified, as, for example, in the use of the soft pink, green, and yellow of saltwater taffy for the Candy Palace; the men's clothing store was decorated in blue, gray, and white so as to suggest with exaggeration a vintage man's suit and tie.[8] This was not a restoration of a village but of its storybook memory, a themed rather than heritage nostalgia.

This nostalgia for a romantic version of small towns was repeatedly reinforced in the movies seen in reruns on TV (think of Carvel, the home of Andy Hardy in the movie series of the late 1930s, or Bedford Falls, in the 1946 Christmas classic *It's a Wonderful Life*). It was a secondhand nostalgia for those born too late to experience the real thing and who instead grew up in featureless suburbs. Disney, at this time in his early sixties, could lecture his customers: "When you visit the apothecary . . . we hope you'll visualize, as I often do, your own home town Main Street, or the one your parents and grandparents have told you about." Disney envisioned that this aspect of the park would promote conversation across the generations that would continue as families entered the storybook "lands."[9] But Main Street USA in fact invited families to adopt a child's imagination—the old to regress and recall their own childhoods sprinkled with "pixie dust" and for the child to revel in a storybook world.

Even if many adults did not grow up in Disney's small town, as over time fewer had, they often adopted Disney's fantasy of his youth as their own. Memory of a mediated past may have been more real than the one that they actually knew. Mobility and marriages across ethnic and neighborhood groups meant that "homesickness" (that is, nostalgia) might not be for a specific place but for a romantic idea, one easily blended and idealized in an all-white, all-American Main Street.[10] Even though set in suburbia (Anaheim, California) and accessible via the newly built Santa Ana Freeway, Disneyland recalled a time before the "placelessness" of modern suburban developments dominated by cars and highways and lacking sidewalks. It offered an alternative to suburban banality and boredom. In effect, Disneyland was a "town" you could actually walk through, even if it was only a fantasy.[11] Disneyland is an evocation of a lost space in modern industrial and automotive culture—the contained, often labyrinthine, and highly featured cultural site of a preindustrial European city. Many things destroyed the walkable towns that once contained and marked daily life: rail and then automotive transportation; the separation of work, shopping, and residential spaces; the emergence of mega-cities; and the shortened lifespan of the built environment. But this eclipse made Disney's nostalgia America's nostalgia.[12]

The secret to the success of Disney was not in the creation of a safe, saccharine sentimentality or even the perpetuation of a sanitized memory of small-town life. It was in making a "memory" of the past into a playground of nostalgia, the memory of a child's play set for young and old alike. This suggests a very different aesthetic than what inspired the (re)constructions of the "streets" of Williamsburg, Old Sturbridge Village, or Greenfield Village.

From the magical wormhole of Main Street USA, Disneyland fans out to four "lands" of memory and fantasy. Again these were reminiscent of Disney's own childhood imaginative life inspired by the pulp fiction (*Tom Swift*, e.g.) and popular magazines (like *St. Nicholas*) of the early twentieth century. Frontierland was full of references to the Wild West and Tom Sawyer, and Adventureland's Jungle Cruise recalled Disney's boyhood pleasures of imagining traveling to mysterious far-off places. By contrast, Tomorrowland evoked the cult of progress and technological advancement promoted in magazines like *Popular Mechanics*. Finally, Fantasyland presented a series of themed circular and scenic rides based on Disney animation, many of which had their origins in the 1930s (the Mad Tea Party from *Alice in Wonderland*). But these too ultimately derived from Disney's childhood exposure to late-nineteenth-century children's literature.

Disney's success was built not only on nostalgia for a fantasy place and Disney's attractive evocation of his own childhood. It was based on a new image and understanding of childhood itself. Not often recognized is the fact that Disney abandoned the freak shows and disaster spectacles of earlier parks and the thrills of rollercoasters and spinning rides for cutesy images of cartoon animals designed to evoke delight in children. Many of the attractions and tame rides of Disneyland were built around upbeat stories, many of which had been previously made into Disney movies. In this way, Disney was following a long trend—the replacement of popular fascination with (and often fear of) the "unnatural" freak (dwarf, giant, bearded lady, Siamese Twin, etc.) with more child-like, elfin creatures that appealed to the imagination of youngsters and to the longing of adults to identify with the child.[13] By 1955, many Disney-raised children had kids of their own with whom to share these very same Disney fantasies when they reappeared on TV and were rerun in movie theaters. These Disney images of Mickey Mouse, Donald Duck, and the rest of the menagerie were at the core of the child-based nostalgia of Disney's empire.

This skillful combination of nostalgia and the cult of the child's delight delivered a family crowd rather than the throngs of single youths that gathered at traditional amusement parks and carnivals. Disney wisely attracted dependent children around which intimate family groups gathered to form a nonthreatening crowd rather than a mob of youth. But as important, the childlike at Disneyland offered adults a way back to their own childhoods.[14]

As a result Disney created a cross-generational appeal that was built on adults evoking delight in children through rituals of giving. Since about 1900, American parents had been experimenting with ways to arouse wonder in their offspring: they began by taking children to seaside resorts and offering them ice-cream cones, teddy bears, and amusement rides; they showered their kids with Santa's gifts, in time largely forgetting the old elf who once had left coal in the stockings of bad boys and girls. This began when increasing affluence led to more tolerant childrearing practices and a fantasy world presumably derived from children's sensibilities. Think, for example, of the popularity of *Peter Pan* with adults as well as children when it appeared in 1904.[15] This production of cross-generational appeal was a long process. Whereas Coney Island visitors rarely brought children in 1900, as much because of the cost as because of lack of interest in playing with their offspring,[16] by 1955 many parents could afford family vacations and happily made the Disney trip an affirmation of love for children.

Whereas the child at Disneyland was to be delighted and the adult nostalgic for that delight, the child at the heritage site was to learn, and the adult was to teach. Not only were the Disney child and adult likely to have more fun, but the Disney way was far easier to achieve because Disney fantasy could be shared by parent and child whereas the memory of heritage was so easily lost from one generation to the next. The appeal both to the child and to the adult's "inner child" is arguably the key to the Disney success—a bridge that crosses generations—and this is Disney's advantage over the heritage site but also over so many other forms of consumed nostalgia that lack this intergenerational link.

But Disney does more. It offers us a magical place, not the everyday world of our hardscrabble ancestors. Disney doesn't ask us to "return" to an alien world, abandon our intensity-adapted senses for a slower-paced sensibility, as do heritage sites. It goes in the opposite direction. It provides a modern pilgrimage site, one adapted to a consumer culture. The Disney visit animates the memory of Mickey in the two-dimensional world of comics and films by creating a gigantic, hyperreal replica of those fantasies, and it invites the "pilgrim" inside the dream, as Hench so ably describes. This was surely a secular update of the medieval pilgrim's desire to enter the cathedral, reputed to contain the relics of saints, the stories about which were embedded in the consciousness of the faithful. And like medieval pilgrimage sites, Disney offered customers returning home souvenirs, often miniatures of sights seen.

NOSTALGIC PILGRIMAGE SITES AFTER WALT: DISNEY WORLD, RESORTS, AND CELEBRATION

Walt Disney's nostalgia business expanded after his death in 1966. Disneyland as a blowup play set of Disney's childhood was repeated in the Magic Kingdom in 1971, the first park of the much larger Florida-based Walt Disney World complex. And nostalgic themes were also central to more innovative Disney projects. Walt had planned to create a model urban utopia, the Experimental Prototype Community of Tomorrow (Epcot). But instead, in 1981, his successors opened another theme park reminiscent of the old American tradition of world's fairs, roughly divided between a permanent exhibition of progress (Future World), with exhibits offering entertaining takes on the history and future of technology, and international exhibits (World Showcase),[17] a semicircle of idealized replicas of tourist sites that was an upscale version of the "villages" depicting African, South Seas, or even European life that had for nearly a century stirred the imaginations of visitors to world's fairs without either the time or money for world travel.[18]

Michael Eisner, who became CEO of Disney in 1984, pursued the nostalgic theme with a string of hotel/resort complexes at Disney World. Abandoning the partnership with Marriot and its generic hotels, Eisner built a series of resort hotels for affluent park goers who might have imagined themselves to be inheritors of traditions of the genteel tourism that dated from the late nineteenth century through the 1920s. The Grand Floridian Beach Resort (1986) was designed to evoke nostalgia for the turn of the twentieth century, when the rich escaped New York and Boston winters for southern Florida beaches. The hotel features a gabled roof and Victorian balustrades befitting the elegance of that era. The Disney Yacht Club and Beach Club Resort adopted a New England theme of late-nineteenth-century nautical elegance, with Newport-style cottages that feature white wicker arched verandas, pennants, and even a small water park built around a ship run aground. Other Disney complexes included the Old Key West Resort (another Florida-themed site suggesting the small islands off the southern Floridian coast), the Wilderness Lodge and Villas (recalling railroad-linked hotels in the Rocky Mountain national parks before 1920, with all the appropriate "Indian" themes like totem poles, teepees, and elegant log-cabin lodgings). These luxury resorts were complemented by a string of more moderately priced resorts beginning with the Caribbean Beach Resort in 1988; followed by Port Orleans in 1991 (with an Old French Quarter look); BoardWalk in 1996, modeled after the Atlantic City and Coney Island of the 1920s; and Coronado Springs in 1997 (with a southwestern American theme). Finally, in 2004, Disney World opened its Saratoga Springs resort, whose clusters of rooms and suites were themed to evoke "memories" of the small town in upstate New York that in the nineteenth century attracted celebrities and thousands of mostly affluent health and fun seekers to its mineral springs and horse racing. Eight of the seventeen Disney World resorts today are nostalgia themed.[19]

Interestingly, few customers had actually any direct memory of these historic sites of elegant leisure, and in none of these resorts was there any attempt actually to build accurate replicas, much less to restore even bits of the historic sites (as did Old World Wisconsin and Colonial Williamsburg). In all of these historically themed Disney resorts a formula seems to be followed: a central lobby and restaurant/bar building with theme-appropriate interiors, exteriors, and even wall and building colors. For example, Disney's Saratoga Springs pulls architectural references out of their original contexts and places them in the Disney schema: The reception and restaurant building (called the Carriage House) features paintings of horse races and the "winner's circle," as well as a large bronze statue of a racing horse (vaguely in reference to the famous racetrack at the real Saratoga Springs). The High Rock Spring is not a source of mineral water (that made the New York site famous in the early nineteenth century) but an artificial water display that empties into a heated pool at the On the Rocks pool bar. Architectural accents include stripes and diamonds (allusions to jockey silks), gingerbread trim and arched openings presumably recalling horse stalls, and the colors and fretwork of late Victorian Saratoga Springs houses.[20] Otherwise, the resort is a replica of the successful Disney family resort: Studios or multibedroomed "villas" offer many comforts of home (full kitchens, washers and dryers). And, instead of the original New York resort town's racetrack, ballrooms, grand wooden hotels, gambling casino, and mineral springs to drink from to cure the cumulative sins of excess, there are four pools, two playgrounds, a modern beauty "spa," a high-tech game room, and tennis and basketball courts, all designed to appeal to suburban families with children (which the original was definitely not).[21]

Considering all the ways that the Saratoga Springs resort is not like the original, one might conclude that all these efforts of themed nostalgia are little more than an attempt to distinguish Disney lodgings from the garden-variety Holiday Inn or Marriot. Disney's historically themed resorts are certainly a variation on the movie-set experience of Epcot's World Showcase's miniatures of the Eiffel Tower and Buddhist pagoda. The superficiality of Disney's "restoration" of the past reflects an ignorance of the past—of both designers and visitors—and the fact that no one wants to return to the culture (and inconveniences) of the past. Still, the success of these Disney resorts suggests that the Victorian worlds of Saratoga, Newport, Key West, and the Rocky Mountain lodges retain an appeal to modern American suburbanites, even if these resorts are in fact manifestations of what replaced that genteel culture—the family lodging complex attached to a theme park. These sites are part of a deeper commercial nostalgia based less on personal memory than on a romanticized "past" derived from vague recollections of scenes from movies, illustrations, and stories.

In fact, the nostalgic lodgings of Disney resorts were linked to the company's re-creation in 1996 of an ideal small town adjacent to the Florida theme-park complex: the planned community of Celebration. Unlike the genteel Victorian exoticism of Disney World's upscale resorts, Celebration was designed as a "perfect" replica of small-town America, a compact community of homes suitable for pedestrian and cycle travel with much space devoted to public recreation, a lively commercial center (with the inevitable Disney "weenie," in this case a stereotypical small town's water tower), and even a town seal (featuring a quaint image of a ponytailed little girl on a bike with her dog). Most of these symbols of a lost paradise are missing from the modern suburbs in which most of the new inhabitants had lived. The town was limited to twenty thousand people and was set far enough away from other developments to assure buyers that their community would remain unique. And, although house design was restricted to six choices (ranging from Colonial Revival to Coastal Classic), they were dispersed to avoid the cookie-cutter appearance of the modern suburban development. Though "neotraditional" planned residential communities were fashionable in the late 1980s and 1990s, Celebration is easily the best known (and most criticized). At least the first generation of home owners were mostly older baby boomers who grew up with Disney and "believed that Disney can do no wrong," even as they sometimes clashed with Disney rules (especially the early program of "progressive education" in the Celebration schools). While porches were designed to encourage neighborliness, they were not used much (while TVs indoors were). Apparently it was hard for ex-suburbanites to break old habits. Still, Celebration was the town that realized the romance of Main Street USA.[22]

A final piece of Disney's nostalgia complex is Disney-MGM Studios, which opened in 1989, a recreation of another romantic memory—the Hollywood of the film industry's Golden Age, the 1930s and 1940s. The general concept was borrowed from Universal Studio's park built near Hollywood in 1964, which combined movie-based rides with tours of stage sets and real movie and TV production facilities. Later renamed Disney's Hollywood Studios, the park dropped the reference to MGM, a great movie company of the past and whose name and movies Disney had licensed for the theme park. By the late 1980s, Eisner realized that Walt's generation—nostalgic for small-town America and Disney's early-twentieth-century vision of adventure, fantasy, and the future—was passing from the scene. Nostalgia had moved up a generation to a group with fond memories of 1930s and 1940s Hollywood and the classical movies of that period. The new park offered a glorification of the Golden Age of movies with a scaled-down (and grossly inaccurate) version of 1940s-era Hollywood and Sunset Boulevards, including movie-star hangouts like the Brown Derby and with a replica of Grauman's Chinese Theater at the center. This classic Hollywood theater was the home of the park's flagship attraction, the Great Movie Ride, featuring exciting video clips from famous movies that visitors watched from cars shaped like soundstage vehicles. In an account of the site in the mid-1990s, "cast members" paraded as starlets and autograph hounds, chatting with the crowd and with one another, loading their conversation with pop-culture references from the days of Clark Gable and Greta Garbo. And the 50s Prime Time Cafe went much further than the standard 1950s-themed soda fountain. It featured TVs continuously playing loops from iconic 1950s TV (*Leave It to Beaver*, *I Love Lucy*, and *Lassie*), offered such fare as "Mom's Meat Loaf," and the waiter even asks guests if they'd washed up before dining. In many ways this was just another version of the reenactments common at Colonial Williamsburg, but with pop culture replacing crafts and social life. But the crowd hardly expected the "real 1950s" but rather the sitcom version of it, as if they were on the set of *Happy Days*. For those with no memory of the 1940s and 1950s or even the movie or TV version of it, Disney bought the rights to Jim Henson's Muppets, a collection of puppets familiar to most American children (and many adults) through their TV and movie appearances in the 1970s and 1980s. Disney's Hollywood Studios offered what the small screen or movie theater (then) could not provide, *Muppet Vision 3-D* in 1991, the first of a new wave of 3-D movies with in-theater special effects.[23]

Perhaps inevitably, the nostalgic theme at Hollywood Studios (and elsewhere at Disney World) has been supplemented since the late 1980s with an increasing emphasis upon thrill rides and water parks. These changes have been designed both to attract older children (and their families) and to compete with Universal Studios in Orlando and other amusement/theme parks, whose new generation of fast, high, and twisting roller coasters have successfully tapped into the desires of excitement seekers. But Disney still remains the best example of the themed nostalgia site.[24]

What Disney and others added to consumed nostalgia was the power of the pilgrimage, the gigantic, "live," and interactive form of childhood fantasy adapted to a multifaceted and changing world of memory. Disney World drew 48.5 million and Disneyland 15.96 million visitors in 2012, despite admission prices doubling in ten years. Like other pilgrimage sites, Disney offers the salve of the souvenir and provides the full range of the miniature to the gigantic in the parks. And far more than heritage sites, Disney and other theme parks often beget repeat returns. To understand this better, let's take a closer look at the theme-park souvenir in the form of "Disneyana" and the theme park's powerful influence on collectors.

RETRO DISNEY: THE COLLECTIBLE SOUVENIR AND THE CULT OF RETURN

Disney Enterprises became the master of the nostalgic collectible. In this Disney built on a well-established collection culture—

assembling diverse objects (paintings, furniture, miniatures, statuary, books) around a common theme (origin, age, material, or topic)—in this case, a Disney character, story, or site. And manufacturing objects to be gathered and displayed as a "complete" collection by consumers was a marketing trick that long preceded Disney. Nineteenth-century makers of dolls, trade cards, celebrity photographs, and ceramic figures attracted a diverse market of mostly women and children collectors. Walt Disney, at first quite unintentionally, took this strategy to a new level. He licensed his cartoon images for sale on merchandise, mostly for children that adults later reassembled into nostalgic collections. In this he followed illustrated storybook and comic-strip artists, like Palmer Cox of *The Brownies*, but also movie stars like Charlie Chaplin. Disney was simply trying to capitalize on an already popular image when he marketed Mickey Mouse dolls in late 1929. The object was to subsidize his costly cartoon enterprise, and quickly this effort expanded to licensing the Mickey character on a wide variety of objects toys, and also handkerchiefs, school supplies, toothbrushes, alarm clocks, Christmas tree lights, ties, and clothing of all kinds. Most notable were cheap Mickey Mouse watches (1933) and for Lionel, the maker of model train sets, a Mickey Handcar (1934).[25]

Most of these products were designed for children, especially toddlers and primary-school kids, and many were gifts from parents, especially at Christmas or birthdays. Interestingly, in the years from the first Mickey cartoons in 1928 until the mid-1930s, the Mouse became both less rodentlike and, especially with the addition of his dog, Pluto, more like the friendly boy next door. Moreover, according to the famed biologist Stephen Jay Gould, this shift in the look of Mickey was an adoption (consciously or not) of the view of Konrad Lorenz that juvenile features in animals (including kids) trigger positive and protective emotional responses in adults.[26] This paid big dividends for decades as Disney characters bore their way into the affections and memories of Americans (and much of the world).

Disney drew on early successes in linking cartoons to merchandising with the 1937 release of *Snow White and the Seven Dwarfs*. He licensed characters from the movie across what merchandisers would later call "multiple platforms" for a wide array of figurines, toys, and other merchandise. This inaugurated the corporate-initiated, multifaceted commercial fad that Disney (and many others) would orchestrate again and again thereafter. As early as the 1930s, half of Disney's profits came from merchandise licensing.[27]

In the generation that grew up in the 1930s, Disney provided childhood memories of wondrous innocence (notable in a period of general hardship). At the same time an adult cult of Disneyana (a precursor to the anti-high-culture attraction of camp) appeared. Recall the whimsically sophisticated lyrics of Cole Porter's 1934 song "You're the Top": "You're a melody from a symphony by Strauss / You're a Bendel bonnet / A Shakespeare's sonnet / You're Mickey Mouse!" Almost everybody loved the Mouse. In fact, in the mid-1930s, Disney cartoon drawings were embraced by "sophisticated" patrons of the Metropolitan Museum of Art. The cels, the original drawings of Disney animators on celluloid plastic, were produced by the thousands, and the ever-enterprising Disney organization sold them through art stores as early as 1938. It's no surprise that the middle aged in the 1960s and 1970s might turn back to Disney.[28]

But Disney and his successors added another ingredient to this powerful nostalgic brew with Disneyland and Walt Disney World. With these sites of the "gigantic," Disneyana became the corresponding miniatures or souvenirs of the pilgrimage of the faithful. As early as 1956, Disneyland's Art Corner store published a mail-order catalogue that sold celluloid inked drawings and character sketches (formerly used in Disney animation) at amazingly low prices (50 cents to $1.47) as well as souvenir gifts of Disneyland pennants, plates, and replicas of the jungle boats of Adventureland, toy guns from Frontierland, and space helmets embossed with Tomorrowland imagery.[29]

Disneyland was not only a radical departure from the entertainment of the traditional amusement park; it was a major extension of cross-marketing or "synergy."[30] Months before the opening of Disneyland in Anaheim, Walt Disney negotiated with ABC to air an hour-long program, *Disneyland*, in December 1954. This compilation of Disney films and documentary footage of the "back-stage" activities of the company was primarily a feature-length advertisement for the upcoming opening of the theme park. One of the early successes of the *Disneyland* show was the serial presentation of Davy Crockett, a highly fictionalized and child-friendly story of a defender of the Alamo in Texas. This led not only a very popular movie but created a fad for Crocket "coonskin caps" in the spring of 1955. Shortly after the opening of the theme park, Disney further exploited the link between TV, Disneyland, and character merchandising with the late afternoon airing of *The Mickey Mouse Club* (October 1955), producing not only a song-and-dance revue of ordinary American kids ("Mouseketeers") but an avalanche of Disney merchandise (beginning with the "mousekeears," a beanie hat with Mickey Mouse ears attached). Within scarcely three months, Benay-Albee Novelty Company had shipped 550,000 of these silly things. A wide assortment of Mickey Mouse Club items followed—the mousegetar music box, shaped like a guitar, and a variety of toddler push toys, many sold to doting parents as impulse purchases sparked by a pleading child near the checkout line of grocery or drug stores.[31] These TV shows were weekly or daily conduits for Disney products, which, along with the theme park and movies, invaded the sensoria of successive generations of American children and families.

By the end of the 1950s, Disney had a thirty-year record of licensing products across a wide range of tastes and age cohorts, but the company (after Walt's death in 1966) had only begun to recognize the attraction of Disneyana as commercialized nostalgia rather than as fad products. But by the later 1960s, old Disney-themed novelties, especially from the 1930s, were already attracting collectors. Stimulated by the pop art of Andy Warhol and Roy Lichtenstein, cartoon drawings from Disney's "golden age" became popular at high-end auctions (at Sotheby's, e.g.). While Disney could not benefit directly from old merchandise, beginning in 1968, the company licensed the sale of porcelain replicas of 1930s Disneyana (Mickey, Snow White, etc.). This was an early example of substituting old collectibles for new ones that shared a common association with childhood memory. The fortieth anniversary of Mickey Mouse's debut on the screen brought a *Life* feature (September 1968) with interviews of Disneyana collectors, and, fostered by the youth counterculture of the day and its taste for camp, there was a revival of Mickey Mouse watches. The Metropolitan Museum of Art in December 1975 featured another exhibition of Mickey Mouse art. Cecil Munsey's thorough 1974 guide to Disneyana (aided by access to the Disney archive in Burbank) helped launch a wave of collecting.[32]

That interest expanded with Disneyana books by Robert Heide and John Gilman (1983) and Tom Tumbusch (1985).[33] Others followed, often linked to memorabilia stores (such as the Disney-only Fantasies Come True of Los Angeles, in business since 1980).[34] In 1980, the *Collector Club Newsletter* (in 1982 renamed *Disneyana Collector*) was published in cooperation with Disney Productions. It featured an array of stories about the figurines, animation cels, and other memorabilia available at Disney theme parks as well as news on the latest fads in collecting. This newsletter also offered folksy stories about old-time Disney insiders (set directors and illustrators like Ward Kimball and Bill Justice) and histories of Disney trivia (like the history of the Mickey Mouse watch), details about the casting methods used in making figurines, and "advanced" news about future attractions at Disney parks. This and later magazines like *Disneyana* and *Toy Box* were mostly thinly veiled vehicles for selling memorabilia, but they also provided collectors and park enthusiasts with a sense of belonging to a community.[35]

All this merchandising and promotion of Disney accelerated the collecting frenzy. Still, the key was the aging of the Disney's children: by the 1980s, collectors' nostalgia for their 1930s and 1940s childhoods made Disney stuff from that era valuable (and in fact too pricey for many); moreover, as old Mouseketeers became middle-aged nostalgiacs, there was a surge in interest in Disneyana dating from the 1950s. The sheer variety of Disneyana (pins, stuffed animals, animation cels, figurines, Christmas ornaments, comics, children's books, and watches) provided a wide range of personal collections. Conventions, clubs, and later the Internet created opportunities for distinct and often very specialized communities of Disney fans.

In 1984, seeking to exploit this and many other markets, Disney's new CEO Michael Eisner initiated licensing agreements, including seven thousand items with the toy-manufacturing giant Hasbro, raising merchandising profits from $100 to $425 million by 1994.[36] Central to this success was the launching of the first Disney Store in Glendale, California, in 1987. Much of the highly profitable floor space of this and subsequent stores (749 by 1999) was devoted to the cross-promotion of current Disney projects, but the Disney Stores also met the growing market for nostalgic collectibles.[37]

While inevitably Disney Enterprises had close ties to Disneyana publications and merchandizing, there were also independent groups of enthusiasts that sometimes clashed with the company. The dominant group was the National Fantasy Fan Club (NFFC), based in Irving, California, which recently has been renamed the Disneyana Fan Club. It was founded in 1984 with conventions from 1985 for buyers and sellers of Disney memorabilia. By 1992 there were nineteen chapters (six in California). The NFFC gathered enthusiasts of Disney parks and of collectibles. Since 1993, the NFFC convention has presented "Legends" awards to notable Disney artists—though interestingly never to the business brass.[38] But this didn't mean that this club embraced everything the company did. In August 1992, the Orlando branch held a "World Chapter's Day of Disneyana" at Walt Disney World. While Disney staff offered special early entrance passes to members, this didn't stop NFFC members from lamenting in their newsletter that the "Walt Disney Story," an exhibit that had attracted visitors for twenty-one years, had "closed with no fanfare" recently.[39]

Not surprisingly, to profit from fan enthusiasm (and perhaps to deflect criticism), Disney organized its own Disneyana Convention, which was first held at Walt Disney World's Contemporary Resort, September 24–27, 1992, drawing 750 fans. Three of the original Mouseketeers—Bobby, Sharon, and Sherry—were on hand to autograph photographs. Speeches from Disney brass, including Dick Nunis, the chairman of Walt Disney Attractions, were heard. And, not surprisingly, Disney staff displayed the full array of Disney enterprises (Disney Art Editions, Disney Stores, the Disney

Vacation Club, etc.). Disney even found room for independent dealers. And for those with deep pockets, there was a Disneyana auction, selling off theme-park props from the Disney vaults (an "original Dumbo attraction unit" in the shape of the famous elephant sold for $16,000). Disney made sure that no stone of nostalgia was left unturned. Still, NFFC members complained that the Disneyana art was plentiful but too expensive.[40]

In 1992, Disney enterprises also launched the Walt Disney Classics Collection to produce and retail "fine Art Animation sculptures" that drew on "archival materials from Disney's original films." The idea was to capture a cinematic climax in porcelain, for example, a "touching moment between Quasimodo and Esmeralda" in the animated *Hunchback of Notre Dame* (1996). By 1998, Disney claimed that sixty-five thousand people had "joined" the Walt Disney Collectors' Society and received promotional literature for classic minisculptures such as the "Magician Mickey" (from the Sorcerer's Apprentice cartoon).[41]

These efforts to co-opt the collecting craze culminated in 2009 with the launching of D-23, a wide-ranging vehicle for capturing Disney park and collectible enthusiasts through a website, convention, magazines, and numerous "special offers" for "members" of D-23. Named for the year (1923) when Walt Disney first went into business, D-23 is committed to the memory and "history" of Disney and everything that the company has done. The magazine for members includes, for example, "Where in D?," a "mystery photo" that subscribers are encouraged to identify, the "Funny Pages" of long-forgotten Disney newspaper comic strips, Disney-themed crafts for the kids, and recipes from Disney's most famous restaurants. There is even a section called "Ask Dave"—Dave Smith, the longtime Disney archivist. Inevitably, the site also includes a "D-23 Boutique," where Disney merchandise can be purchased online. The first convention in Anaheim in 2009 reprised earlier Disney efforts to gather faithful spenders: the Fan Art Gallery offered "Treasures of the Walt Disney Archives," including old props, photos, and cartoon drawings. As at earlier conventions, Disney provided lectures from "Imagineering Legends" on the making of Disney park attractions and the viewing of a "lost" Mickey Mouse cartoon from the 1950s. All this made conventioneers feel special, a kind of aristocracy of Disney fans.[42]

The Disney success story (especially in the era of Michael Eisner) had been built on cross-generational attractions. But that success has long threatened Disney's control over its own creations. To Walt's horror, a web of cheap and often tacky lodgings, eating places, and attractions sprang up adjacent to Disneyland soon after it opened in 1955 (prompting him to buy a far larger tract of land for his Florida enterprise to keep the riffraff at bay). And especially insofar as Disney has been built on nostalgia, the company has unintentionally encouraged a fan culture, whose adherents fervently, perhaps irrationally, embraced all things Disney but also assumed an attitude of ownership of the beloved Mouse. This possessiveness had long characterized fan culture (for example, in the fan clubs of movie stars).

It is no surprise that, in addition to the long-running NFFC, independent websites posted by Disney collectors and park enthusiasts have flourished, offering a seemingly endless array of Disney trivia, "insider" news, and advertising for Disneyana (MiceAge.com, LaughingPlace.com, etc.).[43] And these fans, despite or, from their point of view, because of their love of things and places Disney, have frequently challenged the company for betraying the Disney vision. One abiding concern of enthusiasts is that Disney's lands remain unchanged. Jeff Baham of San Jose, an enthusiast of Disney rides, summed up this point of view succinctly in 2005, as he recalled his frequent childhood visits to Disneyland: "There is something amazing about being able to revisit an immersive experience that has remained, essentially, unchanged, while everything else in life evolves and moves on. . . . It's the closest thing to time travel that there is." But of course this sentiment can lead to dissatisfaction when Disney attractions are closed or updated. Werner Weiss's website, www.yesterland.com, features pictures and stories about Disney rides and sites that have disappeared (for example, the Carousel of Progress, Adventures Through Inner Space, and even the old Disneyland parking lot, now the site of California Adventure). He misses the old Mine Train Through Nature's Wonderland for its slow and artifact-filled view of the old West and wishes he could take his kids on it to experience an alternative to the now standard thrill rides. Steve DeGaetano of Los Angeles was so enamored as a five-year-old by the Disneyland Railroad that circles the park that he founded a newsletter and wrote a book about it.[44]

This sort of obsession with a material memory of childhood is rare, but surely more common is the hurt that frequent visitors feel when something changes. The *Los Angeles Times* reported in 1994 the dismay of park regulars when Tomorrowland's Skyway cable gondolas disappeared. The audience at a Disneyana convention that year booed when Disney staff announced a minor change to Storybook Land (replacing a dated and now obscure scene from "Mr. Toad" with one from the hit movie *Aladdin*). This response has frustrated park officials in plans to modify or replace attractions (even though twenty-one of thirty-eight have been changed or replaced in Disneyland's first forty years, the transformation has been subtle). Still, defenders of the status quo have shot back with a letter-writing campaign to save a not-very-popular "Great Moments with Mr. Lincoln," in which a figure representing the president delivers a speech.[45]

This sense of possession and stakeholding among Disney nostalgiacs might mean an occasional PR headache for Disney executives, but organized fandom has also complicated Disney's management politics. As a publicly traded company, Disney attracts not only institutional and savvy investors but stock purchases from fans. In a power struggle between Roy E. Disney (nephew of Walt) and Michael Eisner in 2004, Roy formed Shamrock Holdings to mobilize small shareholders against Eisner. He used fan websites to campaign against the twenty-year reign of Eisner and launched his own website, savedisney.com. Enthusiasts had long been attentive to signs of shoddy maintenance of the theme parks and overpriced collectibles. Some like Michelle Smith (fabuousdisneybabe.com) of San Diego, who claimed to visit Disneyland one hundred times a year, helped organize a letter-writing campaign against Eisner. This complex story culminated in a mere 45 percent vote of confidence for Eisner by the Disney Board in 2004 and his departure from the company in September 2005, a year before he had planned.[46]

THE GIGANTIC IN THE PILGRIMAGE TO DISNEY, THE MINIATURE IN THE DISNEYANA SOUVENIR

I began this chapter comparing themed and heritage nostalgia and trying to explain why the themed version seems to prevail. I passed over the obvious point that Disneyland is just more fun than Old World Wisconsin and thought it worthwhile to adopt at least a few of the insights of cultural studies—the concepts of the pilgrimage and the souvenir, the gigantic and the miniature—to elucidate the appeal of themed nostalgia through the sites and stuff of Walt Disney Enterprises.[47] Let's follow that theme further by comparing the traditional with the Disney version of the pilgrimage and souvenir.

The gigantic/pilgrimage site must involve a journey with anticipation and "travail" (labor) that brings the visitor to a special place—a sacred site, in fact—across a transitional entrance and into a "blow-up" of the smallness and thinness of memory. The site necessarily is massive, sensuously dense, and often features statues, colored windows, precious building materials, and elaborately decorated structures (as, for example, the gargoyle-covered cathedrals of Europe). The grandeur lets you experience your imagination and memory in real space and time as you traverse the pilgrimage site, making ideas and memory more vivid and alive. The traditional pilgrimage site validates faith—in the divine or in a lost way of life.[48] The journey of believers to the ancient town of Lourdes and its church laden with history and symbolism is very much like the trip of the enthusiast to Disneyland, its dramatic entrance and paths through Main Street USA to the "lands" fanning out from Sleeping Beauty's Castle.

But Disney is not a historical or holy site; instead it is obviously "staged," always an artifice, not a site of miracles or a natural wonder. No one, not even the most ardent Disneymaniac, is deceived. In fact, being "in the know" about the tricks of the show is one of the things that attracts the seasoned customer to attend Disneyana conventions.[49] Disney enjoyed demonstrating the arts of animation on his TV shows, and Eisner opened an elaborately planned Disney Institute in 1996 in part to attract Disney enthusiasts interested in taking short "courses" in animation and in the engineering and design of the theme parks. The Disney Institute provided the "backstage" view of Disney theatrics.[50] Even though it failed to generate the interest Eisner hoped for (and was replaced by the Saratoga Springs resort in 2004), this appeal to enthusiasts seeking an insider's view inside the "magic" was central to the identities of Disney fans.

The Disney pilgrimage, however, is more than a staged show. It gains historical and quasi legitimacy because of its being marked off with berms rather than ancient walls, labeled with distinctive structures like "weenies," spotless, dramatically lit, saturated with happy music, and associated with the sacred time not of miracles but of childhood memory. In fact, the Disney gigantic often is a blow-up of the child's miniature—the play set, toy, or doll. Though playful, really a supersized toy, Disney's evocation of the wondrous innocence of childhood makes it quasi-sacred, a place to go to in order to renew one's "faith" in the innocent delights of childhood.

Thus Disney's lands, like some other theme parks, have become sites of regular return across the life course. Over the years, Disney has encouraged this custom of recurrence by offering "rites-of-passage" venues: special meals with entertainment in Sleeping Beauty's Castle for "Little Princesses" and a Wedding Chapel for grown-up princesses who have met their Prince Charmings. Disney's Wedding Chapel (opened in 1995) offers a glass-enclosed pavilion on its own island with a backdrop of the Magic Kingdom's Castle. Walt Disney World has also appealed to thousands as a honeymoon site.[51] Despite innovations, it is the memory and quest for reassuring continuity that brings people back year after year.

The Disney pilgrim does not journey to a natural setting (like the Grand Canyon) or a historical one (like Gettysburg) but "returns" to a childhood fantasy that not only is commercialized but was always commercial—a nostalgia for a toy or comic book in a store or a cartoon in a theater that came and went in childhood. What makes the Disney parks timeless is that they are the materialization of the ephemeral (often a flicker on the movie or TV screen), fixing the fast capitalism of entertainment; Disney's parks promise not to change (much) in contrast to the ephemerality of the broader consumer culture or the inevitability of growing up. In sum, the Disney site is about a "return" to the Edenic site of first delights, not in nature or in a preindustrial era of skilled work and slow-paced interactions with others but in a return to a commercialized childhood. And that memory is evoked not by grandparents or teachers or even childhood friends but by Mickey Mouse. This may seem paltry and even pathetic, but, as is true with other forms of commercial nostalgia, Disney's lands and the Disneyana that it generates may be one of the few ways that we moderns have of getting in touch with our pasts. At least, it is an easy and popular way.

The souvenir brought back from the religious, natural, and even Disney pilgrimage allows us to extend the memory of the site. At least we think so, in our feverish taking of pictures and gathering of mementos at gift shops in order to possess, control, and confine the ephemeral experience—even though we often forget about them. Tourist and religious souvenirs are often private miniaturizes of public monumental sites (Eiffel Tower paperweights, for example).[52] And in some cases, the miniature expresses, as Susan Stewart notes, "nostalgia for preindustrial labor, nostalgia for craft."[53]

The Disney souvenir miniature shares much with its traditional counterpart, and the company fully understands this in its dozens of well-stocked gift shops located at the exits of rides and attractions. Even in the curious manufacture of cartoon scenes in porcelain figurines, there is an appeal to the rarity and exclusivity of fine "craftsmanship."[54] But the Disney miniature or souvenir goes further because it isn't singular and unique but "additive," gaining value by its multiplication rather than its "authenticity." That's the point of the collectible: the more the better. And, despite the relatively timeless and eventually "hallowed" character of Disney's lands, the souvenir is not just a derivative of the site but really another form of the themed line of products, movies, TV shows, toys, figurines, and embossed goods that return collectors to their particular childhoods.

Old Disney objects are "real," but replica collectibles can also be "real" to the collector because they look like the original. The key is the semblance. Both are representations of an animation or staged action in film, and what counts is the "authentic" effect—the evocation of the memory of the wondrous first viewing of the scene. Disneyana transcends the old constraints on the souvenir—valuable because rare, old and dispersed, hard to get, and necessarily physically linked with the "source"—the tourist or pilgrimage site. Disneyana (and much collectible culture today) can be accessed without a pilgrimage via websites and "remote Disney shrines"—mall-based Disney stores. The special value of "rarity" is retained with "limited editions" (often numbered items). The dreary uniformity of mass commodity production leads many of us to seek human-scale spaces, times, and especially things in nostalgia. In many ways Disney provides these personally relatable places, events, and things, and that is a major reason for its success. But Disney delivers all this in the highly "mediated" or commercial world of Main Streets, old Disney toys, and modern mass-produced cartoon figurines.[55]

There is little evidence that any of this concerns Disneyana collectors, but, in their fashion, some at least try to deepen their nostalgic experience. Ironically, perhaps, they do so by becoming Disney "insiders," making the site and souvenir "context-full," joining Disney clubs to make the Disney experience "communal" and seeing themselves as stakeholders in the Disney enterprise. Others simply complete a set of a Disney collection and "put on" the Disney in an emotional and sensuous immersion in Disney detail at Anaheim and Orlando. This works for some, even crossing the cross-generational barrier that few other forms of consumed nostalgia provide. But might there still be something missing? We'll explore that question in our final chapter.

CONCLUSION

Where We've Been, Where We Might Go

Nostalgia has come a long way. The homesickness that once drove this longing has largely been replaced by a desire to recover the things and experiences of a novelty-driven consumer society. Nevertheless, most critics of nostalgia continue to associate it with the loneliness of the migrant, the distress of those left behind by rapid change, or a people's lost faith in the future, all of whom are pitied by the well-adjusted, rational, and forward looking. This longing for a lost home is, as the historian David Lowenthal says, a "distortion of the past." As the literary scholar Svetlana Boym notes, "There is a deep-seated fear of reflection on history and its blank spots." For her, "Modern nostalgia is a mourning for the impossibility of mythical return, for the loss of an enchanted world with clear borders and values."[1]

This negative assessment of nostalgia contrasts with the positive view of a group of psychologists (led by Constantine Sedikides,

Tim Wildschut, and Clay Routledge). In lab studies they show how nostalgic recollections of volunteer subjects bring forth feelings of belonging, stronger ties between the present and past, and more positive assessments of their lives. These psychologists argue that though nostalgia can be obsessive, it is mostly a resource to help people cope with the stresses of life.[2] The British cultural historian Gaynor Kavanagh adds that we are attracted to the past (as we age) because it helps us reassess and sometimes integrate our lives.[3]

In my view, this debate won't be resolved because the two contenders are not talking about the same thing. Critics like Boym are thinking about a tribal sort of memory that leads to "restorative nostalgia" that distorts the past and blocks dialogue in the present; proponents are talking about immediate psychological responses to recollections of past events and relationships. The first is social/political, embodied in monuments and ideology; the second is personal and an immediate response to a memory. These forms of nostalgia very much survive today, as I noted in the introduction. But after observing and reading about modern nostalgia, I believe that both interpretations miss the special way that much nostalgia is actually "lived" now—through consumed objects and experiences. Trying to understand nostalgia in this way may lead to a different judgment—that it should not be rejected wholly but that, as memory mediated through the fast capitalism of modern consumption, neither should it be understood as an unalloyed psychological asset. Nuance is required, and alternatives need to be posed.

OBJECTS OF OUR MEMORY

Nostalgia today is mostly for things, not home, religion, or politics. Though it may be experienced in reverie, it is evoked and lived through objects and media owned or encountered personally. Of course, the heritage and theme parks considered above are at least partially destinations rather than possessions, but the theme park is artificial (not "sited" historically), and the heritage site is in decline precisely because its authentic location doesn't contain many objects of personal memory—and the theme park does. Perhaps modern people daydream or "introspect" as much as people in the past, but I doubt it; things get in the way. Studies of memory show that long-term recollections are highly subjective and thus usually linked to specific objects. Memories are "context-dependent and highly sensory."[4] For many of us that context is the encounter with a consumer good that is intensely sensuous: a colorful toy, a song with a driving beat, a powerful car.

We need objects to evoke memory, and this was true even in the past, though ritual and reverie sustained it more than today. Artifacts, not abstract representations of the past (like monuments), define heritage sites now, but even these places need gift shops to survive. As anthropologists tell us, objects embody persons and personal relationships as well as ways of life. This is especially true today. Because words, thoughts, and memories are so ephemeral, we need to "fix" them in things that will last at least for a time, in things that matter to us because they are linked to our youths, and this includes cars, playthings, songs, serial teleplays, and a few places and their souvenirs that remind us of the things and fantasies of childhood.

The objects of our nostalgia are different from those of our ancestors in still other ways. Our things of memory are simultaneously mass-produced and ephemeral. Nationally distributed goods and entertainment have undermined regional and local culture and thus traditional nostalgia. Rock and roll may have come from the South, but it became a national (even international) music of youth by 1955 and of mass nostalgia by 1970. These things are often portable and thus individually possessed, but they became accessible to many and later "shared" as common objects of nostalgia across regions, even as they are segmented by age and taste. They consist of multiple lexicons of memory—doo-wop for some, muscle cars for others, Atari cartridges for still others, each making possible minicommunities across the nation and beyond. It is often through these shared consumer experiences rather than through a common involvement in an event (a war, election, revolution, etc.) that we become "tribal" today. One thing that separates us from our ancestors is that we embrace ephemeral, time-bound things and consumed experiences from our unique childhoods (instead of markers of a distant past or the "eternal"). This is inevitable in our world of fast capitalism—mass-marketed consumer goods and experiences that create demand through continuous turnover, novelty, and variety. Moreover, this fast-paced consumption eliminates "old-fashioned longing that took too much time for daydreaming and thinking."[5] Like much of modern consumer culture, nostalgia is about an embrace of fashion, both in the ephemera of one's childhood and in the pursuit of the "latest thing" in memorabilia. As I have often noted in this book, we make things into obsessions that obscure their origins in relationships and social experiences. But these are our experiences, and things of memory, especially in our fast-moving consumer culture, help us cope. The almost inevitable result is that the central act of modern nostalgia is collecting.[6]

COLLECTING MEMORIES

Collecting, for centuries a hobby of rich people that preserved their "heritage" and asserted their cultural superiority, has become a way for the many to recover personal remembrances of childhood and youth.[7] Modern collecting has become progressively childlike in the attempt to create order on a small scale, as Walter Benjamin notes in "Unpacking My Library" (originally written in 1931).[8] This trend has been elaborated more recently by the French postmodernist Jean Baudrillard: "For the child, collecting represents the most rudimentary way to exercise control over the outer world; by laying things out, grouping them, handling them." Thus, kids collect toys and dolls, and adults return to them in regressive nostalgia. Like the pet lover who imposes a personal relationship on the animal, collecting "points to a failure to establish normal human relationships and to the installation of a narcissistic territory—the home—wherein subjectivity can fulfill itself without let or hindrance." Baudrillard continues, "I am able to gaze on [the collection] without its gazing back at me. This is why one invests in objects when one finds it "impossible to invest in human relationships."[9]

Following this characterization, others see a similarity between collecting consumer goods and the behavior of those suffering from Asperger's Syndrome: poor relations with others, an obsessive need for objects that do not change, and command over arcane knowledge about them. And collecting may be a way of finding sanctuary from daily stress, a regression from the responsibilities of maturity, and for some males "a kind of alternative masculinity in which mastery is based around knowledge and discernment."[10] In addition to the apparent puerility and escapism of collecting, it is said to lead to the illusion that an object somehow possesses the aura of a beloved past person or event, as, for example, in the quasi-religious tone of Elvis memorabilia. In the end, collecting can be idolatrous, like the self-delusion of millennia of people who made statues of gods to worship and bargain with. Or as the postmodernist would have it: it is a confusion of the signifier (object) for the signified (the hero or time/place of the past).[11]

A seemingly deeper goal of collectors is to abolish time and deny death: "the organization of the collection itself replaces time," Baudrillard notes, because the collector can return to the past at any time in surveying his or her collection, creating the illusion of the reversibility of time.[12] Collecting memory is a substitute for traditional "machines for the suppression of linear time" as, for example, religious rituals of repetition in a quest for immortality. As the consumption scholar Russell Belk pessimistically concludes: "the ultimate disappointment of realizing that all we hope for is not enough is kept forever at bay through collecting."[13] While much of this assessment may psychologize away the pleasures of collecting, there is a ring of truth to it.

Nostalgic collecting today seems to go further than generic collecting. It not only tries to suppress time but does so by buying a specific time, enlivened by sensuous and material associations. That collecting creates the illusion of a "timeless," life-affirming stage of youth (which, of course, only appears timeless because it has gone and seems to embody the natural world outside of historical change). This purchase of one's own era, catching the brass ring of a particular time, not only denies one an appreciation of what came later but inevitably narrows the possibilities of forming social links across generations.

In addition to collecting objects and experiences of consumer culture, modern nostalgia is also about the quest for "authenticity." This passion is shared equally by Disney fans and Civil War reenactors, consumers of themed parks and patrons of heritage sites. And this longing also is a reaction to and a consequence of fast capitalism. Susan Stewart explains: "Within the development of culture under an exchange economy, the search for authentic experience and, correlatively, the search for the authentic object become critical. As experience is increasingly mediated and abstracted, the lived relation of the body to the phenomenological world is replaced by a nostalgic myth of contact and presence."[14] This quest for the authentic is more than a reaction to the alienation of the market; it is an anxious response to the fleeting. We cope with change (which no longer is just "fate" but the human-driven acceleration of time) not by dreaming of timeless "eternity" but by possessing "our moment," be it in songs, toys, cars, or even personal snapshots. This authenticity satisfies, but, again, it divides people and frustrates those who might want to pass on their "moment" to the next generation. The modern quest for the authentic is a rejection of the symbolic and abstract, at least in part out of the realization that in our secular age of "disenchantment" the symbolic representations of the past in monuments or sacred texts no longer convey the emotion they once did. And attempts to reestablish those emotional links with "authentic" reproductions of the past no longer work for many today. Leaders of heritage sites and museums understand all this as they face declining visitorship and are forced to compromise their mission by substituting the supposed "dull" significance of the past with the "exciting" and "relevant."[15]

But, of course, nostalgic collecting and the quest for the authentic are more than this. Our attraction to things goes beyond our materialism and consumer fetishism. The line is hard to discern, but we need to search for it. First, collecting does not always isolate; it often brings people together. Recall how car shows provide opportunities for collectors to share skills and information. Old-car clubs unite people around their common desire to preserve a legacy, even if it is only the "glory" of 1957 Chevrolet sedans. The seeming "triviality" of this point of unity brought these men together and keeps them together without fighting over religion, politics, or culture. For some, the bonding object may be incidental to the social bonding.

Consumed nostalgia often has been and remains a subtle protest against consumerism. Record collectors, notes Simon Reynolds, are "renegades against the irreversibility of pop-time's flow, taking a stand against the way that styles go out of fashion or run out of steam." Collecting is about the search for a solidity and dependability "that is hard to find in people but that can be projected onto and sought in inanimate objects."[16] Ironically, we may resist the logic of fashion and its essential ephemerality when we purchase the fashionable toy or hit tune of our youth, thereby rejecting today's fashion and making the old novelty "permanent." Consumed nostalgia may in fact be a protest against consumer society insofar as collecting goods and media recall a "naive" simpler time when there were fewer goods that lasted longer and still played an important part in family life. This may be the message of collectors of 1950s living-room TVs or the DVDs of the 1950s sitcoms that were seen on those TVs. The appeal of "camp" in collections of period kitsch, even aluminum Christmas trees, comes from the same disaffection with today's ultraslick, boringly practical, short-lived goods.

And although mass-produced objects lose the "authenticity" of the original,[17] mass-produced collectibles still retain magic through their myriad associations with their historical contexts. As we have seen, the collector wants to know everything about the collectible; the Disneyana newsletters and websites provide the facts and stories that make Mickey in porcelain more than a fetish. Memorabilia is designed to evoke a string of memories.[18] By collecting, we "singularize" the commodity, turning it into something unique to be admired in a world of mass production, conformity, and utility. Nostalgic collectors are also heroic in saving those parts of the past that the rest of us deny or ignore. Modern collecting in a consumer society is a response to the alienated workplace, making skilled "work-like hobbies an appealing source of dignity." Even if fetishistic, nostalgiacs seek an alternative to the soulless materialism of our time.[19]

Moreover, the quest for authenticity may be more than delusion and a replacement of "real history" with superficial sensuality and emotion. It is part of the modern rejection of symbols (like Gettysburg monuments or family portraits) that no longer convey meaning. The authentic is a way of combating the fake—the romantic and airbrushed—as well as a rejection of the soullessness of much history writing. Challenging the meaningless abstraction with the "authentic" is inevitable and often worthwhile, even when it becomes a fetish.[20]

In the final analysis, the simple fact is that we need things of memory. We fill our lived spaces with objects that aren't useful but that "instead serve to stabilize and order the mind," notes the anthropologist Mihaly Csikszentmihalyi. In an unchanging society, one where relationships are continuous, "there may not be a need to secure one's position in the web of kinship through material symbols. But in a highly mobile society like modern America, things play an important role in reminding us of who we are with respect to whom we belong."[21] All this may be understandable and even inevitable, but as the 1960s song goes, "Is that all there is?"

Can we separate memory from consumption, if not from things? And if many of us cannot recollect without collections, are there ways of reducing object fetishism or at least ways of making consumer goods a means rather than an end? Or are we all inherently tied to objects? Maybe the problem isn't just that we "objectify" memory but how our relationship with the objects of recollection obscure or deny us what we need in our nostalgia. I say that consumed nostalgia isn't necessarily a wrong turn, but it is often a truncated one—too isolated from others and from other times.

SOLIPSISTIC NOSTALGIA AND FORGETFULNESS

Over and over, after observing old-car shows, toy and doll collectors, and watching oldies' concerts and retro TV, I have come to the same conclusion: Consumed nostalgia cuts people off from others, even the ones they want to relate to. It negates the broader world of where we came from. The fixation on stuff and experience tends to be radically isolating because we live in an age of radically individualistic consumption. The objects of our nostalgia are mostly parental gifts of delight, personal tokens of liberating moments of youth, essential components of narrow communities of display, and finally the endless quest to be "different." This is confirmed by the collectors that I talked with. The specificity of their "objectness," be it a 1957 Edsel or a googly- eyed doll, assures self-isolation. Of course, we look for peer communities to share our obsessions, but this still separates us into often very narrow comfort zones. This is an odd development considering the widely acknowledged idea of Maurice Halbwachs that all memories are social. Better put, the social group is often constructed through memory. We become a generation not by sharing common values and even trajectories in the present but in the selective recollection of shared memories that otherwise would disappear. Memory is retrieved, Halbwachs claimed in 1950, "with the help of landmarks that we always carry within ourselves," that help us "locate ourselves within the social framework." Halbwachs was probably thinking of something like a generation of veterans similar to the middle-aged Civil War veterans, who erected monuments in the 1890s commemorating their regiments.[22] More recently, Gaynor Kavanagh observed that "older adults get to know each other by drawing from the past in an effort to position themselves in relation to others, taking as reference points life events (children and grandchildren, the onset of infirmities) or broader historical markers (before the war, after the depression)."[23]

But our memories today are much less about collectivities. As the cultural critic Fredric Jameson wrote in 1994, "our entire contemporary social system has little by little lost its capacity to retain its own past."[24] This may be extreme. After all, there still are veterans' organizations, and "you are not forgotten" flags are still flown for the POWs/MIA of the Vietnam War many decades after the conflict. But memories of events and social customs seem no longer to construct generational identity, and the institutions and their rituals (think of the Elks or Women's Clubs) intent on perpetuating these memories are in decline, as famously noted by Robert Putnam.[25] They have been partially replaced by narrow age cohorts built around shared memories of consumption (like those "bench cruisers" that gather at drive-ins to recall their first cars).[26] The reenactors that I met at Old World Wisconsin would find the latter-day cruisers pitiful both because their obsessions were so petty and because their memories were so "short," focused on their own personal recollections, not their "roots" in the deeper past of community.

This brings us to the oft-noted "forgetfulness" that has emerged with modernity and that is so obvious to the reenactors. The geographer Paul Connerton finds shortsightedness in the "decline of [a] stable system of places" experienced by modern people. The rapid change in (and separation of) work and lived spaces and the rise of featureless megacities and unmemorable journeys at rapid speeds has produced trackless lives. The decline of markers and boundaries stands in contrast to the sensuous and social intensity of the walled cities of medieval Europe and the Middle East. But much more broadly, consumer capitalism has made modern life "fast" and thus forgettable. Connerton argues that the roots of this phenomenon are deep: modern consumption entails the separation of goods from production and, with this, the aestheticization of variety and plenty (as exhibited in the Crystal Palace International Exhibition of 1851 in London, which was soon followed by department stores). And with this pile of goods came an acceleration of fashion, which "valorizes and devalues itself simultaneously," producing a rapid turnover of goods as the new is desired and the old shunned. The "growing domination of the market over art" produces a "compulsion to reject" the past that has only been compounded in recent years by the shift from a goods-based consumerism to an experiential one (obvious in the coming and going of digital goods like apps and electronic media and devices).[27]

This is familiar stuff to anyone who has read David Harvey's *The Condition of Postmodernity* or any of its successors.[28] But Connerton adds a point that is especially germane here: the rapidity of the flow of goods and media impedes our ability to hold on to any memory. "Informational overload is one of the best devices for forgetting, the function of the news media being not to produce, nor even to consume, but rather to discard, to consign recent historical experience to oblivion as rapidly as possible."[29] To extend his argument, attachment to ephemeral goods in nostalgia and the loss of past communities go hand in hand. We still remember, but our memories are short.

It is worthwhile noting that a number of early-twentieth-century intellectuals focused on the difficult task of recovering memory in an increasingly fast-paced world. Marcel Proust insisted that creativity comes from building on the past. But recovering past emotions and thoughts was becoming problematic because of the sensory intensification caused by the rise of cinema, popular music, and other fast-changing forms of consumer capitalism around 1900. Freud too found the past elusive. Psychoanalysis was built on the hoary task of recovering repressed emotions and therefore realizing self-understanding and liberation from the dysfunctional impact of that repression. The essayist Walter Benjamin, the sociologist Georges Simmel, the psychologist Henri Piéron, and, of course, Halbwachs all shared the goal of recovering deep and multifaceted memory despite modern forgetfulness. And the massive construction of monuments between 1890 and 1930 was prompted by fears that future generations would forget past glories and sacrifices. But that is what has happened, and the philosophical concern about memory loss has waned with that loss of memory.[30]

The building of monuments as abstract or heroic markers has declined since World War I, especially at the local level. Instead, we see efforts to recover the past in reenacting authentic "moments" from the past. Memory loss and the desire to intensify the "moment" go together. In part, modern historical museums cultivate this longing to recover those lost instants. But as we have seen, heritage sites have lost audiences despite endless efforts to make them authentic, "relevant," and family-friendly recreations of past moments. The core reason for this decline is the general abandonment of distant and shared memory (confirmed by the cultish character of reenactors who remain committed to it).

Again, we come back to the quest for our personal memory in our own "moments." As Walter Benjamin anticipated in the 1930s, as "the worlds of memory replace themselves more quickly, a totally different world of memory must be set up ever faster against them."[31] Forgetting the distant past begets remembering ever new "moments" in nostalgia in our personal lives. What is lost is a perspective on the past, a recognition of historical "distance" and cumulative change. With this loss, fewer are willing to transcend their personal, immediate, and transitory memory for an appreciation of a deeper past, a recognition of what has been lost and what that loss may mean for us today.

Many readers might challenge this argument by noting that the problem is not our forgetfulness but that we don't forget enough, that we don't move forward, and that we can't distinguish between the present and the past. In his review of modern pop music and its seeming inability to transcend its past, Simon Reynolds raises these penetrating questions: "Is nostalgia stopping our culture's ability to surge forward, or are we nostalgic precisely because our culture has stopped moving forward and so we inevitably look back to more momentous and dynamic times? But what happens when we run out of past?"[32] Moreover, today the past is always with us: more and more of it is made available on the Internet, where nothing disappears and where everything is accessible and transferable, making "the past and the present commingle in a way that makes time itself mushy and spongiform." Internet sites like YouTube offer us a nearly infinite access to past images but also reduce the difference between past and present.[33] According to Reynolds, we seem to have entered a deeply unimaginative era. The problem isn't an inability to innovate; it's an incapacity to come up with visionary goals to aim for.[34]

It turns out that Reynolds's argument isn't that different from mine. The problem raised by Reynolds and others is not the fixation on the deep past (indeed, Reynolds would appreciate a recovery of a long musical memory, before the age of rock, to refresh a decadent musical culture). His concern is the obsession with the recent and personal past. We grasp the once new and in the process forget the more distant past. Symptomatic of this trend is the

Rolling Stone list of the five hundred best songs "of all time." It includes only one song from as early as the 1940s; 39 percent are from the 1960s. This reflects the hubris of the magazine's boomer bias but also how many of us, regardless of generation, embrace the wow of the recent now and reject the wow of the distant now.[35]

The problem of "forgetting" and "remembering" may boil down to our obsession with our personal pasts and especially with those "moments of consumption" of the emerging child or the incipient adult. Many of us not only forget all but the recent past; we also repress memory of other points in our or our family's lives. This return to childhood is perhaps an inevitable search for origins and escape into the excitement but also the "simplicity" of youth. But should that be a primary goal? There are good and practical reasons for our selective memories. But is this any reason not to reassess and to expand our moments of memory?

PATHS TO POSITIVE NOSTALGIA

We play lots of games with our recollections—adhering to different accounts of the same events, choosing to meet only happy memories or obsessively dwelling on the hurtful ones, "coming to terms" (or not) with traumatic or guilt-ridden pasts. All this has been the concern of psychologists since Freud, and of the religious far longer, but not usually of historians like me, who are mostly focused on ascertaining and interpreting past public events. Yet, as I have tried to show, there is also a history of the culture of memories, and a dominant form today is shaped by the dynamics of consumed nostalgia. Mostly this book has been about identifying and exploring this particular culture as it has emerged in the twentieth century. It's not for me to offer a guidebook to good nostalgia. I certainly haven't wanted to mock consumed nostalgia or to suggest that we return to a collective memory based on ideology or ethnic or regional identity, much less demand that we turn, unsentimentally and rationally, to the future. In fact, I have found that modern materialistic nostalgia often meets real needs; it is frequently playful, sometimes ironic, and can bring us to a new understanding of ourselves and our world. But, as in much human endeavor, in this we get diverted from our goals in fixing on means rather than ends and thereby miss opportunities for growth.

So in these final pages, let me conclude this journey into modern memory by making a few comments about how we might modify and build on our experience with consumed nostalgia. It's clear that for practically all of us, memory requires things of memory. But these things are means that become ends, that is, fetishes or projections of ourselves. They can and should, I think, instead be instruments to reach fresh insights and understandings. Ultimately, is this not what a collection of old toys or watching old TV should do for us?

This can happen when we use things of memory to engage with the past but not regress into the past, especially into a childhood of lost adventure and/or simplicity. If we converse with that past, bring a full and honest consciousness of our present lives into the encounter with what has gone before, nostalgia can reveal something about ourselves now. And through "repetition"—going back to where we came and thus to whom we have been—we can make our understanding of ourselves clearer and more accurate. This may happen if we are willing to let that past tell us something we hadn't expected, to allow a new standpoint to emerge.[36] Such a return might even lead to an acceptance of self (finally getting over our obsessions with the pains and resentments that go along with many childhoods or longings to return to the good ol' days), and there is no reason why it might not also lead to what the famous psychologist Erik Erikson called "ego integrity," a self at peace with its past selves.[37]

But again this will take place only if we allow those objects of memory to go beyond their materiality and to tell us something about our relationships. I repeatedly saw the revered old car or toy (especially in men) disguise a shared experience with a dad or brother, positive or not. But this need not be the case. Returning to a teenage memory through the teenage car can lead to a deeper self-understanding. And what we may learn about our relationships may take us beyond the tribalism of modern consumption.

This requires that we stand back from our memories, not claim that "our song" is better than the next person's, and instead appreciate a shared pathos and humanity. Another aspect of this "disengagement" is the need to resist the temptation to deny what has truly gone (so evident in the illusion of possessing the past in collections or in recreating an "authentic" historical event or mood)—even as we may *playfully* enjoy a regression now and then into that past. And to recognize the pastness of the past allows us to see the past more "objectively," not as an extension or fulfillment of our self-image today but instead to recognize what is gone and why.

All of this, of course, doesn't condemn nostalgia. Recollecting the past (or "reconsuming" it) often offers a desirable alternative to the ephemerality of the everyday experience of fast capitalism. But by adopting a less burdened, more positive nostalgia, we can see the past differently—not just from when it was our present—but also differently from the last time we visited it. This, we may find, is what can happen when we see TV reruns.

This positive meaning of repetition can also be a function of the reunion. For fifteen years, two friends from college and I have met for two days every August. It is a ritual, and maybe even an obsession, but each year is different. Some years, we talk about a recent change in one or more of our lives—children, marriages, careers; other years, we recall shared memories of college, youth, etc. But the "repetition" of old songs, movies, TV shows, and theme parks can do the same thing, especially if they aren't "reconsumed" too often (a problem for the obsessive collector or for those who will listen only to channel 6 on satellite radio). And this nostalgia can be positive even in the seemingly obsessive collection of the toys of youth. Jeffrey Hammond demonstrates this in his reverie on his homey collection of Marx toys from his 1950s childhood. He weaves his recollection of Roy Rogers and Dale Evans (and their toy figures) with memories of his father; he recalls his boyhood enchantment with dinosaur figures, which compensated for his childish fear of animals. He goes beyond his personal experience as he comes to understand how the world has changed since the days of American triumphalism, when Louis Marx made cowboy and Indian figures celebrating the conquests of the white man. He shows how his playful interlude into a world that has disappeared has helped him understand himself better and grow emotionally as a sixty-year-old man. His obsession with his desktop of toys turns out to be not an escape into immaturity but an encounter with memory that contributes to a new stage of maturity.[38]

If memory work needs to transcend fetishism and self-isolation, it should also require us to look in the past for a world less familiar than our childhoods. This may not only mean engagement with the challenging distant past, of which we have no personal memory, but also with those things that we missed during our formative years (not "our" oldies or sitcoms but perhaps our parents' or older siblings' music and movies). Even more, we might consider recalling those periods of our lives that may not be so wondrous or exciting; returning to places and people that shaped our later lives to seek an understanding of what happened and why since the "golden years" of our youth. Such a memory journey can help us realize both that we can never go back but also that a voyage into the past can help us learn from what is left and what is not. All this might lead us to abandon some of our delusions. It might also offer us new insights and perhaps delights as we take on a wider view of the past and see it from new perspectives. We also may want to find ways of making memory less isolating, less about "me," and perhaps more about a renewal of lost relationships and the creation of new ties across generations. Even more, perhaps we may need to readjust just what we should recall and where and when we need to forget. Like so many other commodities, consumed memory satisfies many of our longings, but it may reveal needs that things purchased can never deliver.

I might argue that we should try to engage our memories beyond the consumer culture in reunions with long-lost friends, especially if we avoid bragging about the accomplishments of our lives. About ten years ago, I found it extraordinarily meaningful to return to the little town I lived in as an elementary-school child where, to my surprise, I met several people who remembered me. I realized that I couldn't go home, but I learned about myself and why I was so nostalgic about that small place. Some day I plan on rereading some of the books that I read and commented on in the margins when I was in college; I am even contemplating going to my fiftieth high-school reunion. And I visit heritage sites wherever I travel. These are all alternatives to commodity nostalgia, but there is no reason to insist on their necessary superiority.

My journey across the nostalgic worlds of today's consumer culture has made me recognize much more about why many of us collect the goods or return to the media of our childhoods. I've come to the conclusion that consumed nostalgia can work if it means psychological and cultural growth, if it transforms or calls into question our identities.[39] Packaged memory can give new meanings to the past, provide us with new perspectives on growing up in the 1950s or 1990s, and sometimes free us from old resentments and distortions. But consumed nostalgia only points in that direction; it can easily short-circuit the potential of recollection. Memory can and might well go beyond our recollection of commercialized life, no matter how central it may be to our past lives. We can find triggers of recollection in many other places. We all live in and are shaped by a world of fast capitalism, and therefore of consumed nostalgia, but we need not be consumed by it.

NOTES

INTRODUCTION. OUR NOSTALGIC NOVELTY CULTURE

1. *Antiques and Collecting Magazine* (Aug. 2000): 14; *Chicago Tribune* (Dec. 26, 2004): 1; *Chicago Tribune* (Oct. 23, 2005): 4; *Antiques and Collecting Magazine* (Nov. 2003): 6.

2. http://en.wikipedia.org/wiki/Barbie#Collecting;http://www.barbiecollector .com/; *Doll Reader* (May 2002): 28; *Antiques and Collecting Magazine* (July 1995): 45.

3. "That's Not Junk. That's Early Tech," *Business Week* (Feb. 21, 2005): 82.

4. *Knight Ridder Tribune Business News* (March 4, 2007): 1; *Knight Ridder Tribune Business News* (Oct. 26, 2006): 1.

5. *Los Angeles Times* (Aug. 31, 2006): F7.

6. *Los Angeles Times* (Dec. 2, 2000): N3; *Los Angeles Times* (Jan. 22, 2003): F1; Carol and Richard Smyth, *Beach Pails: Classic Toys of the Surf and Sand* (Philadelphia: Running Press, 2002); Karen Horman and Polly Minick, *Sand Pail Encyclopedia: A Comprehensive Value Guide for Tin-Litho Sand Toys* (Philadelphia: Hobby House Press, 2002); *Wall Street Journal* (Nov. 8, 1996): B10.

7. *Wall Street Journal* (Aug. 27, 1999): W12; *Wall Street Journal* (July 9, 1999): W12.

8. *Afro-American Red Star* (April 8–April 14, 2006): B4.

9. *Chicago Tribune* (June 27, 1993): 1.

10. *Daily Variety* (April 29, 2005): 20.

11. http://inventors.about.com/library/inventors/bl_trivia_pursuit.htm.

12. Svetlana Boym, *The Future of Nostalgia* (New York: Basic Books, 2001), 3, 6; Johannes Hofer, *Dissertatio Media de Nostalgia* (Basel, 1688), trans. Carolyn Anspach, *Bulletin of the History of Medicine* 2 (1934): 384–390; Jean Starobinski,

"The Idea of Nostalgia," *Diogenes* 54 (1966): 81–103; George Rosen, "Nostalgia: A Forgotten Psychological Disorder," *Clio Medica* 10, no. 1 (1975): 28–51.

13. Starobinski, "The Idea of Nostalgia," 81–103; Peter Fritzsche, "Specters of History: On Nostalgia, Exile, and Modernity," *American Historical Review* 106 (Dec. 2001): 1587–1618.

14. Boym, *Nostalgia*, xiv–xv. Similar is David Lowenthal, *Possessed by the Past* (New York: Free Press, 1996), 8–11; Susan Matt, "You Can't Go Home Again: Homesickness and Nostalgia in U.S. History," *Journal of American History* 94, no. 2 (Sept. 2007): 469–498.

15. Kenneth Woodbridge, *The Stourhead Landscape* (London: The National Trust, 2002); Boym, *Nostalgia*, 11–15; Susan Stewart, *On Longing: Narratives of the Miniature, the Gigantic, the Souvenir, the Collection* (Durham, N.C.: Duke University Press, 1993), 141; David Lowenthal, *The Past Is a Foreign Country* (Cambridge: Cambridge University Press, 1985); Lowenthal, *Possessed*, xi–xii, 13; Joy Kenseth, " 'A World of Wonders in One Closet Shut,' " in *The Age of the Marvelous*, ed. Joy Kenseth (Hanover, N.H.: Hood Museum of Art, 1991), 101; Krystof Pomian, *Collectors and Curiosities: Paris and Venice, 1500–1800* (1987; Cambridge: Polity, 1990), 53; Russell Belk, *Collecting in a Consumer Culture* (London: Routledge, 1995), 29–35.

16. Eric Hobsbawm, *The Invention of Tradition* (Cambridge: Cambridge University Press, 1992); Brian Graham and Peter Howard, "Heritage and Identity," in *The Ashgate Research Companion to Heritage and Identity*, ed. Brian Graham and Peter Howard (Aldershot: Ashgate, 2008), 1–18; B. Graham, G. J. Ashworth, and J. E. Tunbridge, *Geography of Heritage: Power, Culture, and Economy* (London: Arnold, 2000); Andre Huyssens, *Twilight Memories: Marking Time in a Culture of Amnesia* (London: Routledge, 1995), 14; Gaynor Kavanagh, *Dream Spaces: Memory and the Museum* (London: Leicester University Press, 2000), 1–9.

17. Boym, *Nostalgia*, 15. Recent writings on domestic-artifact collections include John Potvin and Alla Myzelev, eds., *Material Cultures, 1740–1920* (Farnam: Ashgate, 2009), 37–52; Pierra Nora, "Between Memory and History: Les Lieux de Memoire," *Representations* 26 (1989); Pierra Nora, *Realms of Memory* (New York: Columbia University Press, 2000); and Charles Scott, "The Appearance of Public Memory," in *Framing Public Memory*, ed. Kendall Phillips (Tuscaloosa: University of Alabama Press, 2004), 147–156.

18. Michael Kammen, *Mystic Chords of Memory* (New York: Vintage, 1991), 42; Boym, *Nostalgia*, 16–18; Susan Matt, *Homesickness: An American History* (New York: Oxford University Press, 2011).

19. Stewart, *On Longing*, 139; Boym, *Nostalgia*, 13, 42–45; Lowenthal, *Possessed by the Past*, 5, 17–19; Hobsbawm, *The Invention of Tradition*; Graham and Howard, "Heritage and Identity"; Graham, Ashworth, and Tunbridge, *Geography of Heritage*; Huyssens, *Twilight Memories*, 14; Kavanagh, *Dream Spaces*, 1–9.

20. Steven Lubar, "Exhibiting Memories," in *Museums and Their Communities*, ed. Sheila Watson (London: Routledge, 2007), 398; James Weeks, *Gettys-*

burg: Memory, Market, and an American Shrine (Princeton, N.J.: Princeton University Press, 2001), chap. 7.

21. Lowenthal, *Possessed*, 60, 85, 193–194.

22. David Harvey, "The History of Heritage," in *The Ashgate Research Companion to Heritage and Identity*, ed. Brian Graham and Peter Howard (Aldershot: Ashgate, 2008), 32.

23. Gary Cross, *The Cute and the Cool: Wondrous Innocence and Modern American Children's Culture* (New York: Oxford University Press, 2004).

24. Mihaly Csikszentmihalyi, "Why We Need Things," in *History from Things: Essays on Material Culture*, ed. Steven Lubar and W. David Kingery (Washington, D.C.: Smithsonian Institution Press, 1993), 20–29. Readable and sensible defenses of this positive take on consumption and identity are in the English anthropologist Daniel Miller's *The Comfort of Things* (Cambridge: Polity, 2008), 6, 287, 293; and his *Stuff* (Cambridge: Polity, 2010), 60–62.

1. *GUYS* TOYS *AND* "GIRLS" *DOLLS*

1. Werner Muensterberger, *Collecting, An Unruly Passion* (Princeton, N.J.: Princeton University Press, 1994); Giuseppe Olmi, "Science-Honour-Metaphor: Italian Cabinets of the Sixteenth and Seventeenth Centuries," in *The Origins of Museums: The Cabinet of Curiosities in Sixteenth- and Seventeenth-Century Europe*, ed. Oliver Impey and Arthur MacGregor (Oxford: Clarendon, 1985), 5–16.

2. Pierre Bourdieu, *Distinction: A Social Critique of the Judgment of Taste* (Cambridge, Mass.: Harvard University Press, 1984); Gary Cross, *The Cute and the Cool: Wondrous Innocence and Modern American Children's Culture* (New York: Oxford University Press, 2004), esp. chap. 3.

3. Dorothy and her daughters Elizabeth and Evelyn Coleman joined forces to publish the bible of doll references, the 697-page *Collector's Encyclopedia of Dolls* (New York: Crown, 1968; updated ed., 1986).

4. From the collection of The Strong (library), Rochester, N.Y.: Stevens and Brown, *Illustrated Price List of Tin, Mechanical, and Iron Toys* (1872), 90–91, 98, 100–101; Ives, *Iron Toys* (1893), 56–58, 60–63; Erlich Brothers, *Toy Price List* (1882), 3–4; Brown and Stevens, *Illustrated Price Catalogue* (1872), 28–31.

5. See Gary Cross, *Kids' Stuff: Toys and the Changing World of American Childhood* (Cambridge, Mass.: Harvard University Press, 1997), chaps. 3, 7; and *Men to Boys: The Making of Modern Immaturity* (New York: Columbia University Press, 2008), 90–102, 192–193.

6. Pat Schoonmaker, *A Collector's History of the Teddy Bear* (Cumberland, Md.: Hobby House, 1981), 227–241, 250–252, 280–282; and Linda Mullins, *A Tribute to Teddy Bear Artists* (Grantsville, Md.: Hobby House, 1994), 74–80.

7. "The Kewpies' Christmas Frolic," *Ladies Home Journal* (Dec. 1909): 28; G. Borgfeldt ad for Kewpies, *Playthings Magazine* (Jan. 1913): 20–21. See also Miriam Formanek-Brunell, *Made to Play House: Dolls and the Commercialization*

of American Girlhood, 1830–1930 (New Haven, Conn.: Yale University Press, 1993), chaps. 4–5; Ralph McCanse, *Titans and Kewpies: The Life and Art of Rose O'Neill* (New York: Vantage, 1968).

8. Cecil Munsey, *Disneyana: Walt Disney Collectibles* (New York: Abrams, 1974), 32, 39–48, 80–99, 109–100; Robert Heide and John Gilman, *Cartoon Collectibles: Fifty Years of Dime Store Memorabilia* (Garden City, N.Y.: Doubleday, 1983), 101–102, 113–115; Cross, *Kids' Stuff*, chap. 4.

9. The original story by Philip F. Nowland, "Armageddon—2419," appears in *Buck Rogers, The First Sixty Years in the Twenty-Fifth Century*, ed. Lorraine Dille Williams (New York: TSR, 1988), 19–46; Crystal and Layland Payton, *Space Toys* (Sedalia, Mo.: Collectors Compass, 1982), 41–42.

10. Coleman, *The Collector's Encyclopedia of Dolls*, 143, 152; Johana Anderton, *Twentieth-Century Dolls: From Bisque to Vinyl* (Des Moines, Iowa: Wallace-Homestead, 1971), 23–27, 225–238. Madeline Merrill, *The Art of Dolls, 1799–1940* (Cumberland, Md.: Hobby House, 1985); Patricia Schoonmaker, *The Effanbee Patsy Family and Related Types* (North Hollywood, Calif.: Doll Research Project, 1971), 1–15, 20–35.

11. "Public Takes Shirley to Its Heart in April," *Toys and Novelties* (April 1936): 83; "Cash in on April's Double Header," *Playthings Magazine* (March 1936): 64. See also Judith Izen, *A Collector's Guide to Ideal Dolls* (Paducah, Ky.: Collector, 1992), 21.

12. The Ginny doll had its origins in Jennie Adler Graves Carlson's Vogue Doll Shoppe of Sommerville, Massachusetts, that opened in 1922. By the time she introduced Ginny in 1948, her business had gone national, and by 1957 she employed eight hundred women as domestic craft workers. Traditional to the core, Jennie Carlson rejected TV advertising, and while popular with mothers, by the end of the 1950s Ginny was too childlike to be seen as "a liberated friend" to girls, notes the doll historian and collector A. Glenn Mandeville. A. Glenn Mandeville, *Ginny: An American Toddler Doll* (Cumberland, Md.: Hobby House, 1991), 85, 88, 95.

13. "Fact Sheet: Hasbro's G.I. Joe, A Real American Hero," Hasbro Press Kit (Feb. 1993), *Toy Fair Collection*, Box 3, Please Touch Museum, Philadelphia; Vincent Santelmo, *The Official Thirtieth-Anniversary Salute to G.I. Joe* (Iola, Wis.: Kreuse, 1994), 17–18, 66–72, 75–97, 325, 343, 412–413; Susan Manos and Paris Manos, *Collectible Male Action Figures* (Paducah, Ky.: Collector, 1990), 20–33, 38–43; Tom Engelhardt, *The End of Victory Culture: Cold War America and the Disillusioning of a Generation* (New York: Basic Books, 1995), 81–86, 300.

14. "Star Wars," *Toys and Hobby World* (June 1983): 24, 26; Chris Taylor, *How Star Wars Conquered the Universe: The Past, Present, and Future of a Multibillion-Dollar Franchise* (New York: Basic Books, 2014).

15. The Toy Fair Collection at the Please Touch Museum include: Coleco Press Kit (June 1986), Box 5/2; Tyco Press Kit (Feb. 1988), Box 8; and Tyco Press Kit (Feb. 1989), Box 9. Note also Sydney Stern and Ted Schoenhaus, *Toyland:*

The High-Stakes Game of the Toy Industry (Chicago: Contemporary Books, 1990), chaps. 5, 11, 14, 17.

16. Ruth Handler, *Dream Doll* (New York: Long Meadow, 1995); Robin Gerber, *Barbie and Ruth: The Story of the World's Most Famous Doll and the Woman Who Created Her* (Collins Business, 2009); A. Glen Mandeville, *Doll Fashion Anthology and Price Guide*, 4th ed. (Cumberland, Md.: Hobby House, 1993), 1–33; M. G. Lord, *Forever Barbie* (New York: Avon, 1994); Tanya Stone, *The Good, the Bad, and the Barbie: A Doll's History and Her Impact on Us* (New York: Viking: 2010); Kristin Noelle Weissman, *Barbie: The Icon, the Image, the Ideal: An Analytical Interpretation of the Barbie Doll in Popular Culture* (n.p., 1999), 19–43; Mary Rogers, *Barbie Culture* (London: Sage, 1999), 37–40, 61–66; Patricia Adler and Peter Adler, *Peer Power: Preadolescent Culture and Identity* (New Brunswick, N.J.: Rutgers University Press, 1998), 39–56.

17. Pleasant Rowland's American Girl collection (1986), a line of expensive full-size dolls in the "New Kid" style that were extensions of a series of historical storybooks, was bought by Mattel in 1998. Though originally considered "anti-Barbie" dolls with little of the emphasis on fashion and beauty, under Mattel's direction, the dolls have adopted a strongly consumerist tone, as witnessed by any visit to the American Girl stores in Chicago, New York, and Los Angeles, even though the storybooks remain popular.

18. Mattel, *Barbie, Teen-Age Fashion Model* (Hawthorne, Calif.: Mattel, 1958); Mattel, *Barbie, Teen-Age Fashion Model and Ken, Barbie's Boy Friend (He's a Doll)* (Hawthorne, Calif.: Mattel, 1960); and Mattel, *Exclusive Fashions by Mattel, Book 3* (Hawthorne, Calif.: Mattel, 1963). The Strong (library), Rochester, N.Y.; Cross, *Kids' Stuff*, 171–175.

19. Cross, *Kids' Stuff*, chap. 6.

20. A. F. Robertson, *Life Like Dolls: The Collector Doll Phenomenon and the Lives of the Women Who Love Them* (New York: Routledge, 2004), 5–10, 9.

21. "Sweethearts of the 1950s," *International Doll World* (Feb. 1996): 20; "Hollywood Collecting," *International Doll World* (Jan.–Feb. 1991): 74–81; "Wax Dolls of Mexico," *International Doll World* (Aug. 1993): 58–59.

22. Jan Foulke, *Focusing on Dolls* (a compilation of articles from *Doll Reader*, 1974–1986), (Cumberland, Md.: Hobby House, 1988), 6–12.

23. Doll museums took off after 1980. "Margaret Woodbury Strong Museum to Open October 1982," *Antique and Toy World* (Sept. 1982): 7–10; See the Strong's website, http://www.thestrong.org/; "Doll Museums," *Doll News* (Aug. 1959): 2; United Federation of Doll Clubs (UFDC), *Convention Journal* (1959): 53; "Doll Museums," *International Doll World* (Aug. 1986): 38–41.

24. Max von Boehn, *Dolls and Puppets* (London: Harrap, 1932); Edith Ackley, *Paper Dolls, Their History, and How to Make Them* (Philadelphia: Lippincott, 1939); Winifred Mills, *The Story of Old Dolls and How to Make New Ones* (New York: Doubleday, 1940); Eleanor St. George, *Dolls of Yesterday* (New York: Scribner's, 1948); Coleman, *Collectors' Encyclopedia of Dolls*.

25. Mary Lewis, editorial, *UFDC Convention Journal* (Jan. 1951): 1; Janet Johl, editorial, *Doll News* (Jan. 1952): 1; Janet Johl, editorial, *Doll News* (March 1954): 2; Nita Loving, editorial, *Doll News* (Aug. 1962): 3; "Mary Lewis," *UFDC Convention Journal* (1987): 20–22, all at the United Federation of Doll Clubs, Kansas City, Mo.

26. For example, club notes and interview with UFDC President Karen Rockwell, in *Doll News* (Spring 2010): 122–123, 20–21.

27. Hazel Snider, "What Is a Doll?" *UFDC Convention Journal* (1959).

28. Photos and captions, *UFDC Convention Journal* (1981), 64–65; UFDC, *Victorian Scrapbook* (1989 Convention), 23; United Federation of Doll Clubs, *Wonder of Childhood* (1986 Convention), 4, 28, all at the United Federation of Doll Clubs, Kansas City, Mo.

29. William Wordsworth, "Ode: Intimations of Immortality from Recollections of Early Childhood," (1804; pub. 1807), in *Complete Poetical Works of William Wordsworth*, ed. Biss Perry (Boston: Houghton Mifflin, 1904), 354.

30. Note, for example, editorials, *UFDC Convention Journal* (1981): 3; *UFDC Convention Journal* (1985); 5; *UFDC Convention Journal* (1993): 1–2; and *UFDC Convention Journal* (1998): 2, all at the United Federation of Doll Clubs, Kansas City, Mo. *Doll News*, various issues on Victorian dolls: Summer 2009, 4; Spring 2007, 16, 30–33; Fall 2010; survey of doll preferences: Winter 1996, 51.

31. In 2012, a woman of sixty-five would have been born in 1947, too old for the first Barbies of 1959. The manager of the UFDC, in a November 20, 2011, interview, told me that when she first was hired in 2004, officials estimated that the average age of members was sixty-five.

32. First sold through mail order and by advertising in magazines, by 1995 these companies had switched to TV infomercials and shortly after that to the Internet. Audrey Dean, *Dolls* (New York: HarperCollins: 1997), 104–107; Robertson, *Life Like Dolls*, 25–29, 36, 54.

33. Robertson, *Life Like Dolls*, 76–87. Ellen Seiter wrote, "boys become their toys in play; girls take care of their toys." Ellen Seiter, *Sold Separately: Children and Parents in Consumer Culture* (New Brunswick, N.J.: Rutgers University Press, 1993), 131.

34. Hamilton Collection ad, *International Doll World* (Dec. 1992): 25; Ashton-Drake Galleries ad, *International Doll World* (Oct. 1992): 3; Danbury Mint ad, *International Doll World* (Dec. 1992): 18.

35. Seiter, *Sold Separately*, 74, 129; Robertson, *Life Like Dolls*, 101–102, 119, chaps. 4–5, esp. for discussion of "dollification." Note G. Stanley Hall and A. Caswell Ellis, "A Study of Dolls," *Pedagogical Seminary* 4, no. 2 (1896): 132–159, for an early psychological analysis of childhood and dolls.

36. Robertson, *Life Like Dolls*, 189, 207 (citing My Twinn catalog [Aug. 1998]), 215.

37. Mattel ad, *UFDC Convention Journal* (1971): 5; Clara Leopold, "Barbie Doll Syndrome," *UFDC Convention Journal* (1974): 73–74; positive statements

on Barbie, *UFDC Convention Journal* (1985): 99–101; *UFDC Convention Journal* (1988): 23; all at the United Federation of Doll Clubs, Kansas City, Mo. "Barbie," *Doll News* (Spring 1996): 8; "Barbie," *Doll News* (Spring 2011): 22–24.

38. Glenn Mandeville, "Trends in Modern Doll Collecting," in *Collecting Modern Dolls, Souvenir Journal of the Third Annual Modern Doll Convention*, ed., John Axe (Cincinnati, Ohio: Modern Doll Convention: 1981), 24; John Axe, ed., *Fiesta of Dolls: Souvenir Journal of the Thirty-Fifth Convention* (San Antonio, Tex.: United Federation of Doll Clubs, 1984).

39. Robertson, *Life Like Dolls*, 133, 148.

40. "2011 National Barbie® Doll Collectors Convention," http://www.barbie convention.com/.

41. 2014 National Barbie® Doll Collectors Convention, http://barbie convention.com/.

42. Beth Summers, *A Decade of Barbie Dolls and Collectibles, 1981–1991* (Paducah, Ky.: Collector, 1996), 1–5; Sybil Dewein and Joan Ashabraner, *Collectors' Encyclopedia of Barbie Dolls and Collectibles* (Paducah, Ky.: Collector, 1992), 2–3.

43. Rhapsody Barbie ad, *International Doll World* (Dec. 1992): 3; A. Glenn Mandeville et al., *Barbie Doll Collectors' Handbook* (Cumberland, Md.: Hobby House, 1997), 23–24.

44. Louis Hertz, *The Toys Collector* (New York: Funk and Wagnalls, 1969), 1–3, 9–11, 21, 27, 45, 274.

45. Harry Rinker, *Guide to Toy Collecting* (New York: HarperCollins, 2008), 1–7; Harry Rinker website: http://harrylrinker.aol.com/hear.html.

46. Cross, *Kids' Stuff*, chaps. 2–3.

47. *Washington Post* (Aug. 6, 1989): W21.

48. Various issues of *Antique Toy World*: Jan.–Feb. 1982, 49; March 1982, 10–13, April 1982, 6, 16–18; May 1982, 1, 8, 13; June 1982, 2; Feb. 1984, 10; June 1983, 1, 97; Oct. 1993, 61.

49. *Pittsburgh Post-Gazette* (Nov. 15, 1996): 2.

50. Jeffrey Hammond, *Little Big World: Collecting Louis Marx and the American Fifties* (Iowa City: University of Iowa Press, 2010); Marx Toy Museum, http://www.marxtoymuseum.com.

51. *Los Angeles Times* (Dec. 18, 2003): A1.

52. *Lexington Herald-Leader* (Dec. 17, 2007); *Chicago Tribune* (April 20, 2009): 21; corporate websites of Jakks Pacific (http://www.jakks.com/), Mezco (http://www.mezcotoyz.com/), and NECA (http://www.entertainmentearth.com/hit list.asp?company=NECA).

53. "Robert Style," *Fortune Small Business* 14, no. 2 (March 2004): 96.

54. Robert Kozinets, "Utopian Enterprise: Articulating the Meanings of *Star Trek*'s Culture of Consumption," *Journal of Consumer Research* 28, no. 1 (June 2001): 67–89; Rebecca Lynne Morrison, "Bringing the Collection to Life: A Study in Object Relations," Ph.D. diss., University of Alberta, 2010.

55. *Daily News Sunday Now* (August 2, 2009): 11; G.I. Joe Club, http://www .gijoeclub.com.

56. *USA Today* (February 6, 2002): 6D; *New York Times* (December 23, 2003): W1; Ravi Chandiramani, "Are Retro Toys Stifling Innovation?" *Marketing* (July 31, 2003): 13.

57. *Chicago Tribune* (April 8, 2001): 1; *Toronto Star* (April 1, 2007): C7.

58. *Christian Science Monitor* (December 6, 2001): 19.

59. Margaret Talbot, "Little Hotties: Barbie's New Rivals," *New Yorker* (Dec. 5, 2006): 15.

60. "President's Message," *Doll News* (Winter 1986): 3; "UFDC, Annual Report," *Doll News* (Fall 2011): 206–210; virtually all regional directors of the UFDC were retired professionals: *Doll News* (Spring 2010): 119; *Doll News* (Spring 2011): 181.

61. "President's Message," *Doll News* (Fall 2010): 205; reports on "Junior Clubs": *Doll News* (Summer 2011): 146; *Doll News* (Spring 2010): 121–125; *Doll News* (Fall 2006): 23; *Doll News* (Fall 2011): 202.

2. LOVIN' THAT '57 CHEVY (OR WHATEVER WAS YOUR FAVORITE CAR AT SEVENTEEN)

1. David Lucsko, *The Business of Speed: The Hot Rod Industry in America, 1915–1990* (Baltimore, Md.: Johns Hopkins University Press, 2008), chap. 5.

2. For insight into the racist implications of the term "rice burners," see Amy Best, *Fast Cars, Cool Rides: The Accelerating World of Youth and their Cars* (New York: New York University Press, 2006), 103–106.

3. Lucsko, *Business of Speed*, 103.

4. Lucsko, *Business of Speed*, 241–243.

5. Harman Keith, *Great American Hot Rods* (Iola, Wis.: Krause, 2005), 7–9.

6. Antique Automobile Club of America, http://www.aaca.org/about /default.aspx. The National Hot Rod Association (NHRA) claims a membership of 80,000 with more than 35,000 licensed competitors in drag races. http:// www.nhra.com/nhra101/about.aspx.

7. Kathleen Franz, *Tinkering: Consumers Reinvent the Early Automobile* (Philadelphia: University of Pennsylvania Press, 2005), 5–23, 41, 45, 55, 108, 147.

8. Lucsko, *Business of Speed*, 16–18, 41–45, 64–68. For the story of the introduction of auto mechanics in public schools, see Kevin Borg, *Auto Mechanics: Technology and Expertise in Twentieth-Century America* (Baltimore, Md.: Johns Hopkins University Press, 2007), chap. 4.

9. Edward Radlauer, *Drag Racing, Quarter Mile Thunder* (New York: Abelard-Schuman, 1966), 28; H. F. Moorehouse, *Driving Ambitions: An Analysis of the American Hot Rod Enthusiasm* (Manchester: Manchester University Press, 1991), 27–32, 42–44; Michael K. Witzel and Kent Bash, *Cruisin': Car Culture in America* (Osceola, Wis.: MBI, 1997), 72–89.

10. "Souped up Speed," *Colliers* (April 5, 1947): 3; "California Gangway," *Time* (Sept. 26, 1949): 24.

11. Moorehouse, *Driving Ambitions*, chap. 2. Most criminality related to hot rods was caused by teens, but not all. A motorcycle gang called the Boozefighters terrorized the small California town of Hollister in 1947, an event fictionalized in the movie *The Wild One*. These predecessors of the Hell's Angels consisted of disgruntled veterans (led by Arvid Olsen, a member of the acclaimed World War II Fighting Tigers). Bill Hayes, *The Original Wild Ones: Tales of the Boozefighters Motorcycle Club* (Osceola, Wis.: Motorbooks, 2005); Lucsko, *The Business of Speed*, 71.

12. Moorehouse, *Driving Ambitions*, 50, 36–38, 45, 63, 78; Wally Parks (President of the National Hot Rod Association), *Drag Racing: Yesterday and Today* (New York: Trident Press, 1966), 2–3, 14–22, 26–27.

13. Moorehouse, *Driving Ambitions*, 50–53, 106, 119, 145, 151, 156, 201; Kevin Nelson, *Wheels of Change: From Zero to 6,000 MPH—The Amazing Story of California and the Automobile* (Berkeley: Heyday, 2009), chaps. 23–24; Lucsko, *Business of Speed*, 2, 4, 1, 76, 83–84; John De Witt, *Cool Cars, High Art* (Tuscaloosa: University of Mississippi Press, 2002); Robert Post, *High Performance: The Culture and Technology of Drag Racing, 1950–2000* (Baltimore, Md.: Johns Hopkins University Press, 2001), x.

14. Tom Wolfe, *The Kandy-Kolored Tangerine-Flake Streamline Baby* (New York: Noonday, 1963), 87–98.

15. Obituaries for Ed Roth: *Baltimore City Paper* (Dec. 12, 2001): 4; *Los Angeles Times* (April 6, 2001): B6; *Washington Post* (April 7, 2001): B7; *New York Times* (April 7, 2001): B6.

16. "The Kids Are All Right: The New Generation of Hot-Rodders," *AutoWeek* (Nov. 9, 1998): 31. "Kids These Days," *AutoWeek* (April 17, 2000): 8.

17. Antique Automobile Club of America, http://www.aaca.org/about; *The Bulletin of the Antique Automobile* 1, nos. 1 and 2 (1937).

18. *Model T Times* (Nov.–Dec. 1990); *Model T Times* (July–Aug. 1991).

19. Richard Lentinello, *It's Only Original Once: Unrestored Classic Cars* (Minneapolis, Minn.: MBI, 2008), 6–7, 108–110, 120–122, 8–9; J. Richardson, *Classic Car Restorer's Handbook* (New York: HP, 1994), vi.

20. Classic Car Club of America, "What Is a Classic?" http://www.classiccarclub.org/grand_classics/what_is_classic_car.html.

21. "Classic Cars," *Crain's Chicago Business* (February 4, 2008): 35.

22. For information on the Old Car Festival at Greenfield Village in Dearborn, see http://www.thehenryford.org/events/oldCarFestival.aspx.

23. *New York Times* (June 14, 2002): F1.

24. Steven Gelber, *Horse Trading in the Age of Cars: Men in the Marketplace* (Baltimore, Md.: Johns Hopkins University Press, 2008).

25. Cotten Seiler, *Republic of Drivers: A Cultural History of Automobility in America* (Chicago: University of Chicago Press, 2008), 60–68.

26. Gary Cross, *Men to Boys: The Making of Modern Immaturity* (New York: Columbia University Press, 2008), chap. 6.

27. *Washington Times* (August 11, 2005): M14; Michael Witzel and Kent Bash, *Cruisin'*, 141.

28. Various announcements of local car cruises, http://www.paysonrim country.com/Activities/SpecialEvents/BeelineCruiseInCarShow.aspx; http://www.bluesc.com/; http://www.hastingsdowntown-mn.com/cruise-in/guidelines .htm; http://www.oldiez96.com/; ClassicCarCruiseIns/tabid/5295/Default.aspx; Rod Reprogle, *The Mother of All Car Books: How to Get More Fun and Profit Buying, Showing, and Selling Vintage and Classic Cars* (Los Alamitos, Calif.: Duncliff's International, 1995), 158–159. Witzel and Bash, *Cruisin'*, 141, 147–148.

29. Cruises in Reno, Nevada: http://www.visitrenotahoe.com/reno-tahoe /what-to-do/events/special-events/08-09-2011/hot-august-nights.

30. Detroit Free Press, *Joy Ride: Ten Years of the Woodward Dream Cruise* (Detroit, Mich.: Detroit Free Press, 2004), 13, 23, 42, 57–61, 67.

31. Best, *Fast Cars, Cool Rides*, 31–55.

32. Witzel and Bash, *Cruisin'*, chap. 1.

33. Robert Genat, *Woodward Avenue: Cruising the Legendary Strip* (North Branch, Minn.: Car Tech, 2010), 12–45; Witzel and Bash, *Cruisin'*, 28–28, 51–55.

34. By 1967, *Drive In Restaurant Magazine* carried "Ordinance Roundup," a column informing tradespeople of laws passed around the country to restrict cruising. Genat, *Woodward Avenue*, 57–61, 77; Witzel and Bash, *Cruisin'*, 56–67.

35. An example of this is the discussion of cruisers from Watts (a black neighborhood) in a road fight in Pacoima (forty miles away from home) and five carloads of Pasadena cruisers into South Los Angeles (white kids in a black neighborhood tossing a gasoline-filled bottle into a car). The extent of race conflict in these accounts is obscured by the press. *Los Angeles Times* (July 5, 1961): B1; see also *Los Angeles Times* (July 3, 1966): A1; Mathew A. Ides, *Cruising for Community: Youth Culture and Politics in Los Angeles, 1910–1970* (Ph.D. diss., 2009), 99–150.

36. *Los Angeles Times* (March 17, 1974): B2; *Los Angeles Times* (July 6, 1975): A1; *Los Angeles Times* (Aug. 5, 1976): SE1; *Los Angeles Times* (Aug. 8, 1979): E1; *Los Angeles Times* (Oct. 21, 1979): B11.

37. *Los Angeles Times* (Aug. 3, 1986): A1; *Los Angeles Times* (Oct. 16, 1986): 2; *Los Angeles Times* (July 17, 1988): OC 16; *Los Angeles Times* (July 24, 1988): OC10.

38. *Los Angeles Times* (Oct. 8, 1981): H1; *Los Angeles Times* (May 14, 1986): A6; *Los Angeles Times* (June 8, 1986): A1; *Los Angeles Times* (Jan. 12, 1989): HD1.

39. "Editorial" and "Letters," *Rod and Custom* (Aug. 1969): 5, 9; "Roadster Roundup" and "40s Limited Scrapbook," *Rod and Custom* (Dec. 1969): 12–13, 20–21.

40. "Car Clubs," *Rod and Custom* (Sept. 1970): 20–22.

41. "Street Rod Nationals," *Rod and Custom* (Nov. 1970): 5, 11, 18; "Bud Bryan," *Rod and Custom* (Feb. 1997): 72–73; "Editorial," *Rod and Custom* (May 1971): 5; "Nationals News," *Hot Rod Magazine* (July 1971): 102–103; "The Fun's

in the Run," *Hot Rod Magazine* (Oct. 1971): 102–105; "Street Rod Nationals," *Hot Rod Magazine* (Nov. 1971): 117. Henry Felsen, *Hot Rod* (New York: Dutton, 1950); Seiler, *Republic of Drivers*, 53.

42. *Los Angeles Times* (May 14, 1986): A6; *Los Angeles Times* (June 8, 1986): A1.

43. *Boston Globe* (August 14, 1999): C1; *Baltimore Sun* (August 17, 2005): 1G; *Los Angeles Times* (Jan. 12, 1980): HD1.

44. *Milwaukee Journal Sentinel* (July 28, 2003): 1E. As we have seen, Hispanic car culture sometimes has been associated with gang and criminal activities. Like the hot rodders a half-century before, lowrider clubs have tried to combat this prejudice. "History of *Low Rider Magazine*," http://www.paigerpenland.com/lowriding/history_of_lowrider_mag.html. For an example of a conflict between a local city council and a lowrider cruise group, see *Yakima Herald-Republic* (Aug. 3, 2010); *Yakima Herald-Republic* (Aug. 30, 2010). *Low Rider Magazine* since 1979 has reported on and promoted this culture from northern California.

45. Tad Tuleja, "Trick or Treat: Pre-Texts and Contexts," in *Halloween and Other Festivals of Death and Life*, ed. Jack Santino (Knoxville: University of Tennessee Press, 1994), 88–90.

3. (RE-)LIVING THAT GOLDEN DECADE

1. The result is a "Potemkin village of a historical kind." Fredric Jameson, *Postmodernism, or, The Cultural Logic of Late Capitalism* (Durham, N.C.: Duke University Press, 1991), 279–282.

2. Mary Burnside, "Centre Hall Fair Attendees 'Stake' Claim to Tradition," *Amusement Business* 115, no. 33 (Aug. 18, 2003): 9.

3. Stephanie Coontz, *The Way We Never Were: American Families and the Nostalgia Trap* (New York: Basic Books, 1992).

4. Tom Hine, *Populuxe* (New York: Knopf, 1986).

5. "Sha Na Na, 'The Unreal Fifties,'" *Vogue* (Nov. 1969): 126; *New York Times* (Nov. 1, 1970): C12; Daniel Marcus, *Happy Days and Wonder Years: The Fifties and the Sixties in Contemporary Cultural Politics* (New Brunswick, N.J.: Rutgers University Press, 2004), 12. Fred Davis, *Yearning for Yesterday: The Sociology of Nostalgia* (New York: Free Press, 1979), 49.

6. Marcus, *Happy Days*, 16–17; "Back to the '50s," *Newsweek* (Oct. 16, 1972): 78–82; "The Nifty Fifties," *Life* (June 16, 1972): 38–42; Barbara Ribakove and Sy Ribakove, *The Happy Years* (New York: Award, 1974).

7. Marcus, *Happy Days*, 25–30; Lynn Spigel, "From the Dark Ages to the Golden Age: Women's Memories and Television Reruns," *Screen* 36, no. 1 (Spring 1995): 317–335.

8. Stephen Fenichell, *Plastic: The Making of a Synthetic Century* (New York: HarperCollins, 1996), chap. 3. Kenneth R. Berger, *A Brief History of Packaging*

(New York: Morris, 1958), 56–58; Packaging Today website, http://www.pack agingtoday.com/introcelluloid.htm.

9. Fenichell, *Plastic*, chap. 5; Georg Borgstrom, "Food Processing and Packaging," in *Technology in Western Civilization*, ed. M. Kranzberg and C. W. Pursell (New York: Oxford University Press, 1967), 2:386–402; Hyla Clark, *Tin Can Book: The Can as Collectible Art, Advertising Art, High Art* (New York: New American Library, 1977); Morris, "Management and Preservation of Food," in *A History of Technology*, ed. C. Singer et al. (Oxford: Clarendon, 1958), 5:26–52; Robert Opie, *Art of the Label* (New York: New American Library, 1977), chap. 3.

10. Sylvia Katz, *Plastics: Common Objects, Classic Designs* (New York: Abrams, 1984), 11–15, 70–71, 77–78.

11. Leslie A. Piña, *Fifties Furniture* (Atglen, Penn.: Schiffer, 2005), 7, 13, 31.

12. Amy Ortega, *Designing the Creative Child: Playthings and Places in Mid-century America* (Minneapolis: University of Minnesota Press, 2013), chap. 3; Elaine Tyler May, *Homeward Bound: American Families in the Cold War Era* (New York: Basic, 1988).

13. Hine, *Populuxe*, 3; for quotation, 8.

14. Typical are "A Designer's Home of His Own," *Life* (September 11, 1950): 148, featuring Charles Eames; and "Four Rooms: $1,800," *Life* (May 14, 1951): 89.

15. Betty Friedan, *The Feminine Mystique* (New York: Norton, 1963), chaps. 1–3.

16. Brian Alexander, *Atomic Kitchen: Gadgets and Inventions for Yesterday's Cook* (Portland: Collectors Press, 2004), 8–9.

17. Cynthia Lee Henthorn, *From Submarines to Suburbs: Selling a Better America, 1939–1959* (Athens: Ohio University Press, 2006); Kathleen Parkin, *Food Is Love: Food Advertising and Gender Roles in Modern America* (Philadelphia: University of Pennsylvania Press, 2006); quotation from Jan Lindenberger, *The '50s and '60s Kitchen* (Atglen, Penn.: Schiffer: 2003), 6–7.

18. Alexander, *Atomic Kitchen*, 17, 32–34, 69, 88, 97, 120, 175; Whitney Matheson, *Atomic Home: A Tour of the American Dream* (Portland: Collectors Press, 2004), 13, 27, 48–49; Lindenberger, *'50s and '60s Kitchens*, 23–56.

19. Will Brooker, *Batman Unmasked: Analyzing a Cultural Icon* (London: Continuum, 2000), 171–248. Madeleine Marsh, *Miller's Collecting the 1950s* (London: Mitchell Beazley, 1997).

20. "Appeal of the Camp," *Knight Ridder Tribune Business News* (Oct. 26, 2006): 1. William L. Bird Jr., *Paint by Number: The How-to Craze That Swept the Nation* (Washington, D.C.: Smithsonian Institution, National Museum of American History, in association with Princeton Architectural Press, 2001).

21. *Chicago Tribune* (June 21, 1998): 10; Betty and Bill Newbound, *Collector's Encyclopedia of Figural Planters and Vases* (Paducah, Ky.: Collector, 1996); Kathy Deel, *Figural Planters: A Pictorial Guide with Values* (Altglen, Penn.: Schiffer, 1996).

22. Travis Smith, *Kitschmasland* (Altglen, Penn.: Schiffer, 2008), 6, 7, 10, 14–15, 90–91, 160.

23. *Los Angeles Times* (Aug. 8, 1998): 4S; Mark Young, Steve Duin, and Mike Richardson, *Blast Off: Rockets, Robots, Ray Guns, and Rarities from the Golden Age of Space Toys* (Milwaukee: Dark Horse Comics, 2001); James H. Gillam, *Space Toys of the 60s: An Illustrated Collector's Guide to Major Matt Mason, Zeroid Robots and Star Team, and Colorforms Outer Space Men* (London: CG, 1999).

24. *Chicago Tribune* (Sept. 23, 1988): 3.

25. Baby Boomer Memories, http://www.squidoo.com/baby-boomer-memories -and-gifts.

26. Marcus, *Happy Days*, 104–105.

27. Rae Corelli, Larry Black, and Jane O'Hara, "Nostalgia Trips," *Maclean's* (March 21, 1988): 44; *New York Times* (Feb. 17, 1991): C2.

28. *Wall Street Journal* (April 18, 1985): 1; Timothy Taylor, *The Sounds of Capitalism: Advertising, Music, and the Conquest of Culture* (Chicago: University of Chicago Press, 2013), chaps. 6–8.

29. Marcus, *Happy Days*, 112.

30. Francine Prose, "Trying On the 60's," *New York Times Magazine* (Aug. 11, 1991): 618; Nina Darton, "Feelin' Groovy on 7th Avenue," *Newsweek* (July 9, 1990): 618.

31. Madeleine Marsh, *Miller's Collecting the 1960s* (London: Octopus: 1999), 42–44, 78, 88, 102.

32. Cleveland *Plain Dealer* (Aug. 30, 1993): C1; *Hamilton Spectator* (Nov. 11, 2003): G16.

33. Antony Slide, *Collector's Guide to TV Memorabilia* (Des Moines, Iowa: Wallace-Homestead, 1985); Jan Lindenberger, *Fun Collectibles of the 1950s, 60s, and 70s* (Altglen, Penn.: Schiffer, 1999), 116–121; *Times Union* (Albany) (April 10, 1995): 1.

34. *Atlanta Journal-Constitution* (Aug. 14, 2011): 1.

35. *Daily Breeze* (Torrance, Calif.) (Sept. 28, 1986): 1.

36. "The Magic of a Rearview Mirror," *Maclean's* (March 21, 1988): 42.

37. *Chicago Tribune* (Feb. 11, 1990): 1; *Chicago Tribune* (July 31, 1994): 3; *Chicago Tribune* (March 4, 2007): 10, 9; *New York Times* (April 15, 1990): 2, 28; Michael Goldberg, *The Collectible 70s* (Iola, Wis.: Krause, 2001), 11, 13, 25, 40.

38. Pagan Kennedy, *Platforms: A Microwaved Cultural Chronicle of the 1970s* (New York: St. Martin's, 1994), 1, 5, 22, 3.

39. Kennedy, *Platforms*, 14–15.

40. *Chicago Tribune* (Sept. 23, 1993).

41. *Wall Street Journal* (Dec. 12, 2001): A1.

42. An accessible website on "decade nostalgia" is http://www.search.com /reference/Decade_nostalgia.

43. James Twitchell, *Where Men Hide* (New York: Columbia University Press, 2006).

44. *Pittsburgh Post-Gazette* (Sept. 9, 2003): B1.

45. *Columbus Dispatch* (Ohio) (Dec. 24, 2001): 1D.

46. F. F. Schwarz, "The Patriarch of Pong," *American Heritage of Invention and Technology* 6, no. 2 (1990): 64; Barry Atkins, *More Than a Game: The Computer Game as Fictional Form* (Manchester: Manchester University Press: 2003), chap. 1; Henry Lowood, "A Brief Biography of Computer Games," in *Playing Video Games: Motives, Response, and Consequences*, ed. Peter Vorderer and Jennings Bryant (Mahwah, N.J.: Lawrence Erlbaum, 2006), 28–32; Stephen Kline, Nick Dyer-Witheford, and Grieg De Peuter, *Digital Play: The Interaction of Technology, Culture, and Marketing* (Montreal: McGill-Queen's University Press, 2003), 84–108.

47. Lowood, "A Brief Biography," 35–36; "Computer Games," *Boston Globe Magazine* (December 10, 2000): 16; Herman Leonard, *Phoenix: The Fall and Rise of Videogames* (Springfield, N.J.: Rolenta, 2001), 89–99; Steven Malliet and Gust de Meyer, "The History of the Video Game," in *Handbook of Computer Games Studies*, ed. Joost Raessens and Jeffrey Goldstein (Cambridge, Mass.: MIT Press, 2005), 26–28.

48. Barry Smith, "The (Computer) Games People Play: An Overview of Popular Game Content" and G. Christopher Klug and Jesse Schell, "Why People Play Games: An Industry Perspective," both in *Playing Video Games*, ed. Vorderer and Bryant, 43–56, 91–100.

49. Kline, *Digital Play*, 128–150.

50. Entertainment Software Association (2011), http://www.theesa.com /facts/pdfs/ESA_EF_2011.pdf.

51. Will Wright, "Foreword," in David Freeman, *Creating Emotion in Games* (Indianapolis, Ind.: New Riders, 2004), xxxii.

52. Certainly, the digital generation has developed new ways of communicating, learning, and displaying self. One manifestation of this is certainly a decrease in viewing TV, listening to pop radio, and interest in cars as compared to previous generations, for whom television, music radio, and car culture were defining experiences of youth. Cell phones and laptops have opened up new and far more diverse ways of accessing video and audio culture and new ways of socializing, ways that TV, radio, and cars (through cruising, for example) once provided. Don Tapscott, *Growing Up Digital: The Rise of the Net Generation* (New York: McGraw Hill, 1998); Jack Neff, "Is the Digital Revolution Driving a Decline in America's Car Culture?" *Advertising Age* 81, no. 22 (May 31, 2010): 1–22.

53. Susan Stewart, *On Longing: Narratives of the Miniature, the Gigantic, the Souvenir, the Collection* (Durham, N.C.: Duke University Press, 1993), 168.

4. LEAVING IT TO BEAVER AND RETRO TV

1. *Buffalo News* (Oct. 21, 2011): 1.

2. See, for radio series collected by nostalgiacs, "Old Time Radio," http:// www.otrnow.com/.

3. Analysis of the role of reruns in meeting the emotional need for predictability include Percy H. Tannenbaum, "Play It Again Sam: Repeated Exposure to Television Programs," in *Selective Exposure to Communication*, ed. D. Zillman and J. Brants (Hillsdale, N.J.: Erlbaum, 1985), 225–241;Todd Gitlin, *Inside Prime-Time* (New York: Pantheon, 1985), chap. 1.

4. Samantha Barbas, *Movie Crazy: Fans, Stars, and the Cult of Celebrity* (New York: Palgrave, 2002), 15–28, 35–57; Richard DeCordova, *Picture Personalities: The Emergence of the Star System in America* (Urbana: University of Illinois Press, 1990), 85–90.

5. David Zinman, *Saturday Afternoon at the Bijou* (New Rochelle, N.Y.: Arlington House, 1973), 288–300; Jim Harmon, *Great Movie Serials: Their Sound and Fury* (Garden City, N.Y.: Doubleday, 1972), 2–5; Kalton Lahue, *Continued Next Week: A History of the Moving Picture Serial* (Norman: University of Oklahoma Press, 1964), 5–6, chaps. 4–10.

6. Susan Douglas, *Listening In: Radio and the American Imagination* (New York: Times, 1999); Bruce Lenthall, *Radio's America: The Great Depression and the Rise of Modern Mass Culture* (Chicago: University of Chicago Press, 2007), especially chap. 3.

7. Cobbett Steinberg, *TV Facts* (New York: Facts on File, 1985), 86–87.

8. Note especially Derek Kompare, *Rerun Nation: How Repeats Invented American TV* (New York: Routledge, 2005).

9. Gary Edgerton, *The Columbia History of American Television* (New York: Columbia University Press, 2007), 113–130, 139, 144–155, 163; James Baughman, *Same Time, Same Station: Creating American Television, 1948–1961* (Baltimore, Md.: Johns Hopkins University Press, 2007), 17–19, 82–83, 101.

10. Timothy Day, *A Century of Recorded Music* (New Haven, Conn.: Yale University Press, 2000), 19; Mark Coleman, *Playback: From the Victrola to MP3, One Hundred Years of Music, Machines, and Money* (New York: Da Capo, 2003), 39, 59–68, 76–85; Tom Anderson, *Making Easy Listening: Material Culture and Postwar American Recording* (Minneapolis: University of Minnesota Press, 2006), 7–12, 24, 34–37, 44, 111.

11. Kompare, *Rerun Nation*, introduction, 43, 45, 55; William Boddy, *Fifties Television: The Industry and Its Critics* (Urbana: University of Illinois Press, 1990), 169–180; Baughman, *Same Time, Same Station*, 131–135, 140–145.

12. Kompare, *Rerun Nation*, 72–84.

13. Occasionally, somebody will try to sell DVDs of Dean Martin's celebrity roast shows—featuring Lucille Ball, Phyllis Diller, George Burns, Johnny Carson, and others familiar to the middle aged in the 1970s when they were aired. See, for example, "The Best of the Dean Martin Celebrity Roasts," http://www.imdb.com/title/tt0300989/.

14. Horace Newcomb, *TV: The Most Popular Art* (New York: Anchor, 1974), 31–33, 41.

15. David Marc, *Demographic Vistas: Television in American Culture*, rev. ed. (Philadelphia: University of Pennsylvania Press, 1984), 65.

16. *Father Knows Best* TV episodes: "Big Sister," 1958, UCLA Film and Television Archive (FTA), VA5815T; "The Big Test," 1955, FTA, VA5815T; "Betty Goes Steady," 1956, FTA, VA729T; "The Homing Pigeon," 1956, FTA, VA5811T; Nina Liebman, *Living Room Lectures: The Fifties Family in Film and Television* (Austin: University of Texas Press, 1997), 124; Gerald Jones, *Honey, I'm Home! Sitcoms: Selling the American Dream* (New York: Grove Weidenfeld, 1992), 98–101.

17. Susan Cheever, "Father Knows Best," in *Prime Times: Writers on their Favorite TV Shows*, ed. Douglas Bauer (New York: Crown, 2004), 45–51.

18. Rick Mitz, *The Great TV Sitcom Book*, exp. ed. (New York: Perigee, 1988), 134–136; 199–220; *My Three Sons* episodes: "Birds and the Bees," 1962, FTA, VA1741T; "Almost the Sound of Music," 1963, FTA, VA 214T; "Adjust or Bust," 1960, FTA, VA1752T.

19. Jones, *Honey, I'm Home*, 105–106.

20. A late example is the successful movie series "Ma and Pa Kettle" from the late forties, where a simple farm couple and their large family prevail over city sharpies and the modern world in general. See Anthony Harkins, *Hillbilly: A Cultural History of an American Icon* (New York: Oxford University Press, 2004).

21. Marc, *Demographic Vistas*, 39–63. Don Rodney Vaughan, "Why *The Andy Griffith Show* Is Important to Popular Cultural Studies," *Journal of Popular Culture* 38, no. 2 (Nov. 2004): 397–423.

22. David Marc, *Comic Visions: Television Comedy and American Culture* (Boston: Allen Unwin, 1989), 129–139; Edgerton, *American Television*, 242–248, 326–327.

23. Edgerton, *American Television*, 274–278; Marc, *Comic Visions*, 63, 166–187.

24. Marc, *Comic Visions*, 187–199.

25. Jill McCorkle, "The Andy Griffith Show," in Bauer, *Prime Times*, 61–63.

26. The 1980s also reproduced pseudofamily comedies like *Taxi* (1978–1983), which offered a burlesque of a goofy family of characters; *Three's Company* (1977–1984), the relatively mild sexual innuendo of a man and two women sharing an apartment; and *Cheers* (1982–1993), a more sophisticated collection of dysfunctional but mostly loveable barflies. Alex McNeil, *Total Television*, 4th ed. (New York: Penguin, 1996), 181–182; Vincent Terrace, *Television Sitcoms* (Jefferson, N.C.: McFarland, 2000), 145–148; Kompare, *Rerun Nation*, 201.

27. James Baker, *Teaching TV Sitcom* (London: British Film Institute, 2003), 48–49.

28. Sitcoms like *Modern Family* (from 2009) find humor in the diversity of modern family units and relationships (including a gay couple with an adopted daughter). Marc, *Comic Visions*, 100–118, 166–174; Jones, *Honey, I'm Home*, 193–202, 235–236; Thomas Hibbs, *Shows About Nothing: Nihilism in Popular Culture from* The Exorcist *to* Seinfeld (Dallas: Spence, 1999), chap. 6.

29. Lee Siegel, *Not Remotely Controlled: Notes on Television* (New York: Basic Books, 2007), 96.

30. Christine Bold, *Selling the Wild West: Popular Western Fiction* (Bloomington: Indiana University Press, 1987), 3–5, 10–15, 33, and chap. 3; Jeffrey Wallmann, *The Western: Parables of the American Dream* (Lubbock: Texas Tech University, 1999), 69–71, 95, 125, 128, 137; Jane Tompkins, *West of Everything* (New York: Oxford University Press, 1992), 23–45; McNeil, *Total Television*, 159.

31. Gary Yoggy, "James Arness: Television's Quintessential Western Hero," in *Back in the Saddle: Essays on Western Film and Television Actors*, ed. Gary Yoggy (Jefferson, N.C.: McFarland, 1998), 177–199.

32. Gary Yoggy, "When Television Wore Six-Guns: Cowboy Heroes on TV," in *Shooting Stars: Heroes and Heroines of Western Films*, ed. Archie McDonald (Bloomington: Indiana University Press, 1987), 123–156.

33. Newcomb, *Popular Art*, 96–97.

34. Newcomb, *Popular Art*, 84, 92; Thomas Leitch, *Perry Mason* (Detroit, Mich.: Wayne State University Press, 2005); Marc, *Demographic Vistas*, 67; Siegel, *Not Remotely Controlled*, 33.

35. The 1970s brought a number of picture books about the early years of TV with heavy doses of sentimental remembrances of favorite shows seen while growing up. Kompare, *Rerun Nation*, 117. Irving Settel and William Laas, *Pictorial History of Television* (New York: Grosset & Dunlap, 1969); Arthur Shulman and Roger Youman, *The Television Years* (New York: Popular Library, 1973); Vincent Terrace, *The Complete Encyclopedia of Television Programs, 1947–1976* (New York: Barnes, 1976); and Donald Glut and Jim Harmon, *The Great Television Heroes* (New York: Doubleday, 1975), are full of nostalgia and references to childhood.

36. *NBC: The First 50 Years*, 1976, FTA, DVD 10894-10898 T.

37. *ABC Silver Anniversary Celebration*, 1978, FTA, VA10483.

38. *CBS of the Air*, 1978, FTA, VA1806–10 T. Note also the *Father Knows Best Reunion*, 1977, FTA, VA14261 T, which brought back the cast of the 1950s show with the Anderson parents wistfully reflecting on their empty nest but still managing to "help out" their grown-up children at a Thanksgiving reunion: Bud is a race-car driver with a marriage on the rocks, Betty is a clothing buyer still unmarried but with a prospect back home in an old boyfriend, and Kathy is marrying a doctor. This touching story was a perfect nostalgic fit for "greatest generation" couples and their adult boomer children in 1977.

39. So successful was the Museum of Broadcasting's nostalgic displays and public viewings of archived TV shows that a sister museum was opened in 1996 in Hollywood. Kompare, *Rerun Nation*, 101, 106, 120–122.

40. Edgerton, *American Television*, 300–304, 314, 320–322, 332; Christopher Sterling, *Stay Tuned: A History of American Broadcasting* (Mahwah, N.J.: Lawrence Erbaum, 2002), 871; Mavis Scanlon, *2006 Industry Overview* (Washington, D.C.: National Cable and Telecommunications Association, 2006), 14.

41. Megan Mullen, *The Rise of Cable Programming in the United States* (Austin: University of Texas Press, 2003), 155–162.

42. Edgerton, *American Television*, 340–345.

43. By 2014, Disney-ABC owned ESPN, A&E, Lifetime, the Disney channels, ABC Family, and the History channels. Viacom held Nickelodeon, TV Land, Spike, Comedy Central, MTV, VH1, and the BET networks. Time Warner ran HBO, Turner Classic Movies, TNT, TBS, CNN, the Cartoon Network, and Adult Swim; NBCUniversal (acquired partially by Comcast in 2009) owned USA, CNBC, MSNBC, Oxygen, E!, and the Weather Channel. Kompare, *Rerun Nation*, 189; Edgerton, *American Television*, 350–351; Scanlon, *2006 Industry Overview*, 14. "Comcast $16.7bn Buyout of NBCUniversal," *Financial Times* (Feb. 12, 2013).

44. Kompare, *Rerun Nation*, 171, 175–177; Joseph Turow, *Breaking Up America: Advertisers and the New Media World* (Chicago: University of Chicago Press, 1997).

45. Mullen, *Cable Programming*, 163; Turow, *Breaking Up America*, 104–106.

46. Sarah Banet-Weiser, "The Nickelodeon Brand: Buying and Selling the Audience," in *Cable Visions: Television Beyond Broadcasting*, ed., S. Banet-Weiser, C. Chris, and A. Freitas (New York: New York University, 2007), 234–255; Sarah Banet-Weiser, *Kids Rule! Nickelodeon and Consumer Citizenship* (Durham, N.C.: 2007).

47. Disneyland's anniversary show of 1985 was scarcely more than an opportunity to hype the Disney brand. And the *Happy Days Reunion* of 1992 was a love fest, with the whole TV family boasting of their enduring friendships. The *Honeymooner's* reunion (1985) was even sillier, with lots of clips of the familiar "Pow, right in kisser!" and "To the Moon, Alice!" along with "beloved" spats between Ralph and his wife. *Disneyland Thirtieth Anniversary*, 1985, FTA, VA 21707T; *Happy Days Reunion*, March 3, 1992, Paley Media Center (Los Angeles), T25713; *Jackie Gleason Presents: Honeymooner's Reunion*, May 13, 1985, Paley Media Center, Los Angeles, T85.902.

48. *Still the Beaver*, March 19, 1983, Paley Media Center, B12393.

49. *Daily Breeze* (Torrance, Calif.) (Feb. 19, 1988): 1; *Post-Tribune* (Indiana) (February 2, 1988): 2; *Baltimore Sun* (January 20, 1991): C1.

50. In March 2004 there was still another spate of movie remakes of vintage TV, including the 1970s cop show *Starsky & Hutch*, the 1960s sitcoms *Bewitched* (with Nicole Kidman in the lead), and *I Dream of Jeanie*, the Saturday-morning cartoon *Scooby-Doo*, and the adventure series *Mission Impossible*. *New York Post* (November 11, 1999); *Charleston Daily Mail* (W.V.) (May 7, 2002); *Pittsburgh Post-Gazette* (May 25, 2002); *Miami Herald* (September 29, 2002); *USA Today* (March 4, 2004).

51. The PBS *Pioneers of Television* (2008) has produced programs built around entertaining genres, for example, "Acting Funny," "Doctors and Nurses," "Superheroes," and "Sitcoms," with a lot of nostalgic footage. http://www.pbs.org/wnet/pioneers-of-television/pioneering-programs/.

52. *San Francisco Chronicle* (July 8, 1990): 12.

53. *Los Angeles Times* (Jan. 13, 1991): 80; *New York Times* (Oct. 21, 1992): H2; *New York Times* (Dec. 4, 1988): H33.

54. *San Francisco Chronicle* (July 8, 1990): C1; *New York Times Magazine* (May 6, 2007): 76.

55. Kompare, *Rerun Nation*, 181–182; *PR Newswire* (May 11, 2000): 1.

56. Kompare, *Rerun Nation*, 18.

57. TV Land Schedule Archive, 1996–2004, http://www.freewebs.com /tvlandarchives/.

58. Kevin Downey, "Boomer Hit Parade," *Broadcast and Cable* 136, no. 12 (March 20, 2006): 22.

59. *PR Newswire* (New York: Sept. 17, 2008): 1.

60. "TV Land Renews Hit Original Reality Series High School Reunion for a Second Season," *Culvert Chronicles* 3, no. 12 (April 3–April 9, 2008): 16; "TV Land Unveils New Look, Original Television Series," *SNL Kagan Media & Communications Report* (May 10, 2012): 1.

61. Nielsen Corporation, "Introducing Boomers: Marketing's Most Valuable Generation," http://www.nielsen.com/us/en/insights/reports/2012/intro ducing-boomers--marketing-s-most-valuable-generation.html; see also Market ing Charts, http://www.marketingcharts.com/television/baby-boomers-control -70-of-us-disposable-income-22891/.

62. Through the 1990s, the Nostalgia Channel struggled, and between 2001 and 2009, it was owned by the Unification Church, after which it was purchased by Robert A. Schuller, the son of Crystal Cathedral founder Robert H. Schuller. By late 2011 it was called Youtoo TV, shifting to a "social media" format and offering viewers the opportunity to air their own videos with limited retro pro gramming: http://en.wikipedia.org/wiki/YoutooTV.

63. Weakened by the loss of its contract with NBCUniversal Television Dis tribution in June 2011, RTV had to scramble to get access to programming from smaller distributors. As of May 2012, RTV was carried as a digital "subchan nel" by roughly seventy-one local American TV stations, down from ninety- five the year before. "ValCom, Inc. Announces Joint Venture with Luken Com munications," *Marketwire* (March 22, 2011); Retro Television Network, http:// en.wikipedia.org/wiki/Retro_Television_Network; "Heim to Leave Nostalgia," *Broadcasting & Cable* (March 11, 1996): 64.

64. *Chicago Tribune* (November 22, 2010): 34; Me-TV, http://en.wikipedia. org/wiki/Me-TV; http://en.wikipedia.org/wiki/This_TV; "MGM to Handle National Distribution of Weigel's Me-TV Classic TV," *Digital Network Marketing Weekly News* (Jan. 22, 2011): 663, for quotation from Sabin.

65. "Tribune Set to Launch Antenna TV," *Radio & Television Business Report* (December 1, 2010): 1; "Antenna TV Launch Schedule Starting January 2011," *Sitcoms Online* (October 21, 2010): 2; Antenna TV, http://en.wikipedia .org/wiki/Antenna_TV.

66. An interesting effort to reach the emerging class of retirees is Retirement Living TV (from 2006), none-too-subtly rechristened in 2012 as Redefining Living, to avoid sounding too old. It features informational programming about health, exercise, and relationships for the boomer generation who are "redefining" the life course as they enter their "golden years," with programming partially coproduced by AARP. *New York Times* (Dec. 9, 1996): D9; "Centric Finds a Niche," *Multichannel News* (Oct. 3, 2011): 26.

67. Fred Davis, *Yearning for Yesterday* (New York: Free Press, 1979), 12, 44.

68. Fredric Jameson, *Postmodernism, or the Logic of Late Capitalism* (London: Verso, 1991), 18.

69. Paul Grainge, "Nostalgia and Style in Retro America, Moods, Modes, and Media Recycling," *Journal of American and Comparative Cultures* 20, no. 2 (Spring 2000): 27–34; Paul Grainge, *Monochrome Memories: Nostalgia and Style in Retro America* (Westport, Conn: Praeger, 2002), chaps. 1–2; Megan Mullen, "Surfing Through 'TVLand': Notes Toward a Theory of 'Video Bites' and Their Function on Cable TV," *The Velvet Light Trap* 36 (1995): 60–68.

70. *Christian Science Monitor* (July 9, 1999): 13.

71. Cristel Antonia Russell and Sidney J. Levy, "The Temporal and Focal Dynamics of Volitional Reconsumption: A Phenomenological Investigation of Repeated Hedonic Experiences," *Journal of Consumer Research* 39, no. 2 (August 2012): 341–359.

5. GIVE ME THAT OLD-TIME RADIO

1. John Runowicz, *Forever Doo-Wop: Race, Nostalgia, and Vocal Harmony* (Amherst: University of Massachusetts Press, 2010), chap. 1.

2. "PBS Extends Partnership with 'MY MUSIC' Producer T. J. Lubinsky," *PR Newswire* (July 23, 1999), http://www.prnewswire.com/news-releases/pbs-extends-partnership-with-my-music-producer-tj-lubinsky-99111749.html; *New York Times* (March 13, 2011): 3.

3. "Rock and Roll Hall of Fame and Museum Timeline: 1995–2010," http://rockhall.com/pressroom/announcements/hall-in-rolling-stone.

4. Matthew Schulkind, Laura Kate Hennis, and David C. Rubin, "Music, Emotion, and Autobiographical Memory: They're Playing Your Song," *Memory and Cognition* 27, no. 6 (1999): 948–955; Amee Baird and Séverine Samson, "Memory for Music in Alzheimer's Disease: Unforgettable?" *Neuropsychology Review* 19 (2009): 85–101; Matthew D. Schulkind, Patrik N. Juslin, and Daniel Västfjäll, "Emotion in Music: The Need to Consider Underlying Mechanisms," *Behavioral and Brain Science* 31 (2008): 559–621; Patrik Juslin, "Music and Emotion," in *Music and the Mind*, ed. Irène Deliège and Jane Davidson (New York: Oxford University Press, 2011), 113–138.

5. David Hertz, "Memory in Musical Form," and Barbara Tillmann, Isabelle Peretz, and S. Samson, "Neurocognitive Approaches to Memory in Music," both

in *The Memory Process: Neuroscientific and Humanistic Perspectives*, ed. Suzanne Nalbantian, Paul Matthews, and James McClelland (Cambridge, Mass.: MIT Press, 2011), 359–376, 377–394; quotation at 382.

6. Tim Taylor, *The Sounds of Capitalism: Advertising, Music, and the Conquest of Culture* (Chicago: University of Chicago Press, 2012).

7. David Allan, "Effects of Popular Music in Advertising on Attention and Memory," *Journal of Advertising Research* 46, no. 4 (Dec. 2006): 434–444.

8. Morris B. Holbrook and Robert M. Schindler, "Men Relate to Cars of Teens and Women to Songs," *Journal of Consumer Behaviour* 3, no. 2 (Dec. 2003): 107.

9. Edison's competitor Victor embraced the same strategy: "Watch the shadows of emotion flit over the faces of your family," a 1913 ad declared, when you play recordings of sentimental favorites like "Silver Threads Among the Gold." *National Phonograph Co. Catalogue* (1899), 41; *National Phonographic Co. Catalogue* (1904), 12 (both in Hagley Museum Archives); Edison ad, *Colliers* (March 28, 1908): back. Victor ad, *Ladies Home Journal* (Dec. 1913): back for quotation.

10. Michael Chanan, *Repeated Takes: A Short History of Recording and Its Effects on Music* (London: Verso, 1995), 12–13, 19–20; Mark Katz, *Captured Sound: How Technology Has Changed Music* (Berkeley: University of California Press, 2010), 29, 66–70.

11. David Jansen, *Tin Pan Alley: The Composers, the Songs, the Performers, and Their Times* (New York: Donald Fine, 1988), xv, xvi.

12. John Shepherd, *Tin Pan Alley* (London: Routledge & Kegan Paul, 1982), 4–7; Jansen, *Tin Pan Alley*, 40–42.

13. Shepherd, *Tin Pan Alley*, 24; Sheldon Patinkin, *"No Legs, No Jokes, No Chance": A History of the American Musical Theater* (Evanston, Ill.: Northwestern University Press, 2008); Arthur Wertheim, *Vaudeville Wars: How the Keith-Albee and Orpheum Circuits Controlled the Big-Time and Its Performers* (London: Palgrave, 2006); Robert Lewis, *From Traveling Show to Vaudeville: Theatrical Spectacle in America, 1830–1910* (Baltimore, Md.: Johns Hopkins University Press, 2003).

14. Jansen, *Tin Pan Alley*, xx, 3.

15. Ethnic European and African American music was often modified to adapt to Tin Pan Alley imperatives—easy to play and sing and "acceptable" (in the view of publishers) to a mass audience. Thus, the Alley whitened African American innovations like the cakewalk, rag, blues, and jazz. Irving Berlin's "Alexander's Ragtime Band" (a song of 1911 about rag rather than a ragtime song) was promoted instead of Scott Joplin's authentic "Maple Leaf Rag" (1899). Jansen, *Tin Pan Alley*, 45, 36–37; Shepherd, *Tin Pan Alley*, chap. 3.

16. Victor's 1903 catalog offered those "dear old Southern melodies" of the old-time minstrel show that promised to "bring back the old-time thrill." Victor also presented a vast array of dance music and instrumental solos for middlebrow taste. *Victor Catalogue* (1903), Hagley Museum Archives; Victor ad, *Ladies'*

Home Journal (Oct. 1906): 79; *Voice of the Victor* (May–June 1911): 1–4; *Voice of the Victor* (May 1908): 7; *Victor Victrola Catalogue* (1910); *Victor Catalogue* (1918) (All in the Hagley Museum Archives).

17. Though first conceived as a business machine for recording office correspondence (like a Dictaphone) when invented by Thomas Edison in 1877, subsequent improvements (like Emile Berlin's phonograph) abandoned Edison's cylinder records for discs that were easier to reproduce and store, which in turn led to factory-recorded music for entertainment. Though first adapted to coin-operated arcade phonographs (1890 to around 1908), personally owned machines played in the home emerged around 1895 and quickly dominated. See Gary Cross and Robert Proctor, *Packaged Pleasures* (Chicago: University of Chicago Press, 2014), chap. 5.

18. A. J. Millard, *America on Record* (New York: Cambridge University Press, 1995), 136–157; Roland Gelatt, *The Fabulous Phonograph, 1877–1977* (New York: Macmillan, 1977), 218, 245–267; Michael Chanan, *Repeated Takes: A Short History of Recording and Its Effects on Music* (London, Verso, 1995), 38–39.

19. Shepherd, *Tin Pan Alley*, 72; Sungook Hong, *Wireless: From Marconi's Black Box to the Audion* (Cambridge, Mass.: MIT Press, 2001); Steven Wurtzler, *Electric Sounds: Technological Change and the Rise of Corporate Mass Media* (New York: Columbia University Press, 2007); Christopher Sterling, *The Rise of American Radio*, vol. 1 (New York: Routledge, 2007).

20. Mark Coleman, *Playback: From the Victrola to MP3, One Hundred Years of Music, Machines, and Money* (New York: Da Capo, 2003), 39, 59–68, 76–85; Greg Milner, *Perfecting Sound Forever: An Aural History of Recorded Music* (London: Faber and Faber, 2009), 109–112.

21. Erik Barnouw, *A Tower in Babel: A History of Broadcasting in the United States to 1933* (New York: Oxford University Press, 1966), 217.

22. Shepherd, *Tin Pan Alley*, chaps. 8 and 10; Tom Anderson, *Making Easy Listening: Material Culture and Postwar American Recording* (Minneapolis: University of Minnesota Press, 2006), 7–12, 24, 34–37, 44, 111; Jacques Attali, *Noise: The Political Economy of Music* (Minneapolis: University of Minnesota Press, 1985), 87, 128; David Suisman, *Selling Sound: The Commercial Revolution in American Music* (Cambridge, Mass.: Harvard University Press, 2012), 282.

23. Susan Douglas, *Listening In: Radio and the American Imagination* (New York: Times, 1999), chap. 9.

24. This nostalgia continues with reruns of the *Lawrence Welk Show*, featuring stock performers like Norma Zimmer, Bob Ralston, and the Lennon Sisters singing standards. Jansen, *Tin Pan Alley*, 213–215; Arnold Shaw, "Sinatrauma: The Proclamation of a New Era," in *The Frank Sinatra Reader*, ed. Steven Petkov and Leonard Mustazza (New York: Oxford University Press, 1995), 15.

25. Glen Jeansonne, David Luhrssen, and Dan Sokolovic, *Elvis Presley, Reluctant Rebel* (Santa Barbara, Calif.: Praeger, 2011), 122–126. Kerry Segrave, *Anti-Rock: The Opposition to Rock 'n' Roll* (Hamden, Conn.: Shoe String, 1988).

26. Jansen, *Tin Pan Alley*, 280–288.

27. Marc Fisher, *Something in the Air: Radio, Rock, and the Revolution That Shaped a Generation* (New York: Random House, 2007), 69.

28. Fisher, *Something in the Air*, 5–15.

29. Bill Brewster and Frank Broughton, *Last Night a DJ Saved my Life: The History of the Disc Jockey* (New York: Grove, 2000), 25–30.

30. Fisher, *Something in the Air*, chap. 2; Brewster and Broughton, *DJ*, 31–41; *New York Times* (Sept. 24, 1972); Arnold Passman, *The Deejays* (New York: Macmillan, 1971); John Jackson, *Big Beat Heat: Alan Freed and the Early Years of Rock & Roll* (New York: Schirmer, 2000).

31. PBS, "Conversation with Wolfman Jack, June 21, 1995," videotape, Paley Media Center, Beverly Hills, Calif., T39073; Wolfman Jack and Byron Laursen, *Have Mercy: Confessions of the Original Rock-and-Roll Animal* (New York: Warner Books, 1995).

32. Fisher, *Something in the Air*, 60, 88; *Orlando Sentinel* (April 22, 1988): C1.

33. Ad for Schafer Electronics computer programmer, *Broadcasting* (Aug. 24, 1970): 2.

34. Bruce Morrow felt even more out of place when sent by WABC to the Woodstock music festival in the summer of 1969. "I was not a hippie, but I want to be accepted," he recalled. Fisher, *Something in the Air*, chap. 8; Bruce Morrow, *Cousin Brucie: My Life in Rock 'n' Roll* (New York: Beech Tree, 1987), 88 for quotation; *Orlando Sentinel* (April 22, 1988): C1.

35. Richard Goldstein, "Sha Na Na, 'The Unreal Fifties,'" *Vogue* (Nov. 1969): 126; Daniel Marcus, *Happy Days and Wonder Years: The Fifties and the Sixties in Contemporary Cultural Politics* (New Brunswick, N.J.: Rutgers University Press, 2004), 12; Simon Reynolds, *Retromania: Pop Culture's Addiction to Its Own Past* (London: Faber and Faber, 2011), 283–285; Fred Davis, *Yearning for Yesterday: The Sociology of Nostalgia* (New York: Free Press, 1979), 49.

36. Various articles on retro rock concerts: *New York Times* (Dec. 3, 1972): 45; *New York Times* (June 16, 1974): 43; *New York Times* (July 15, 1973): 46; *New York Times* (Sept. 2, 1977): 19; *New York Times* (Nov. 19, 1978): 87; *New York Times* (July 17, 1982): 43; *New York Times* (Sept. 11, 1981): C23.

37. *New York Times* (Dec. 9, 2009): A41.

38. Note the letter written by the leader of the Sex Pistols, John Lydon, calling the Rock and Roll Hall of Fame "piss" in 1996. http://www.lettersofnote .com/2010/09/rock-and-roll-hall-of-fame-is-piss.html.

39. Reynolds, *Retromania*, chaps. 8–9. Legs McNeil and Gillian McCain, *Please Kill Me: The Uncensored Oral History of Punk* (New York: Penguin, 1997).

40. *New York Times* (July 5, 2009): A4.

41. *New York Times* (Sept. 24, 1972): D15.

42. Wolfman Jack and Laursen, *Have Mercy*; Wolfman Jack, *Let's Cruise*, vol. 1 [CD of radio shows] (Big Ear Music, 1998), http://www.cduniverse.com

/search/xx/music/pid/1142593/a/wolfman+jack%27s+let%27s+cruise%3A+
vol.+1.htm; http://en.wikipedia.org/wiki/Wolfman_Jack.

43. Runowicz, *Forever Doo-Wop*, 3–4, 1, 11–14; Robert Pruter, *Doowop: The Chicago Scene* (Urbana: University of Illinois Press, 1997), 250–252; Anthony Bribin and Matthew Schiff, *The Complete Book of Doo-Wop* (Iola, Wis.: Krause, 2000), 13–15.

44. Runowicz, *Forever Doo-Wop*, 26, 30–39, 56; Bruce Morrow, *Doo Wop: The Music, the Times, the Era* (New York: Sterling, 2010); Paul Friedlander, *Rock & Roll: A Social History* (Boulder, Colo.: Westview, 2006), chap. 5; Mitch Rosalsky, *Encyclopedia of Rhythm & Blues and Doo-Wop Vocal Groups* (Lanham, Md.: Scarecrow, 2000); Anthony Gribin, *Doo-Wop: The Forgotten Third of Rock 'n' Roll* (New York: Krause, 1992).

45. Runowicz, *Forever Doo-Wop*, 69, 76–77.

46. Runowicz, *Forever Doo-Wop*, 97.

47. George Lee, *Beale Street: Where the Blues Began* (New York: Robert Ballou, 1934); Jeansonne et al., *Elvis Presley*, 17–43; Karal Ann Marling, *Graceland: Going Home with Elvis* (Cambridge, Mass.: Harvard University Press, 1996), 52; Charles Wolfe, "Presley and the Gospel Tradition," in *The Elvis Reader: Texts and Sources on the King of Rock 'n' Roll*, ed. Kevin Quain (New York: St. Martin's, 1992), 15–18.

48. Peter Guralnick, *Last Train to Memphis: The Rise of Elvis Presley* (New York: Little, Brown, 1994), 64–65. Jeansonne et al., *Elvis Presley*, 72–73, 109–136; Marling, *Graceland*, 133–148, 184–197.

49. Marling, *Graceland*, 80–86, 63–67.

50. Peter Guralnick, *Careless Love: The Unmaking of Elvis Presley* (New York: Little, Brown, 1999).

51. George Lipsitz, *Time Passages: Collective Memory and American Popular Culture* (Minneapolis: University of Minnesota Press, 1990), xiv; Erika Doss, *Elvis Culture: Fans, Faith, and Image* (Lawrence: University Press of Kansas, 1999), 116–161.

52. Doss, *Elvis Culture*, 4, 16,17, 22, 48–54, 167, 188, 214–215, quotation on 13; Bill DeNight, Sharon Fox, and Girs Rijff, eds., *Elvis: The Commemorative Edition* (New York: Beekman House, 1991), 78–79.

53. Doss, *Elvis Culture*, 42–44, 61, 63, 77, quotation on 81.

54. In addition to this shrine to Elvis, there are Elvis "churches"—for example, the First Presleyterian Church of Elvis the Divine. They are online, mostly tongue in cheek, but their founders are really fans (appealing to a Gen-X sensibility of camp). Doss, *Elvis Culture*, 89, 97, 104; Gregory Reece, *Elvis Religion: The Cult of the King* (London: I. B. Tauris, 2006), 10–21.

55. Reece, *Elvis Religion*, chap. 2; R. Serge Denisoff and George Plasketes, *True Disbeliever: The Elvis Contagion* (New Brunswick, N.J.: Transaction, 1995).

56. *Wall Street Journal* (April 13, 1982): 1; *Chicago Tribune* (June 27, 1983): B1; *Globe and Mail* (Canada) (June 14, 1986): D3; *Dallas Morning News* (June 3, 1990): H22; *New York Times* (May 20, 1990): F10.

57. *Globe and Mail* (Canada) (June 14, 1986): D3.

58. *Washington Post* (Nov. 23, 1988): D7; *Wall Street Journal* (April 18, 1985): 1.

59. Sean Ross, "Music Radio—the Fickleness of Fragmentation," in *Radio: The Forgotten Medium*, ed. Edward Pease and Everette Dennis (New Brunswick, N.J.: Transaction, 1995), 95–105.

60. *Washington Post* (May 15, 2001): C1.

61. "Rock and Roll Forever," *Newsweek* (July 5, 1993): 48.

62. Fred Setterberg, "Cruising with Donny on the San Leandro Strip," in *The Automobile and American Culture*, ed. David Lewis and Laurence Goldstein (Ann Arbor: University of Michigan Press, 1980), 320.

63. Reynolds, *Retromania*, 198, 200.

64. Tamara Livingston, "Music Revivals: Toward a General Theory," *Ethnomusicology* 43, no. 1 (Winter 1999): 66–85.

65. Coleman, *Playback*, 159–63.

66. Runowicz, *Forever Doo-Wop*, 142; Jon Coleman, "Oldies Insights Winter 2003: Is Newer Music Helping or Hurting?" http://www.colemaninsights.com; Fisher, *Something in the Air*, 277, 279, chap. 11.

67. Reynolds, *Retromania*, 196–197, for quotation, 409.

68. Reynolds, *Retromania*, xv, for quotation, vi–xix, 386–389, chap. 2.

6. DILEMMAS OF HERITAGE IN AN ERA OF CONSUMED NOSTALGIA

1. Richard Perrin, *Historic Wisconsin Buildings: A Survey in Pioneer Architecture, 1835–1870* (Milwaukee, Wis.: Milwaukee Public Museum, 1981); Richard Perrin, *The Architecture of Wisconsin* (Madison, Wis.: State Historical Society of Wisconsin, 1967); John Krugler, *Creating Old World Wisconsin: The Struggle to Build an Outdoor History Museum of Ethnic Architecture* (Madison: University of Wisconsin Press, 2013).

2. The site has long struggled with costs and limited audience appeal. Perhaps more than at other heritage sites, the expense of maintaining mostly wooden (and very old) structures through years of Wisconsin winters has been a burden on the site's limited budget. Hundreds of period objects (from a long wooden bread trough to simple kitchen bowls) have to be cleaned and stored every winter (as the site is closed mostly from November to May), and the heirloom vegetables have to be planted with special seeds annually (using a greenhouse for early germination). And, with the critical help of volunteers, period garments have to be handmade regularly for interpreters. "Wisconsin Historical Site Captures Old-Fashioned Rural Life," *McClatchy—Tribune Business News* (May 22, 2010).

3. American Association of State and Local History, http://www.aaslh.org/; Association for Living History, Farm, and Agricultural Museums, http://www.alhfam.org.

4. Jay Anderson, *Time Machines: The World of Living History* (Nashville, Tenn.: American Association for State and Local History, 1984), 17–30.

5. Anders Greenspan, *Creating Colonial Williamsburg: The Restoration of Virginia's Eighteenth-Century Capital*, 2nd ed. (Chapel Hill: University of North Carolina Press, 2002), 35, 40–41, 47, 49; Michael Kammen, *Mystic Chords of Memory* (New York: Knopf, 1991), 358–370; Thomas Taylor, "The Williamsburg Restoration and Its Reception by the American Public: 1926–1942," dissertation, George Washington University, 1989, chap. 2; Warren Leon and Margaret Piatt, "Living-History Museums," in *History Museums in the United States*, ed., W. Leon and R. Rosenzweig (Urbana: University of Illinois Press, 1989), 64–97; John D. Rockefeller Jr., "The Genesis of the Williamsburg Restoration," *National Geographic* 71 (April 1937): 401.

6. Richard Handler and Eric Gable, *The New History in an Old Museum: Creating the Past at Colonial Williamsburg* (Durham, N.C.: Duke University Press, 1997), 5.

7. Daniel Boorstin, "Past and Present in America: A Historian Visits Colonial Williamsburg," *Commentary* 25 (Jan. 1958): 1–7; Ada Louise Huxtable, *The Unreal America: Architecture and Illusion* (New York, 1997), chap. 1, quotation on 35; Greenspan, *Creating Colonial Williamsburg*, 128, 143; David Lowenthal, "The American Way of History," *Columbia University Forum* 9 (Summer 1966): 31.

8. *Colonial Williamsburg: Official Guidebook and Map* (Colonial Williamsburg Foundation, 1972), v–vi.

9. Greenspan, *Creating Colonial Williamsburg*, 133, 151; Eric Gable and Richard Handler, "The Authority of Documents at Some American History Museums," *Journal of American History* 8 (June 1994): 119, 121.

10. Colin Campbell, *Colonial Williamsburg Foundation: Seventy-Five Years of Historic Preservation and Education, A Newcomen Address* (New York: Newcomen Society of the United States, 2001), 10, 24.

11. Alicia Griswold, "Colonial Williamsburg in Review," *Adweek* (June 18, 2001): 4.

12. David Kiley, "Shaking off the Dust," *Brandweek* (June 1, 1998): 20–21; "Williamsburg Is Getting Top-to-Bottom Makeover to the Tune of $100M," *Meeting News* 25, no. 12 (Aug. 6, 2001): 54.

13. Eric Gable and Richard Handler, "Notes from the Ethnography of Colonial Williamsburg, Virginia, U.S.A.," in *Defining Memory: Local Museums and the Construction of History in America's Changing Communities*, ed. Amy Levin (Lanham, Md.: AltaMira: 2007), 47–48, 53.

14. William Greenleaf, *From These Beginnings: The Early Philanthropies of Henry and Edsel Ford, 1911–1936* (Detroit, Mich.: Wayne State University Press, 1964), 96; Kammen, *Mystic Chords*, 352–358; Anderson, *Time Machines*, 17–30; The Henry Ford, http://www.thehenryford.org.

15. Henry Ford Museum Staff, *Greenfield Village and the Henry Ford Museum* (New York: Crown, 1972), 15, 21, 57; *A Guide Book for the Henry Ford Museum*

(Dearborn, Mich., 1956). Tony Bennett, "Museums and the People," in *The Museum Time-Machine*, ed. Robert Lumley (London: Comedia, 1988), 63–86; C. B. Hosmer, *Presence of the Past: A History of the Preservation Movement in the United States Before Williamsburg* (New York: Putnam, 1965), 6–10.

16. Kerstin Brandt, "Fordist Nostalgia: History and Experience at the Henry Ford," *Rethinking History* 11, no. 3 (Sept. 2007): 385; David Lowenthal, *The Past Is a Foreign Country* (Cambridge: Cambridge University Press, 1985).

17. Alexander Cook, "The Use and Abuse of Historical Reenactment: Thoughts on Recent Trends in Public History," *Criticism* 46, no. 3 (2004): 487–496, esp. 491; Vanessa Agnew, "Introduction: What Is Reenactment?" *Criticism* 46, no. 3 (2004): 334; Andreas Huyssen, *Present Pasts: Urban Palimpsests and the Politics of Memory* (Stanford, Calif.: Stanford University Press, 2003), 2; James Weeks, *Gettysburg: Memory, Market, and an American Shrine* (Princeton, N.J.: Princeton University Press, 2003), chap. 8, for a discussion of Civil War reenactors.

18. Larry Lankton, "Something Old, Something New: The Reexhibition of the Henry Ford Museum's Hall of Technology," *Technology and Culture* 21, no. 4 (Oct. 1980): 594–613.

19. Geoffrey C. Upward, *A Home for Our Heritage: The Building and Growth of Greenfield Village and the Henry Ford Museum, 1929–1979* (Dearborn, Mich.: Henry Ford Museum, 1979); William Simonds, *Henry Ford and Greenfield Village* (New York: Frederick A. Stokes, 1938); Brandt, "Fordist Nostalgia," 385–386.

20. More money and programs have been added to The Henry Ford since the 1980s (including a new tour of the revamped River Rouge factory, famed for its historic role at Ford and its display of the Wright Brothers' first airplane); L. Lankton, "Made in America," *Technology and Culture* 35, no. 2 (April 1994): 389–395; "Descendants of Wright Brothers and Henry Ford to Unveil Historic Plane at Henry Ford Museum, Today," *PR Newswire* (March 19, 2004): 1.

21. Brandt, "Fordist Nostalgia," 394–395, 400–401; Scott Mallwitz, "Experience Design," Presentation at the Museum Studies Proseminar, University of Michigan (2004), 9, cited in Brandt, "Fordist Nostalgia," 400; Joseph Pine and James Gilroy, *The Experience Economy: Work Is Theatre and Every Business a Stage* (Boston: Harvard Business School Press, 1999).

22. Sherri Begin, "The Henry Ford Plans 'Digestible' Exhibits," *Crain's Detroit Business* 23, no. 52 (Dec. 24, 2007): 10.

23. Catherine Kennelly, *Life in an Old New England Country Village: An Old Sturbridge Village Book* (New York: Thomas Y. Crowell, 1969), 2–3, 6–12, 22–23; Charles Van Ravenswaay, *The Story of Old Sturbridge Village* (New York: Newcomen Society in North America, 1965), 2–9; Samuel Chamberlain, *A Tour of Old Sturbridge Village* (New York: Hastings House, 1972); Kent McCallum, *Old Sturbridge Village* (New York: Abrams, 1996); Laura Abing, "Old Sturbridge Village: An Institutional History of a Cultural Artifact," dissertation, Marquette University, 1997.

24. *Telegram and Gazette* (Worcester, Mass.) (July 27, 1989): A2; *Telegram and Gazette* (Worcester, Mass.) (Jan. 2, 1990): A2; *Telegram and Gazette* (Worcester, Mass.) (July 2, 1999): C3.

25. Kennelly, *Old Sturbridge Village Book*, 2–3; Ravenswaay, *The Story of Old Sturbridge Village*, 8.

26. Kevin Walsh, *The Representation of the Past* (London: Routledge, 1992), 96–97; Barbara Kirshenblatt-Gimblett, *Destination Culture: Tourism, Museums, and Heritage* (Berkeley: University of California Press, 1998), 194–195; and especially Weeks, *Gettysburg: Memory*.

27. Nicholas Zook, *Museum Villages USA* (Barre, Mass.: Barre Publishers, 1971); Walter Knott, "The Enterprises of Walter Knott, Oral History Transcript" (interviewed by Donald J. Schippers in 1963), Oral History Program, University of California, Los Angeles (1965), UCLA Library, Special Collections, 13.

28. "Colonial Williamsburg Site in Virginia Reports Increase in Revenue," *Knight Ridder Tribune Business News* (Feb. 9, 2002); "Colonial Williamsburg, Va., Reports 10 Percent Decline in Visitors in 2002," *Knight Ridder Tribune Business News* (March 26, 2003); "Summer Tourism in Williamsburg, Va., Less Than Expected," *Knight Ridder Tribune Business News* (July 31, 2003); "Colonial Williamsburg, Va., to Cut 95 Jobs in Historic Area," *Knight Ridder Tribune Business News* (Sept. 3, 2003); "Colonial Williamsburg Is Eliminating 95 Jobs in the Historic Area," *Knight Ridder Tribune Business News* (March 13, 2004); "Colonial Williamsburg in Virginia Sees 3 Percent Decline in Visitors," *Knight Ridder Tribune Business News* (Jan. 20, 2005).

29. "Attendance Sinks to a 47-Year Low," *McClatchy—Tribune Business News* (Nov. 6, 2008); "Cutting Costs Was Harsh but Effective," *McClatchy—Tribune Business News* (Feb. 13, 2010); *Richmond Times Dispatch* (Dec. 12, 2013): 1.

30. *Telegram and Gazette* (Worcester, Mass.) (Feb. 1, 2006): A8; *Wall Street Journal* (Aug. 22, 1997): B1, 3.

31. "Old World Wisconsin Looks for New Life After Tornado," *McClatchy—Tribune Business News* (July 7, 2010); *Milwaukee Journal* (May 1, 2011): C1.

32. "Some Fear Colonial Williamsburg Will Have to 'Disnify' to Attract Tourists," *Knight Ridder Tribune Business News* (Sept. 5, 2004).

33. *Telegram and Gazette* (Worcester, Mass.) (Feb. 1, 2006): A8.

34. *Wall Street Journal* (April 15, 1998): NE1.

35. "Keeping Them Coming Back to the Past," *Knight Ridder Tribune Business News* (Feb. 13, 2005).

36. *Gazette* (Montreal) (Sept. 9, 2009): E3.

37. The Sturbridge museum not only expanded its program of school children's field trips (more than 60,000 in 2008, up 8 percent for the year) but also sent interpreters to classrooms in the "History on the Road" program. "Old Sturbridge Village Attendance up 8 Percent in 2008," *Business Wire* (Jan. 19, 2009); "Old Sturbridge Village Museum on Track for Best Year in Decade," *Education Letter* (Sept. 9, 2009): 69.

38. Keith Miller, "Williamsburg Flex Co-Op Brings Positive Tourism Results to Area," *Amusement Business* (March 25, 2002): 6; "Interactive History: British Actors Skilled at Improvisation Are Consultants for a New Dramatic Program at Colonial Williamsburg," *Knight Ridder Tribune Business News* (April 19, 2006); "Colonial Williamsburg Adding New Programs to Draw Visitors," *McClatchy— Tribune Business News* (Oct. 16, 2011).

39. *Wall Street Journal* (Aug. 22, 1997): B1: "Old Sturbridge Village Museum on Track for Best Year in Decade," *Education Letter* (Sept. 9, 2009): 69.

40. Miller, "Williamsburg Flex," 6; *Wall Street Journal* (Aug. 22, 1997): B1.

41. "CW Store Opens Near D.C.," *McClatchy—Tribune Business News* (April 16, 2008).

42. "Henry Ford Museum Catches Boogie Fever With 'Disco: A Decade of Saturday Nights,'" *PR Newswire* (Nov. 18, 2003); "Lego-Lovers Marvel at the Henry Ford Museum's New Lego Castle Adventure Exhibit," *PR Newswire* (Oct. 19, 2009).

43. *Telegram and Gazette* (Worcester, Mass.) (Jan. 23, 2009): D1.

44. "Wisconsin Tourist Attraction Returns to Full Schedule Despite Cuts," *Knight Ridder Tribune Business News* (April 15, 2003); "Old World Wisconsin Trying New Approach," *Knight Ridder Tribune Business News* (May 7, 2006); *Milwaukee Journal Sentinel* (July 16, 2009): 3.

45. Christina Goulding, "Romancing the Past: Heritage Visiting and the Nostalgic Consumer," *Psychology and Marketing* 18, no. 6 (June 2001): 565–592.

46. Barbara Franco, "The Communication Conundrum: What Is the Message? Who Is Listening?" *Journal of American History* 8, no. 11 (June 1994): 151–164; Gary Kulik, "Designing the Past: History-Museum Exhibitions from Peale to the Present," in *History Museums in the United States: A Critical Assessment*, ed. Warren Leon and Roy Rosenzweig (Urbana: University of Illinois Press, 1989), 6.

47. Stuart Hannabuss, "Postmodernism and the Heritage Experience," *Library Management* 20, no. 5 (1999): 295–302.

7. PILGRIMAGES, SOUVENIRS, AND MEMORY AT DISNEY

1. Walter Knott, "The Enterprises of Walter Knott: Oral History Transcript" (interviewed by Donald J. Schippers in 1963), Oral History Program, University of California, Los Angeles (1965), UCLA Library, Special Collections; "Calico Ghost Town, Southern California's Greatest Silver Camp," Orange County Archives, Smart Family Collection; Various clippings, Orange County Archives, Knott's Berry Farm Papers, Clippings Box; Knott's Berry Farm and related websites: http://www.knotts.com/coinfo/history/index/shtml; http://www.knotts.com/park/index.shtml; http://www.narrowgauge.org/nge/html /kbfarm/kbfarm-main.html; Roger Holmes and Paul Bailey, *Fabulous Farmer: The Story of Walter Knott and His Berry Farm* (Los Angeles, 1956), 1–14, 145–149; Gary Cross, "Knott's Berry Farm: The Improbable Amusement Park in the

Shadow of Disney," in *The Amusement Park: History, Culture, and the Heritage of Pleasure*, ed. Jason Woods (Aldershot: Ashgate, forthcoming).

2. Gary Cross and John Walton, *The Playful Crowd: Pleasure Places in the Twentieth Century* (New York: Columbia University Press, 2005).

3. According to Susan Stewart: "Whereas the miniature represents closure, interiority, the domestic, and the overly cultural, the gigantic represents infinity, exteriority, the public, and the overly natural. Miniatures focus on detail, on the individual in control, on timelessness. We find the miniature at the origin of the private, individual history, but we find the gigantic at the origin of public and natural history." Susan Stewart, *On Longing: Narratives of the Miniature, the Gigantic, the Souvenir, the Collection* (Durham, N.C.: Duke University Press, 1993), 70.

4. Mike Barrier, *Animated Man: A Life of Walt Disney* (Berkeley: University of California Press, 2007), 235–236; Kathy Jackson, *Walt Disney Conversations* (Jackson: University Press of Mississippi, 2006), 74; Karal Ann Marling, "Imagineering the Disney Theme Parks," in *Designing Disney's Theme Parks*, ed. Karal Ann Marling (New York: Flammarion), 35, 39, 40–41, 45–47; Martin Sklar, *Walt Disney's Disneyland* (Anaheim, Calif.: Walt Disney Productions, 1969).

5. John Hench, *Designing Disney: Imagineering and the Art of the Show* (New York: Disney Editions, 2003), 2, 67, 56. Later, John Lasseter, another "imagineer," noted that each attraction "must create an immersive and intriguing world . . . touching all the senses." The Imagineers (John Lasseter), *Walt Disney Imagineering: A Behind the Dreams Look at Making More Magic Real* (New York: Disney Editions, 2010), 28, 29–30, 33–40, 75, 84–85, 103.

6. Hench, *Designing Disney*, 23, 37, 39 (quotation), 50, 57, 86 (quotation); Lasseter, *Walt Disney Imagineering*, 75.

7. Marie Louise Gothein, *History of Garden Art: From the Earliest Times to the Present Day* (London: J. W. Dent, 1928), 1:25–30; Julia Berral, *The Garden: An Illustrated History from Ancient Egypt to the Present Day* (London: Thames & Hudson, 1966), 35–39; Karen Jones and John Wills, *The Invention of the Park* (Cambridge: Polity, 2005), 9–25.

8. Hench, *Designing Disney*, 50, 57.

9. *Walt Disney's Guide to Disneyland* (Anaheim, Calif.: Walt Disney Productions, 1964), 4. Note also Elizabeth and Jay Mechling, "The Sale of Two Cities," *Journal of Popular Culture* 15 (Spring 1981): 166–179; Raymond Weinstein, "Disneyland and Coney Island: Reflections on the Evolution of the Modern Amusement Park," *Journal of Popular Culture* 26 (Summer 1992): 131–142.

10. Jean Starobinski, "The Idea of Nostalgia," *Diogenes* 54 (Summer 1966): 81–103; Peter Fritzsche, "Specters of History: On Nostalgia, Exile, and Modernity," *American Historical Review* 106 (Dec. 2001): 1587–1618; Susan Matt, *Homesickness: An American History* (New York: Oxford University Press, 2011).

11. Marling, "Imagineering," 81.

12. Paul Connerton, *How Modernity Forgets* (New York: Cambridge University Press, 2009), 5, 23.

13. The fairy that was both powerful and often harmful in Elizabethan England became domesticated by Victorian times, and the "fairy-like child" was a common image (picked up by Disney in Tinkerbell in *Peter Pan*). Stewart, *On Longing*, 112–113; Emily Watson, *Fairies of Our Garden* (Boston: Tilton, 1862). Katharine Briggs, *The Fairies in English Tradition and Literature* (Chicago: University of Chicago Press, 1967); Leslie Fiedler, *Freaks: Myths and Images of the Secret Self* (New York: Simon and Schuster, 1978), 24–36; Robert Bogdan, *Freak Show: Presenting Human Oddities for Amusement and Profit* (Chicago: University of Chicago Press, 1988), 134–142, 158–160; Rachael Adams, *Sideshow U.S.: Freaks and the American Cultural Imagination* (Chicago: University of Chicago Press, 2001), 7, 9.

14. Gary Cross, *The Cute and the Cool: Wondrous Innocence and Modern American Children's Culture* (New York: Oxford University Press, 2004), chap. 3.

15. Jacqueline Rose, *The Impossibility of Children's Fiction* (London: Macmillan, 1984), 1–9.

16. Woody Register, *Kid of Coney Island: Fred Thompson and the Rise of American Amusements* (New York: Oxford University Press, 2001); Cross and Walton, *Playful Crowd*, chap. 2.

17. Fred Guterl, and Carol Truxal, "The Wonderful World of Epcot," *IEEE Spectrum* 19, no. 9 (Sept. 1982): 46–55; Irwin Ross, "Disney Gambles on Tomorrow," *Fortune* (Oct. 4, 1982): 62–69; Walt Disney Productions, *Project Florida: A Whole New Disney World* (Burbank, Calif., 1967), 10–11.

18. M. Sorkin, "See You in Disneyland," in *Variations on a Theme Park* (New York: Noonday, 1992), 216.

19. "Grand Floridian," *Disney News* (Fall 1986): 4; "Dolphins and Swans and More," *Disney News* (Winter 1989): 29; "Disney's Board Walk," *Disney News* (Winter 1995): 19–23; *Disney Magazine* (Spring 1994): 8; Dave Smith, *Disney A to Z* (New York: Hyperion, 1998), 12–24; Kerry Smith, *Mature Traveler's Guide to Walt Disney World* (Boston: Mercurial, 1997), 33–47.

20. Mark Goldhaber, "Saratoga Springs Disney Versus Reality," *Mouse Planet* (October 29, 2004), http://www.mouseplanet.com/7125/Saratoga_Springs_Disney_vs_Reality.

21. Saratoga Springs Resort and Spa, http://disneyworld.disney.go.com/resorts/saratoga-springs-resort-and-spa/.

22. Douglas Frantz, *Celebration, U.S.A.: Living in Disney's Brave New Town* (New York: Henry Holt, 1999), 21–31, 35, 43–49, 117–120, 185–200; Andrew Ross, *The Celebration Chronicles: Life, Liberty and the Pursuit of Property Values in Disney's New Town* (New York: Ballantine, 1999), for a critical academic view; Michael Lassell, *Celebration: The Story of a Town* (New York: Disney Editions, 2004), for an illustrated Disney account.

23. "A Tour Is Born," *Disney News* (Summer 1989): 17; Michael Eisner (with Tony Schwartz), *Work in Progress* (New York: Hyperion, 1999), 224; The Project on Disney, Jane Keens, Susan Willis, and Sheldon Welder, eds., *Inside the Mouse: Work and Play at Disney World* (Durham, N.C.: Duke University Press, 1996), 46, 95, 150.

24. Todd Trogmorton, *Roller Coasters* (Jefferson, N.C.: McFarland, 1993), 32–33; Scott Rutherford, *The American Roller Coaster* (Osceola, Wis.: MBI, 2000), 102–103; Cross and Walton, *The Playful Crowd*, 185–202.

25. Norman Kline, *Seven Minutes: The Life and Death of the American Animated Cartoon* (London: Verso, 1993), 17, 53, 91–95; Cecil Munsey, *Disneyana: Walt Disney Collectibles* (New York: Abrams, 1974), 29–39, chap. 9; Bevis Hillier, *Walt Disney's Mickey Mouse Memorabilia* (New York: Hawthorn, 1986), 14.

26. Munsey, *Disneyana*, 100–102; Stephen Jay Gould, "Mickey Mouse Meets Konrad Lorenz," *Natural History* (May 1979): 30–36.

27. "Walt Disney Contributes to the Toy Industry," *Toys and Bicycles* (April 1938): 122–123; "Snow White Triumphant," *Playthings* (March 1938): 48–52; Alan Bryman, *Disneyization of Society* (London: Sage, 2004), 84.

28. Robert Heide and John Gilman, *Cartoon Collectibles* (Garden City, N.J.: Doubleday, 1983), 201–208.

29. "Disney catalogs" folder, Disney Resort Room, Anaheim Public Library.

30. Andi Stein, *Why We Love Disney* (New York: Peter Lang, 2011), 216; Frank Roost, "Synergy City," in *Rethinking Disney*, ed. Mike Budd and Max Kirsch (Middletown, Conn.: Wesleyan University Press, 2005), 262–266.

31. Munsey, *Disneyana*, 288–294; Heide and Gilman, *Cartoon Collectibles*, 233–235; Gary Cross, *Kids' Stuff: Toys and the Changing World of American Childhood* (Cambridge, Mass.: Harvard University Press, 1997), 164–165.

32. Bryman, *Disneyization*, 85; Heide and Gilman, *Cartoon Collectibles*, 9–17, 23, 27; Munsey, *Disneyana*, preface.

33. Tom Tumbusch, *Tomart's Illustrated Disneyana Catalog and Price Guide*, 3 vols. (Dayton, Ohio: Tomart, 1985).

34. "Fantasies Come True Stocks 6,500 Different Products and Ships Worldwide," http://www.fantasiescometrue.com; "Finding Neverland," *Daily Variety* (April 29, 2005): 20; David Longest, *Collecting Disneyana (Identification & Values)* (Paducah, Ky.: Collector, 2008); Ken Farrell (owner of Just Kids Nostalgia), *Warman's Disney Collectibles Field Guide: Values and Identification* (Iola, Wis.: Krause, 2006).

35. *Disneyana Collector* (1982–1984), Disneyana folder, Disney Resort Room, Anaheim Public Library; *Disneyana Magazine* (Fall 1994); *Toy Box* (Feb. 1993), Disney Ephemera Collection, Special Collections, University of Central Florida.

36. Disney Productions, *Annual Report* (1984), Disney Ephemera Collection, Special Collections, University of Central Florida; Eisner, *Work in Progress*, 248–250.

37. The Disney stores were outsourced to Children's Place in 2004 but returned to Disney management in 2008, when the stores specialized in sales to the twelve-years-and-under crowd; articles for older consumers and collectors were mostly distributed through department stores and at Disneyana fairs and conventions. Stein, *Why We Love Disney*, 229–233.

38. Included among the "Legends" awarded were Bill Justice, a veteran animator at Disney, in 1993; the "imagineers" John Hench and Martin Sklar in 1994 and 1995; and Roy E. Disney (for his art, I presume) in 1999. Disneyana Fan Club Legends Awards, http://disneyanafanclub.org/legends; Mouse Planet, http://www.mouseplanet.com/9899/Birth_of_Disney_Fandom_Part _One_The_Mouse_Club.

39. *Mouse Club* (July 1986); *Fantasy Line* (of the National Fantasy Fan Club, NFFC) 1, no. 1 (1985); *World Tales and Mouse Review* (NFFC, World Chapter in Orlando) (Dec. 1992), all in Disneyana folder, Disney Resort Room, Anaheim Public Library; *Chicago Tribune* (March 7, 1986): A&E 1; *Orange County Register* (Jan. 18, 2004); Disney clippings, Disney Resort Room, Anaheim Public Library.

40. Disney News (Winter 1992), republished in D23 Archives, http://d23 .disney.go.com/archives/a-first-for-disneyana-collectors/; *World Tales and Mouse Review* (NFFC, World Chapter in Orlando) (Dec. 1992), Disney Resort Room, Anaheim Public Library.

41. *Joy of Collecting* (Sept. 1997); Walt Disney Collector's Society *News Flash* (Feb. 1994), both in Disneyana folder, Disney Resort Room, Anaheim Public Library.

42. The D-23 website is https://d23.com; the press release announcing the organization is at http://www.prnewswire.com/mnr/disney/37333/; "Expo, the Ultimate Disney Fan Experience" (September 10–13, 2009), Anaheim, Disneyana Folder, Disney Resort Room, Anaheim Public Library; *Los Angeles Times* (Sept. 10, 2009); *Anaheim Bulletin* (Aug. 11, 2011); *Los Angeles Times* (Sept. 19, 2011); *Orange County Register* (Aug. 13, 2012), all in the Disneyana Clippings Folder, Disney Resort Room, Anaheim Public Library; Stein, *Why We Love Disney*, 2–3.

43. Disney fan sites: http://MiceAge.com; http://LaughingPlace.com.

44. Steve DeGaetano, *Welcome Aboard the Disneyland Railroad!* (Wake Forest, N.C.: Steam Passages, 2004). DeGaetano edited the "Carolwood Chronicle," the newsletter of the Carolwood Pacific Historical Society (in reference to Disney's name for his first miniature railroad in his own home).

45. Attractions have been closed because of low attendance (for example, the House of the Future and the Mickey Mouse Circus). Others disappeared because they were too costly to operate (like mule rides or the Flying Saucers, each with major maintenance problems). *Los Angeles Times* (Nov. 23, 1994): 1A.

46. *Financial Times* (Dec. 10, 2005): 6; *New York Times* (March 4, 2005): B1; Mark Goldhaber, "Michael's Legacy: Reflecting on the Twenty-One-Year Tenure

of Disney's Outgoing Chief," *Mouse Planet* (Sept. 30, 2005), http://www.mouse planet.com/dan/bm050930mg.htm.

47. I am particularly referring to Stewart's *On Longing*.

48. Tourist consumption is modern, but it is also an expression of "primitive religiosity and righteous journeys such as pilgrimages" and thus sacralizes travel and the souvenir, notes Jon Goss, "The Souvenir and Sacrificed in the Tourist Mode of Consumption," in *Seductions of Place: Geographical Perspectives on Globalization and Touristed Landscapes*, ed. C. Cartier and A. A. Lew (London: Routledge: 2005), 60. S. Buck-Morse, *The Dialectics of Seeing: Walter Benjamin and the Arcades Project* (Cambridge, Mass.: MIT Press: 1989), 189–191; Nelson H. H. Graburn, "The Anthropology of Tourism," *Annals of Tourism Research* 10, no. 19 (1983): 9–33; Eric Leed, *The Mind of the Traveler: From Gilgamesh to Global Tourism* (New York: Basic Books, 1991).

49. The appeal of finding out just "how they did that" was well established in nineteenth-century American crowds at magic and freak shows. See James Cook, *The Arts of Deception: Playing with Fraud in the Age of Barnum* (Cambridge, Mass.: Harvard University Press, 2001), 73; Adams, *Sideshow U.S.A.*, 7, 9.

50. "Learn and Live," *Disney Magazine* (Sept. 1996): 36–43; "Disney Institute," *Disney Magazine* (March 1995): 23; both in the Disney Resort Room, Anaheim Public Library.

51. "New Wedding Pavilion," *Eyes and Ears* (July 13, 1995): 1; "Magical Matrimony," *Eyes and Ears* (Oct. 16, 1997): 3; both in the Disney Resort Room, Anaheim Public Library.

52. Stewart, *On Longing*, 135; Dean MacCannell, *The Tourist* (New York: Schocken, 1976), 42, 148–149.

53. Goss, "Tourist Mode of Consumption," 56–71; Stewart, *On Longing*, 69, 145.

54. Stewart, *On Longing*, 69.

55. Stewart, *On Longing*, 133.

CONCLUSION. WHERE WE'VE BEEN. WHERE WE MIGHT GO

1. Similarly, nostalgia is dismissed by Michael Kammen as "history without guilt" or the equivalent of "kitsch." Michael Kammen, *Mystic Chords of Memory* (New York: Vintage, 1991), 688; David Lowenthal, *Possessed by the Past: The Heritage Crusade and the Spoils of History* (New York: Free Press, 1996), 74, 115, 121–122, 142, 155; Svetlana Boym, *The Future of Nostalgia* (New York: Basic, 2001), xiv–xv, 38; Ada Louise Huxtable, *The Unreal America: Architecture and Illusion* (New York: New Press, 1997); Brian Graham and Peter Howard, "Heritage and Identity," in *The Ashgate Research Companion to Heritage and Identity*, ed. Brian Graham and Peter Howard (Aldershot: Ashgate, 2008), 1–18; B. Graham, G. J. Ashworth, and J. E. Tunbridge, *Geography of Heritage: Power, Culture, and Economy* (London: Arnold, 2000).

2. M. Vess, Clay Routledge, Constantine Sedikides, and Tim Wildschut, "Nostalgia as a Resource for the Self," *Self and Identity* 3 (2012): 273–284; Clay Routledge, Jamie Arndt, Tim Wildschut, Constantine Sedikides, Claire Hart, and Jacob Juhl, "The Past Makes the Present Meaningful: Nostalgia as an Existential Resource," *Journal of Personality and Social Psychology* 101, no. 3 (Sept. 2011): 638–652.

3. Gaynor Kavanagh, *Dream Spaces: Memory and the Museum* (London: Leicester University Press, 2000), 175; S. Pinker, *How the Mind Works* (Harmondsworth: Penguin, 1999).

4. Kavanagh, *Dream Spaces*, 10–15.

5. Boym, *Future of Nostalgia*, 39.

6. Mihaly Csikszentmihalyi, "Why We Need Things," in *History from Things: Essays on Material Culture*, ed. Steven Lubar and W. David Kingery (Washington: Smithsonian Institution Press, 1993), 20–29.

7. John Elsner and Roger Cardinal, *The Cultures of Collecting* (Cambridge, Mass.: Harvard University Press, 1994), 3.

8. Walter Benjamin, "Unpacking My Library: A Talk About Book Collecting," in *Illuminations: Essay and Reflections*, ed. Hannah Arendt (1931; New York: Harcourt, 1968), 60.

9. Jean Baudrillard, *The System of Objects* (1968; London: Verso, 1996), 87–91.

10. Simon Reynolds, *Retromania* (New York: Faber and Faber, 2011), 101, 116; Will Straw, "Sizing up Record Collections," in *Sexing the Groove: Popular Music and Gender*, ed. Sheila Whiteley (New York: Routledge, 1997), 3–16.

11. Russell Belk, *Collecting in a Consumer Culture* (London: Routledge, 1995), 146.

12. Baudrillard, *System of Objects*, 95.

13. Daniel Miller, "Buying Time," in *Time, Consumption, and Everyday Life*, ed. Elizabeth Shove, Frank Trentmann, and Richard Wilk (Oxford: Berg, 2009), 157–169; Belk, *Collecting in a Consumer Culture*, 153.

14. Susan Stewart, *On Longing: Narratives of the Miniature, the Gigantic, the Souvenir, the Collection* (Durham, N.C.: Duke University Press, 1993), 133–135.

15. Umberto Eco, *Travels in Hyperreality* (New York: MBJ, 1986), 30.

16. Reynolds, *Retromania*, 93.

17. Walter Benjamin, "The Work of Art in the Age of Mechanical Reproduction," in *Illuminations: Essay and Reflections*, ed. Hannah Arendt (1931; New York: Harcourt, 1968), 246.

18. Alan Tomlinson, "Consumer Culture and the Aura of the Commodity," in *Consumption, Identity, and Style*, ed. A. Tomlinson (London: Routledge, 1990), 1–9.

19. Igor Kopytoff, "The Cultural Biography of Things: Commoditization as Process," in *The Social Life of Things: Commodities in Cultural Perspective*, ed. Arjun Appadurai (Cambridge: Cambridge University Press, 1986), 80.

20. Ackbar Abbas, "Walter Benjamin's Collector," *New Literary History* 20 (Autumn 1988): 148–149; Belk, *Collecting in a Consumer Culture*, 64; Russell Belk and Melanie Wallendord, "Of Mice and Men: Gender Identity in Collecting," in *Interpreting Objects and Collections*, ed. Susan Pearce (London: Routledge, 1994), 251.

21. Csikszentmihalyi, "Why We Need Things," 22, 27, 28.

22. Maurice Halbwachs, *On Collective Memory* (Chicago: University of Chicago Press, 1950), 80, 175; John R. Gillis, *Commemorations: The Politics of National Identity* (Princeton, N.J.: Princeton University Press, 1994), 5; Keith Basso, *Wisdom Sits in Places* (Albuquerque: University of New Mexico Press, 1996), 6.

23. Kavanagh, *Dream Spaces*, 27–28.

24. Fredric Jameson, "Postmodernism and Consumerism," in *The Anti-Aesthetic: Essays on Postmodern Culture*, ed. H. Foster (Port Townsend, Wash.: Bay, 1983); Frederic Jameson, *Postmodern Culture* (London: Pluto, 1994), 125.

25. Robert Putnam, *Bowling Alone: The Collapse and Revival of American Community* (New York: Simon and Shuster, 2001).

26. Gary Cross, "Consumption Patterns as Generational Markers: American Examples/Comparative Possibilities," in *History by Generations: Generational Dynamics in Modern History*, ed. Christina Lubinski (New York: Palgrave, 2012), 68–81.

27. Connerton concludes that in the shift from a capitalism based on manual labor to one generated by fast markets, our "job" has moved from being "well-ordered machines" of self-disciplined workers to becoming "omnivorous children," consumers, who adapt readily to ever-shorter cycles of fashion/obsolescence. Today, kids learn not lifelong trades but to be adaptive consumers, especially of popular music, and this tools them to ever-changing desire, excellent training for fast capitalism. Paul Connerton, *How Modernity Forgets* (Cambridge: Cambridge University Press, 2009), 17, 6–7, 62, 64, 66; Antoine Compagnon, *The Five Paradoxes of Modernity* (New York, 1994), 62–64.

28. David Harvey, *The Condition of Postmodernity* (Cambridge: Blackwell, 1990), 210–211, 229–231, 270–271.

29. Connerton, *How Modernity Forgets*, 84.

30. Marcel Proust, *Remembrances of Things Past* (New York: Random House, 1934), 298; Henri Pieron, *L'évolution de la mémoire* (Paris, 1910), 41; David Gross, *Lost Time: On Remembering and Forgetting in Late Modern Culture* (Amherst: University of Massachusetts Press, 2000), 17–22, 29, 41, 46, 50; Connerton, *How Modernity Forgets*, 27, 29; Robert S. Nelson and Margaret Olin, *Monuments and Memory, Made and Unmade* (Chicago: University of Chicago Press, 2003), 103–105; Graham and Howard, "Heritage and Identity," 1–18.

31. Walter Benjamin, *Gesammelte Schriften* (Frankfurt, 1972), 5:596, cited in Connerton, *How Modernity Forgets*, 66, also 86.

32. Gross, *Lost Time*, 57–59; Reynolds, *Retromania*, 404, xiv.

33. David Shenk, *Data Smog: Surviving the Information Glut* (New York: Harper, 1997); Reynolds, *Retromania*, chap. 2, quotations on 372, 398; Nicholas Carr, *Shallows: What the Internet Is Doing to Our Brains* (New York: Norton, 2010).

34. Reynolds, *Retromania*, 404; Alvin Toffler, *Future Shock* (New York: Random House, 1970).

35. *Rolling Stone*, "500 Greatest Songs of All Time," 2010, http://www.rollingstone.com/music/lists/the-500-greatest-songs-of-all-time-20110407; http://en.wikipedia.org/wiki/Rolling_Stone's_500_Greatest_Songs_of_All_Time#2010_update.

36. Brian Gregor, "Selfhood and the Three R's: Reference, Repetition, and Refiguration," *International Journal for Philosophy of Religion* 58, no. 2 (2005): 63–94.

37. E. H. Erikson, *Childhood and Society* (New York: Norton, 1963).

38. Jeffrey Hammond, *Little Big World: Collecting Louis Marx and the American Fifties* (Iowa City: University of Iowa Press, 2010).

39. Daniel Miller, *The Comfort of Things* (Cambridge: Polity, 2008); Cristel Antonia Russell and Sidney J. Levy, "The Temporal and Focal Dynamics of Volitional Reconsumption: A Phenomenological Investigation of Repeated Hedonic Experiences," *Journal of Consumer Research* 39, no. 2 (August 2012): 341–359.

INDEX